What Poetry Brings to Business

What Poetry Brings to Business

Clare Morgan

with Kirsten Lange & Ted Buswick

The University of Michigan Press • Ann Arbor

Published in the United States of America by
The University of Michigan Press
Manufactured in the United States of America
♾ Printed on acid-free paper

2013   2012   2011   2010   4   3   2   1

A CIP catalog record for this book is available from the British Library.

Library of Congress Cataloging-in-Publication Data

Morgan, Clare.
    What poetry brings to business / Clare Morgan ; with Kirsten Lange
and Ted Buswick.
       p.   cm.
    Includes bibliographical references and index.
    ISBN 978-0-472-07086-2 (cloth : alk. paper) — ISBN 978-0-472-
05086-4 (pbk. : alk. paper)
    I. Lange, Kirsten.   II. Buswick, Ted.   III. Title.

PN6110.B9M67   2010
809.1'93553—dc22   2009047787

Foreword: Poetry and Business

BY JOHN BARR

At best they have been viewed in America as odd bedfellows; at worst there has been a history of attitudinal sparring between them. W. H. Auden caught the general attitude of poets toward businessmen when he wrote that poetry "survives in the valley of its making where executives would never want to tamper." For the businessman's part, the major American poet Hart Crane was born to a father, the inventor of Life Savers, who thought God had played an outrageous joke by giving him a poet for a son. Closer to home, my own father, a railroad man and a good man, had this advice when I announced that I intended to become a poet: "At least go to college. Then if you become a poet people will think you are an eccentric and not just a beach bum." Sound advice in 1961.

Having listened to my father but also to myself, I have pursued parallel careers in both business and poetry. The experience has persuaded me that the connections between the world of business and management and the world of the arts and humanities are manifold, profound, and resistant to easy conclusions. It also has convinced me that those connections are terribly important. If the province of the businessman (by which I mean businesswoman as well, here and in what follows) is as large as all external reality, then the province of the poet is as large as the world of internal reality within us all. The life of action versus the life of contemplation—the "man of affairs" versus the "man of letters"—is an opposition as old as literature. It is the tension between "doing" and "knowing." And the somewhat insistent desire of each of these ways of living to establish a validity and sufficiency independent of the other runs directly out of the human condition. Are we better able to deal with the imperfection of reality by controlling, to an extent, the world around us, or by making sense, through art and contemplation, of the world within us?

The secret, of course, is that choosing one need not mean excluding the other. As Clare Morgan's book shows, the special kinds of knowledge that poetry discovers can enhance and animate a life in business. And vice versa. Art that is not rooted in the whole of human experience—call that "art for art's sake"—is doomed to be ephemeral, peripheral, because it cannot enrich the life of a general reader. Conversely a business career that has not been informed by art's power of seeing, by poetry's hallmark openness to ambiguity and risk, may not achieve its full potential. This is so because business and poetry are more alike than either knows.

The business of both is to create order out of a chaotic universe. True, the venues of business and poetry are different. The businessman delights in making sense of things in the *external* world, achieving his order by making a sale, building a plant, or similar commercial success. The poet, on the other hand, delights in making sense of things in the *internal* world, achieving order by creating a perfect poem. Robert Frost calls a poem "a clarification of life—not necessarily a great clarification such as sects and cults are founded on, but . . . a momentary stay against confusion." For both, then, creativity is a means of controlling chaos, finding order. Business and poetry draw their waters out of the same well.

The agent for this work is the imagination. Poetry gets a lot of attention for its creativity; it is called one of the "creative arts." But people not in business often miss the point that business is also a creative art. Ben & Jerry's Ice Cream was certainly a creative act on the part of Ben and Jerry. A new company, a new product, even a solution to a mundane business problem requires an idea. And an idea is an act of the imagination.

The modern CEO, I have come to think, is one of the finer products of Western civilization. Not that every business leader we know is a perfect human being, of course, but the CEO of my imagination is a marvel of internal balances. He is comfortable with risk if not in love with it; pragmatic but not at the expense of principles; willing to act and be judged by the results, and, in all the above, refreshingly free of hypocrisy or self-pity. Oh, and he has probably read some poetry.

JOHN BARR *has pursued parallel careers as a poet and investment banker. As a businessman, he has been a managing director at Morgan Stanley, a managing director of Société Générale, founder and chairman of the Natural Gas Clearinghouse (now Dynegy Corporation), and founding partner of Barr Devlin Associates. As a poet, he has published six collections and has taught poetry in the master of fine arts program at Sarah Lawrence College. He has served on the boards of the Poetry Society of America, Yaddo, and Bennington College. Currently, he is president of the Poetry Foundation.*

Contents

Introduction

BOLKO VON OETINGER

Poetry?

I must confess that I was a skeptic when a few years ago Clare Morgan and her coauthors brought me—as director of The Strategy Institute of The Boston Consulting Group (BCG)—a proposal for a book exploring the value of poetry to strategic thinking.

Certainly, the beauty of poetry elevates the mind, but can that higher consciousness go beyond the aesthetic? Aren't these two fields so distant from each other as to have no opportunity for cross-pollination? Can an argument really be made that a manager should read poetry *for the good of his business?*

The book in your hands is proof that I was convinced. Not entirely on that first day—although Clare's answer was certainly plausible enough to justify exploring the idea further—but increasingly as the project evolved. While I never found the "hard" proof I'd initially thought essential, over time it was reading and working with the poems themselves that won me over.

In particular, it was William Stafford's poem "Traveling through the Dark" (p. 59) that made me a believer in the value of poetry to business thinking. (For you, it may well be a different one.) It's a poem about road-kill. A pregnant deer lies dying by the side of the road. What to do?

During the course of this project, I have participated in at least half a dozen discussions of this poem with clients and BCG colleagues in the United States, England, Germany, and Japan. Clare told the participants only that she wanted to discuss and interpret the poem. Yet despite the significant cultural differences, the discussions were remarkably similar. (If you haven't already, go to page 59 and read it quickly now. You may be surprised to find that it's hard to read quickly, so engaging is the dramatic situation.)

Each time the discussion felt almost surreal: the dying doe, the unborn faun, the darkness of the night, the danger on the road, and the relationship of human to animal. The readers quickly and intensely found themselves in the shoes of the narrator who has found the deer. Every participant was drawn into the dilemma, the ambiguity of the situation, and the struggle to find the moral response.

In one of these gatherings—with engineers from a major automaker—the discussion brought the group together in the way that intense shared experiences do but in a fraction of the time. We started out superficially acquainted, but after living together for two hours inside the narrator's head we suddenly knew one another in a completely different, deeper way. How and why would a person behave this way or that? The answers given and suggestions made offered deep insights into the character of each member of the group. We discovered that we were ready to take another look at our own views, recognized the weight of others' arguments, and struggled with them and ourselves. We had all left our comfort zones and were together in a liminal situation looking for a way out.

Over the course of this effort, I've realized a number of things about the power of poetry, especially lyric poetry, to sharpen and open the mind. Three in particular:

Reading poetry is worth it in and of itself. This was not unexpected, and no doubt many readers will share this sentiment. Yet the pleasure we get from a poem may be its price of admission into our psyche. But private pleasure is one thing and commercial benefit another, so I suspect the following two arguments will be more important for the curious but as yet unconvinced reader.

Poetry forces you to find meaning in ambiguity. The language of poetry is like the future, full of vague hints, a mixture of fact and opinion, unclear forms, and incomplete models. It is open and emotional, accommodates multiple meanings, and is frequently controversial. It allows a multitude of paths, detours, and escapes. Different readers will not necessarily agree on what the poem is about, but they will be able to discuss the different assumptions that underlie their conclusions.

The language of business, by contrast, seems clear. In the operational and financial spheres, terms are tightly defined to enable efficient communication and effective collaboration within and beyond the global enterprise. Poetry has little to add here. It will not help you make new calculations, build better projections, increase throughput, minimize scrap, balance a budget, or locate a factory in China.

But when it comes to the sphere of strategy, executives can often find themselves (as is said of the British and the Americans) divided by a common language. Despite, or perhaps because of, the manifold frameworks that try to pin the concept of strategy down, words become buzzwords and are never questioned. Recipients of directives interpret them in their own way and act accordingly. A well-developed poetic competence, as argued in this book, can help executives look behind the words to find, weigh, and resolve alternate meanings.

Beyond its value in clarifying *semantic ambiguity*, poetry can also help develop both a tolerance for and a facility with *situational ambiguity*. The reader/manager will be able to traverse Carl von Clausewitz's "fog of uncertainty" with both greater courage and greater impact. By understanding the multiple meanings at the heart of ambiguity, the manager's ability to make appropriate decisions "on the fly" is enhanced.

Poetry fosters interpersonal understanding. This insight was perhaps the most surprising to me. In a group discussion of poetry—as happened with the auto engineers—people reveal themselves and, since few aspects of a poem are black and white, develop real empathy for the thoughts and ideas of others.

This ability to see the world through the eyes of others is a critical and all too rare management skill. If you can sit inside people's heads, it's easier to convince them. If your people aren't afraid to replay and test their interpretations of your directives, you'll ensure greater strategic alignment. And this kind of empathy can be achieved only to a limited extent through more "rational" approaches. In a world where we need to ensure that strategies are commonly understood, well-defended, responsive, and consistently implemented, poetic competence may represent a new sine qua non for strategic alignment.

But if poetry is so critical, why haven't tens of thousands of managers—me included—known this for ages? Why isn't it taught in business schools? And do I need to read a whole book to get the gist? Couldn't it all be summarized in three pages with bullet points? Perhaps it could, but there's no way of getting around the poems. They entice. They demand attention. They invite interpretation and discussion.

The authors are well aware of the reader's likely skepticism. Consequently, they have made it easier for the reader to be taken along on the trip. The book isn't a theoretical tome; it's a book about writing a book about poetry for executives. At the heart of the book are poems and an imagined dialogue between Clare and an engaged yet skeptical reader. Poetry, doubt, theory, and whimsy coexist, and poetry and doubt are not bad travel companions.

If my experience is any guide, discerning the value of poetry to business is one of those rare gifts that only once you have been given it do you realize you'd always wished for it. I thank Clare, Kirsten, and Ted deeply for giving it to me. I wish a similar experience for you.

On behalf of The Strategy Institute of BCG, I'd like to express my sincere thanks to those colleagues who have assisted the team. They were sometimes more in number, sometimes fewer, but they were always entirely convinced that poetic competence is a truly valuable business skill.

Bill Matassoni, BCG's longtime marketing head, again and again (and even after his retirement!) encouraged us to bring managers closer to poems. In December 2005, he, Clare, Ted, and Gary Callahan, BCG's director of design and publishing operations, developed an edition of poems—read aloud by BCG staff—that was distributed as a holiday gift to clients. Then in December 2007 BCG's Marketing Team, led by Antonella Mei-Pochtler, Massimo Portincaso, and Federico Fregni, selected four chapters from this book as a holiday gift for BCG consultants to give to their clients.

Tiha von Ghyczy, a fellow of The Strategy Institute and strategy lecturer at the Darden School of Business at the University of Virginia, encouraged the team and warned it not to debase poetry by treating it as a "tool" but instead to emphasize its indirect impact on enhancing communication and mutual understanding. Matthew Clark, who runs marketing for BCG's global strategy practice, helped make the book clearer, simpler, and more distinct, and to have no fear of the encounter of economics and poetry.

I am, of course, particularly grateful to and proud of the team of Clare Morgan, Kirsten Lange, and Ted Buswick and also Matthew Wikswo, a team member during the early stages. During this project, they received more "advice" than they'd bargained for. They persevered. Indeed, the stronger the storms of doubt they faced ("Is poetry really useful for businesspeople?") the harder they worked on their message. At the Institute, we are always grateful for doubts and criticism. They enliven thought, sharpen arguments, and show us where the connection to practice has to be strengthened. The Institute thrives on this energy. Also I thank the many poets, businesspeople, and professors who helped the team with their opinions and advice.

BOLKO VON OETINGER *recently retired as a senior partner and managing director in the Munich office of The Boston Consulting Group. He was also director of BCG's Strategy Institute, which he founded in 1998, until his retirement.*

ᥬᥲ **Part 1** ᥫᥰ

What Is Not—Yet

You can never know all there is to know about a situation. To be successful, you have to be able to take the right decisions on insufficient information. In order to do this you have to envision what is not—yet.

Prologue

What Socrates Didn't Like about Poets

Imagine a warm day, spring in the year 399 BCE. Socrates is on trial for his life in the Stoa Basileios. The charge against him is corrupting the youth of Athens. According to the prosecutors, he has undermined the authority of the state. As well as being mixed up with the worst of the Tyrants in the troubles of 404, his ideas about the gods are suspect. He is said to have sympathized with Anaxagoras, who was driven from the city for declaring that the sun was a red-hot stone.

Socrates has conducted himself throughout the trial with his usual composure. He is to be judged by five hundred citizens; they are ranged around him, listening to his defense. He has never set himself up, he insists, as a man of wisdom. When his friend Chaerephon asked the oracle at Delphi, "Is there anyone wiser than Socrates?" and she replied, "Socrates is the wisest of men," he immediately set out to disprove it.

"Knowing I have no wisdom," he says, "I reflected that if I could only find a man wiser than myself, then I might go to the god with a refutation in my hand."

First of all he went to this and that politician, hoping he would find in them such ways of thinking, such fine conclusions, that it would be shown straightaway that the politician was much wiser than he. But when he pressed first one and then the other with questions, it soon became clear that they weren't wise at all. And he managed to alienate some powerful men into the bargain.

Next he went to the poets, thinking to himself, you will be detected; now you will find out that you are more ignorant than they are. He took them some of the most elaborate passages in their own writings and asked what the meaning of them was, thinking that they would teach him something.

"Will you believe me?" he asks his jurors. "There is hardly a person present [here] who would not have talked better about their poetry than they did themselves. That showed me in an instant that not by wisdom do poets write poetry but by a sort of genius and inspiration; they are like diviners or soothsayers who also say many fine things but do not understand the meaning of them. And the poets appeared to me to be much in the same case."

Socrates' five hundred jurors find him guilty by a majority of sixty. The prosecution demands the death penalty, while Socrates is eventually induced to propose for himself the penalty of a fine. The vote is for death by an increased majority of eighty. Perhaps some of his judges were poets themselves, or rhapsodes (poetry reciters). His critique of the poets certainly can't have done him much good for poetry was held in great esteem as a vital part of any valuable citizen's education. A month later Socrates drinks the appropriate measure of hemlock and joins that eternity which (he consoles friends with the thought) may turn out to be "only a single night."

Lines from "Under Which Lyre"
by W. H. AUDEN

Thou shalt not be on friendly terms
With guys in advertising firms,
   Nor speak with such
As read the Bible for its prose,
Nor, above all, make love to those
   Who wash too much.

Thou shalt not live within thy means
Nor on plain water and raw greens.
   If thou must choose
Between the chances, choose the odd;
Read the *New Yorker,* trust in God;
   And take short views.

Poetry in Practice

And as imagination bodies forth
The forms of things unknown, the poet's pen
Turns them to shapes and gives to airy nothing
A local habitation and a name.

High-Tech in Downing College

Cambridge is about sixty miles from London; you can get there in an hour on the English definition of a fast train. The day was sunny, and Downing College would be looking beautiful and regal, set just away from the slightly surreal center of that archetypal English university town.

It was not an academic occasion that I was on my way to. The well-known forms of a particular kind of intellectual debate were not what I was heading for. I had spent the hour on the train with my laptop rather precariously balanced on the drop-down table that was just too small for it. I was making adjustments to my presentation.

At Downing College it was not a more or less eager group of literature students that was waiting for me. True, I was going to talk about poetry. But it was poetry wearing a very different kind of hat. What was waiting for me among the courts and lawns and high-ceilinged rooms of the college was the executive team of a high-tech start-up company. I was running a workshop on strategic thinking. Reading poetry, I was going to say, could be vital to your future. My session was scheduled at the end of a two-day strategy seminar. The executive team was made up of fourteen men and women from London, Belfast, New York, and Minneapolis. They had been working intensively on the future of their company ever since their arrival. They would be tired and already thinking about drinks and dinner. I was on for the last two hours of their final evening. Mine had been billed as an "experimental" slot.

The "So What?" Factor

How could you meet an executive team on its own ground to talk about poetry? This was a vital question not only for the workshop but also for the development of the book I was writing. Because the workshop came out of the idea of a book, which itself came out of the notion—rather startling to some people—that poetry and business strategy have something vital in common.

What might that something be? Among other things, the poem is a unit characterized by strategic intent. It is a language utterance that wishes to communicate through a subtle balance of rhythm, rhyme, imagery, and other mechanisms. There is a lot in common between a poem and a marketable product. Here is my output, the poet says. I would like to share it. Poets are interfacing with consumers in terms of reaching a readership. They have to intersect with the prevailing market forces via the publishing industry. They have to grapple with questions of utility, addressing the relevance of the work to the needs of contemporary moment. They have to establish a niche for a particular work through channels that will enable each individual voice, among many competing ones, to be heard.

The idea of the poem as a marketable entity is not new. Some of the most successful poets have created market niches for their avant-garde or unusual poetry. T. S. Eliot and Ezra Pound did precisely this in the 1920s. They were writing avant-garde poetry that was reaching, at the time, only a tiny audience of friends and poetry aficionados. Their aim was to revolutionize what poetry was doing in the twentieth century: to rid poetry of what they saw as the taint of the Victorian. They needed, desperately needed, a wide audience if they were to be successful. So they began writing reviews of their kind of avant-garde poetry in an important little periodical called *The Dial*, which everybody who was anybody read. They praised the new poetry to the skies, justified its idiosyncrasies, suggested in all kinds of ways that it was a "must have." Pretty soon, with the audience for this new poetry expanding, Eliot and Pound began thinking about setting up their own periodical. The idea was brought to fruition by Eliot, who founded the *Criterion*. As editor, he published all the up-and-coming writers and artists whose work reflected the new tendencies. He and Pound between them had helped kick-start a movement in literature that had an enormous impact on twentieth-century culture, not just in Britain but throughout many parts of the Western world.

Whether my audience in Cambridge would care about Eliot or Pound was open to question. How many people care about poetry anyway? Isn't it an old-fashioned mode that deals in airy-fairy utterances? At the beginning of the twenty-first century, isn't it pretty much an irrelevance unless you are an academic with a vested interest in what Eliot himself called "a periphrastic study in a worn-out poetical fashion"? *Periphrastic:* who needs it?

The project I had embarked on was flying in the face of any such skepticism. I wasn't just taking on the factions that believe YouTube has more to offer the contemporary individual than does Seamus Heaney. I was taking head-on the false (for so I believe it to be) opposition between art and commerce. Between the beauty and power of poetry in all its mystery and the rather more naked exigencies of the bottom line.

I needed a strong argument that would demonstrate what I knew, and had always known and believed in passionately: that poetry is a living, breathing entity that is of extreme relevance to us in the twenty-first century. And that "us" doesn't exclude the executive at his desk, the CEO taking her place in the boardroom, or the eager MBA graduate riding the elevator up to the thirty-sixth floor on the first morning. It doesn't exclude the city trader, the real-estate entrepreneur, or the N.G.O. facilitator on a plane to Zimbabwe. Because reading poetry requires—demands—a very particular way of thinking. And that way of thinking is vitally important in addressing the complexities of the economic, social, and political world we live in.

Wittgenstein, in his *Philosophical Investigations,* states outright that anyone who doesn't understand poetry is "meaning blind." The ability to think the way poetry demands you think is a real differentiator. A complex world requires complex responses, and a poem is its own little engine of complex meanings. Like the world itself, it lures and frustrates and evades and teases. And then, when you start to really reach out toward it, it can come down over you in a shock.

Poetry, Power, and (Business) Possibility

All poets have some common strategies that make their work more or less identifiable under the banner POETRY as opposed to the banner of prose or painting or music or sculpture or a PowerPoint presentation or an annual financial report or a strategic plan. Central to these common strategies is *indirection*. Precision is vital to a poet, precision of language, of image, of nuance, of tone. But the indirection poetry deals in has to do with is rejection of "facts" as the basis of its utterance. A poet isn't trying to tell you something. He isn't trying to *tell* you anything. The poet is taking you on a journey of exploration, and where you arrive in the end, and the nature of the journey, will be different for each person. There are no maps, no certainties. Even the nature of the territory you are covering in reading a poem is open to discussion. This does not imply that a poem can mean absolutely anything. It is not a ground where you can indulge in reckless conjecture. But it is an arena of checks and balances, of starts and stops and realignments. It is a ground where questions are more important than answers and answers do not necessarily negate each other. It is also a territory where there may be no "answer," at least in the way we usually understand that word. There may be, purely, a freshly discovered space for observation. The ability to read a poem—to really read it, not just to look it over—may provide you not only with a new view of something you were considering: it may provide you with new skills in approaching that consideration. Skills you didn't know you needed but which are infinitely useful in engaging with the myriad uncertainties of our fast-moving, twenty-first-century world.

The indirection of poetry, its nonreliance on facts and the cause-and-effect logic that generally goes with the factual, was one of the things that troubled Socrates. He was intent on establishing the importance of definition. Things should—shouldn't they?—be subject to delineation. Boundaries were important: where did one thing end and another begin? If you couldn't get some kind of answer to that, you couldn't progress anywhere.

But the poets thought otherwise. They wanted to *dissolve* the boundaries between things, not delineate them. Wasn't that dangerous, though? Couldn't that lead you into who knows what kind of difficulty?

One of the aspects of poetry's power is what's referred to technically as *mimesis* (as opposed to *diegesis*). This—the power of representation over narration (akin to the idea of showing over telling)—was one of the things that troubled Plato about poetry and after him Aristotle.[1] Poetry was a danger to the state because of its charm and magic. The "what might happen," either possibly or probably, imperiled the well-brought-up citizenry on which the state was founded. Aristotle, in the ninth chapter of the *Poetics*, argued that poetry was more philosophical and serious than history. He set out poetry's "general" truths (what we might call timeless truths) against what he saw as the particular facts of history. On this basis he made the following plea.

We will beg Homer and other poets not to be angry if we cancel those and all similar passages [that is, "false" stories about the gods], not that they are not poetic and pleasing to most hearers, but because the more poetic they are the less are they suited to the ears of boys and men who are destined to be free.

Aristotle could see that poetry was a potent means of usurping established power; it could seriously undermine the authority of even a strong state.

Could this be why so many people—people you would never expect to be interested in poetry—are covert poetry readers and writers? Not necessarily because they want to usurp the state but because they want to get to grips freshly with the *state of things?* My investigations had already led me to talk to a lot of people, and I'd discovered that closet poetry reading—and writing—were rife. Some of the most successful thinkers and inventors wrote poetry. Whether their poetry was "any good" or not didn't matter. What mattered was the significance of scientists, politicians, and inventors feeling the need to adopt the mode that allowed—encouraged—them to eschew facts and move in what has been termed the realm of fancy. To embroil themselves in the mechanisms of uncertainty and conjecture, to immerse themselves in the slippery complications of language. What did this espousal of the "other" world of poetry offer them? It was surely the very indirectness of poetry, the obliqueness of its power compared to the direct, factual worlds they generally inhabited, that exercised such a strong hold on them. But it had to be more than that. In that offering there had to be some form of *enabling.* Poetry freed up something in these exceptional people that the ordinary modes of fact and definition did not.

Rhyme and Reason: Why Facts Aren't Enough Anymore

A colleague sent me the following Internet extract from a *New York Times* newspaper article.

> *Marketing Departments Are Turning to Poets to Help Inspire Their Companies' Clientele*
>
> Flight attendants at American Airlines hand out a poetry anthology. DaimlerChrysler sponsored poetry readings in five cities, AT&T, Deloitte & Touche, Blue Cross, and others have had poets speak to their marketing teams. Doubletree Hotel, Volkswagen, Lanc and Target distribute poetry anthologies to customers.

Poetry was already out there in the marketplace, fairly low key, perhaps to many people invisible, but there as an embryonic presence, bubbling under the surface, addressing something other than the bare facts. If part of my mission was to increase its visibility, another part was to investigate, account for, and capitalize on its importance. The executive team waiting for me at Downing College would want substance. To the spoken or unspoken question "Why are we doing this?" I would provide not answers but a journey. That journey would need to provide outcomes that were justifiable in terms of the priorities of the corporation. What poetry offered had to be tangible and specific, not just general and universal. It had to address in a new way the challenges that the contemporary executive faces.

I was drawn to an essay on my shelf by Wolfgang Iser called "The Reading Process: A Phenomenological Approach." Iser, one of the foremost thinkers of the twentieth century in the field of literary and cultural theory, proposes that reading literary texts fosters an ability vital to the aims of the executive team I was going to speak to: the asking of questions and the making of connections.

"We look forward, we look back, we decide, we change our decisions, we form expectations, we are shocked by their nonfulfillment, we question, we muse, we accept, we reject" is how he describes the process. Because of this, he believes that "reading literature gives us the chance to formulate the unformulated." In other words, Iser is suggesting that engaging with literature can develop the reach of the mind in certain specific respects.

Iser's assertions in relation to literature in general apply, I intended to argue, with particular force in relation to poetry. Poetry, perhaps more than any literary form, thrives on the unstated and so encourages what Iser refers to as "the dynamic process of recreation," which demands so much of its readers.

But why should this "dynamic process of recreation" be of importance to my audience at Downing? William Shakespeare, in a famous passage about a leader who is in danger of losing control of his domain, points to some reasons.

Duke Theseus, in *A Midsummer Night's Dream*, is a strong ruler. He rules his domain by enforcing the logical relations of power and assessing the facts of existence that confront him. He can be seen as a bit of a cold fish, but there's no doubt that he's a powerful leader. However, in the mysterious precincts of the forest, outside but adjacent to the ordered realm of the duke's rational rule, mayhem, on one long night in the middle of summer, breaks out.

In act 5, scene 1, of *A Midsummer Night's Dream*, Shakespeare has Duke

Theseus reflect skeptically on the story that the lovers Demetrius, Helena, Hermia, and Lysander tell of the previous night's strange happenings in the disorderly realm of the forest. This is how the duke comments on the strange and illogical and—to a leader keen on keeping a tight rein on what's happening within his sphere of authority—threatening events that have occurred in the nonrational realm.

> The lunatic, the lover and the poet
> Are of imagination all compact: *[have the same kind of imaginations]*
> One sees more devils than vast hell can hold,
> That is, the madman: the lover, all as frantic,
> Sees Helen's beauty in a brow of Egypt: *[sees Helen of Troy in a dark, ugly man]*
> The poet's eye, in fine frenzy rolling,
> Doth glance from heaven to earth, from earth to heaven;
> And as imagination bodies forth   *[brings into being]*
> The forms of things unknown, the poet's pen
> Turns them to shapes and gives to airy nothing
> A local habitation and a name.

Smack at the heart of the duke's reaction is the poet. Poets, he says, like lunatics and lovers, see the world through a different set of lenses. This makes the world they see, in effect, a different world with different relations. So the things that happen, or can happen, in that world are also different. The poet's world is not bound by the rule of cause and effect; it is not constrained by logic. Poets have the ability to give to "airy nothing" (what is not—yet) "a local habitation and a name" (substance). They conjure something, so to speak, out of nothing.

Is this good or bad? For Theseus at first it is negative and threatening. The conjuring of something out of nothing seems initially to make the world uncontrollable. And leaders have to control their worlds, don't they, through the collection and analysis of facts, through the logical, cause-and-effect ordering of information?

The need to order and control through these means is incontrovertible. It is a vital and undeniable principle of developed economies. It underpins many of the structures of Western civilization. But on its own it is not enough. Complex situations require complex solutions. Or at least, since solutions in the overall sense may not always be possible, far-reaching and insightful ways of addressing the issues are required. Shakespeare knew this four hundred or so years ago. He causes Duke Theseus to find out in the course of the play that the wise leader is someone who can make strategic capital out of a realization that reliance on the facts is not a sufficient answer. Theseus discovers that the powerful man, if he is to retain his power, has to be at home not only with the facts but with the undifferentiated realm of uncertainty that lies beyond them. What might or could be is as important as what is. What we can't tie down is often of vital use to us.

Poets don't focus on facts. Poetry readers have to deal in something other than logic. A poem is made up of words, but it is also made up of other elements. Grappling with the relationship between these elements, immersing oneself in this mode of expression, can be of significant benefit to leaders and strategists, to executives facing infinite complexity and armed with finite resources in a changing world.

This proposition was fundamental to what I would be saying to my audience in Cambridge. It was fundamental to why I had already been approached by a secretive and unnameable government ministry in the United Kingdom to run a series of poetry sessions on a development program for their high-flyers. What they were seeking was a more open and flexible mind-set, referred to by some commentators as "open-mindedness." That mind-set has the very specific emphasis of an unusual tolerance for uncertainty, ambiguity, and complexity. Not just tolerance, but an ability to relish and capitalize on the very states that are often seen as inimical to effective strategic operation.

Generating the emphasis on this mind-set is an increasing awareness that what differentiates people's abilities is the breadth and subtlety not of the facts at their fingertips but of the skills and tools they can bring to the process of interpretation. The differentiating powers an individual brings to bear on a given situation are the crucial factor in determining how successfully that situation is handled. Information is, by definition, always incomplete and insufficient. You can never know all there is to know about a situation. To be successful, you have to be able to make the right decisions based on insufficient information. In order to do this you have to envision what is not—*yet.*

Could reading a poem or two achieve all this, a change in the mind-set? Of course not. But by helping executives begin to develop the skills and approaches needed to come to grips with the intricacies of a poem, by enabling them to begin to enjoy and profit from the circuitous journeys that reading poetry would necessarily take them on—by these means a beginning would have been made on the necessary rebalancing of their reliance on the factual. That is why I had decided that the title of the workshop I would hold in Downing College was Thinking Beyond the Facts.

You Reading This, Be Ready

by WILLIAM STAFFORD

Standing here, what do you want to remember?
How sunlight creeps along a shining floor?
What scent of old wood hovers, what softened
sound from outside fills the air?

Will you ever bring a better gift for the world
than the breathing respect that you carry
wherever you go right now? Are you waiting
for time to show you some better thoughts?

When you turn around, starting here, lift this
new glimpse that you found; carry into evening
all that you want from this day. This interval you spent
reading or hearing this, keep it for life—

What can anyone give you greater than now,
starting here, right in this room, when you turn around?

Feeling for the Light Switch

. . . there is the sound
Of all the atoms whirling round
That one can hear if one is wise

Thinking Beyond the Facts: Where Poetry Takes You

The best way to draw people into poetry is by working with a poem. I had decided to start with a poem about what poetry demands of you. Billy Collins's "Introduction to Poetry" sets out the basics.

Introduction to Poetry
by BILLY COLLINS

I ask them to take a poem
and hold it up to the light
like a color slide

or press an ear against its hive.

I say drop a mouse into a poem
and watch him probe his way out,

or walk inside the poem's room
and feel the walls for a light switch.

I want them to waterski
across the surface of a poem
waving at the author's name on the shore.

But all they want to do
is tie the poem to a chair with a rope
and torture a confession out of it.

They begin beating it with a hose
to find out what it really means.

I would get the group to talk about how many ways we're asked to look at a poem in these few lines, lines that—on the surface at least—are pleasingly simple. I'd done this already in a Knowledge Management forum at one of the UK's leading business schools. With an audience of around forty sitting at six tables, the constituent parts of the poem had divided up nicely, one for each table. Because the poem is divided into six metaphors: the color slide, the hive, the place where the mouse is, the room, the lake/sea, and the torture chamber. I asked the participants at each table to identify the metaphor and then come up with what the metaphor was suggesting a poem might demand of them when they read it. I had allowed fifteen minutes for this, but the discussions went on longer. I went round the tables listening in on the exchanges and putting in a question here and there when I felt the discussion needed to dig deeper. This is what the groups came up with.

Color Slide

A color slide only has meaning or communicates in any way when you take active steps to engage with it. If you don't hold it up to the light in an appropriate way, it stays dark and unavailable. And when you do get the light shining through it, you're looking at images, pictures, relationships between things in a spatial medium. You're employing one of your key senses, the sense of sight.

Hive

A hive is a world of its own within very specific boundaries. It's an ordered world with lots of intricate interrelationships. It's rather mysterious, with methods of communication as complex as the organization they serve. The sound of the hive is the sound of life itself in microcosm. Might there be an element of danger in putting one's ear so close to this engine of action and energy? Perhaps. In any case, you have to listen intently, and you aren't expecting to hear something in a language that's straightforward. Part of the means of communication is through the sense of hearing, but there's an element of humming, too, that intense activity, going right down into you through the bones in your head and neck, getting right down into your being.

Place Where the Mouse Is

The metaphor is inverted here. You don't engage with the poem, you enter it; it surrounds and encloses you. But what is it that you are entering? The poem is a world akin, perhaps (the image of the mouse suggests), to a maze, that "probe" bringing to mind the pointed nose of the rodent sniffing and seeking, heading into dead ends and snouting round blind corners, a process of trial and error, of experimentation, of investigating an unknown territory where all the senses are attuned to discovering a pathway, and when the pathway has finally been discovered there is a release into a wider, sought-after world.

The Room

The poem as a room builds on the image of the mouse in the maze. The reader is asked to enter the poem as if it were a space half known. We all know the general shape and disposition of "a room." It has walls (usually four), a floor, a ceiling, in general it has windows, and we expect furniture to be disposed in it in some relatively logical layout. In exploring this room, in the dark, the sense of touch is paramount. You have to make close contact with the walls, exploring a space that you're not certain of, risking, perhaps, bumping into things or tripping over something that lies unexpectedly in your way. So you take the room—and the poem—on trust while you feel around blindly for some means of illumination. You're not sure whether there is a light switch, but you hope you'll touch something that will enable you to make sense of what it is that surrounds you. You'll be able to see the constituent parts in relation to each other. You'll be able to identify elements that you didn't know were there.

The Lake/Sea

Activity is a key element here. Once again the need to engage with the poem in a wholehearted way is emphasized. The water skier isn't bogged down in investigative minutiae. What's proposed is swift, exciting, and demanding of poise and balance, of energy and a joyful pitching-in to the experience. A water skier is aware of the depths underneath her but rides the glittering immediacy of the surface waves. You need skill and a degree of fearlessness. You need the right conditions and someone who knows how to handle the boat that's towing you. You may fall as you negotiate a corner. The freedom and exhilaration of the experience is what's important.

And what about that waving at the author's name? Is it an acknowledgment, a friendly greeting, or a "look at me, aren't I doing well with this" gesture? It could be all or any of these things. They don't cancel one another out; they can all be true at the same time or at different times. Perhaps what the lines point to is that the poem becomes as much the reader's as the writer's. There it is, to explore and enjoy, a great new territory, depth and surface, a real part of the world to contend with.

Torture Chamber

What do torturers want to find out? The facts about something they believe the subject of their torture knows. In contrast to the delicacy of exploration suggested by the rest of the poem, these closing lines address the dulling and destruction of the senses rather than their opening-up. Concentrating on the extraction of facts alone is a brutal process. More than that, confessions are often made out of desperation; they may be misleading or bear little or no relation to any kind of truth.

So the final lines of the poem seem to be a warning, quite a stark warning, not to treat a poem as if it were the container of a single meaning, as if it followed the cause-and-effect rules of the factual and could in some way be reduced to something less, or something simpler, than the sum of its parts.

Poetry versus Business Think

I have been cheating, a little. Not all the points that I've raised in discussing Billy Collins's poem came from the Knowledge Management forum. They came from many discussions with many different groups. But what's important here is the *difference* in what poetry demands of you. Poetry demands a wholeness of response; all the senses must be employed, and employed nimbly and delicately. Reading a poem is not a singular enterprise of logical deduction. If you try to cut to the chase, the poem will elude you. If you seek closure, you will be disappointed. If you cannot handle ambiguity, you will be frustrated. If, like Socrates, you seek definition and delineation, you will go away empty-handed.

The week before the Downing workshop I'd done an Internet trawl of back topics in the *Harvard Business Review* and been struck by the ready currency of concepts such as "managing meaning" and "refining interpretive outlook." Strategists, leaders, and executives were gradually being given the choice, in the journal's pages, of doing something other than, and complementary to, increasing the facts at their fingertips. The emphasis was shifting onto developing *modes of interpretation* as a differentiating factor in the success or failure of an enterprise. It was clear that the utility and interest of what I was offering were placed at the point of intersection with concerns and issues that were already the subject of accelerating debate in the global business community.

I could approach the importance of this difference, and the role poetry can play in harnessing it, from any number of standpoints. Ivan Fonagy, a language theorist, had famously conducted an experiment that revealed poetry to be highly effective in preventing "automatic perception," that is, making assumptions about what things mean or are going to mean.

I could begin from George Lakoff and Mark Johnson's work on metaphor. The idea of a metaphor as an engine constantly in motion that charges and recharges itself is potent and had already been widely taken up by business theorists. It was an increasingly popular means among consultants and facilitators for generating added breadth to executive development initiatives.

But I wasn't going to take either of these approaches. I had already gone a considerable way to formulating my theory: *Poetry is a process, a mechanism, a unit of meaning, that operates differently from the kinds of units of meaning that usually inform business situations. It is in precisely its* difference *that the value of poetry lies for the business strategist.*

There were further significant linkages to be teased out before that theory could address the "so what?" factor to my clients'—and prospective readers'—satisfaction. So I stepped back and rehearsed my argument. This is how it went.

1. Reading poetry generates conceptual spaces that may be different from the spaces usually available to (business) strategists.
2. These spaces are different because they

   - are associative rather than causal
   - are imaginative rather than deductive
   - offer new ways of assessing relations between things
   - encourage a radical skepticism about the nature of "fact."

This formulation was beginning to make sense in terms of treating an area that directly overlapped the interests of my listeners and readers. The question that remained unanswered was: How can poetry (as opposed to novels or paintings or music or yoga or a host of other possible opportunities) foster the skills necessary to develop or access these spaces?

Billy Collins had already made the frame for answering this question. I synthesized and expanded the points "Introduction to Poetry" raises and focused them to address the needs of the executive audience. I came up with the list in table 1.

TABLE 1

The poem is	Which develops ability to
Multidimensional	• Detect different modes of meaning • Deal with ambiguity and uncertainty
Not offering closure Not based in a logical deductive mode	• Handle nonresolution • Make associative connections
Showing the ordinary as extraordinary	• Question givens • Raise awareness of complexity
Almost infinitely interpretable	• Consider other views • Recognize that "meaning" is unstable • Examine and revise current insights and perceptions
Operating at different levels of accessibility	• Detect weak as well as strong signals • Seek less obvious linkages
Full of coexistent complements and contradictions	• Time judgements carefully • Be aware that binary thinking is not enough
Drawing attention to human needs and motivations	• Make decisions in a more comprehensive context • Address ethical issues
Exploring emotional complexity	• Offer wholeness of response

The need to "recognize meaning as unstable" took on the aspect of a willful eccentricity as the cab wended its way through the narrow lanes of Cambridge, and round every corner there rose up before me the ancient certitudes of scholarship and grandeur embodied in the elegant architraves and mantels of the college buildings. Their angles of honey-colored stone seemed very sure of themselves. What boundaries are you crossing here? they whispered. Or maybe it was just the sneaky east wind you always get in Cambridge.

We were there, and the wrought iron gates swung open. The cabbie wound down the window and spoke to the porter. "Welcome to Downing," the porter said, and handed me my room key. The gates were now fully open. He waved us in.

✺ *Jim Desterland*

by HYAM PLUTZIK

As I was fishing off Pondy Point
Between the tides, the sea so still—
Only a whisper against the boat—
No other sound but the scream of a gull,
I heard the voice you will never hear
Filling the crannies of the air.

The doors swung open, the little doors,
The door, the hatch within the brain,
And like the bellowing of a ruin
The surf upon the thousand shores
Swept through me, and the thunder-noise
Of all the waves of all the seas.

The doors swung shut, the little doors,
The door, the hatch within the ear,
And I was fishing off Pondy Pier.
And all was as it was before,
With only the whisper of the swell
Against the boat, and the cry of a gull.

I draw a sight from tree to tree
Crossing this other from knoll to rock,
To mark the place. Into the sea
My line falls, with an empty hook,
Yet fools the world. So day and night
I crouch upon the thwarts and wait.

There is a roaring in the skies
The great globes make, and there is the sound
Of all the atoms whirling round
That one can hear if one is wise—
Wiser than most—if one has heard
The doors, the little doors swing wide.

My New Colleagues in The Strategy Institute

We are the music makers,
And we are the dreamers of dreams

Big Themes in Common

It is three years, almost to the day, before the Downing College workshop. I have been approached by one of the world leaders in business consultancy, The Boston Consulting Group. More specifically, I've been approached by BCG's Strategy Institute. The Strategy Institute is a kind of think tank, deliberately bringing together unlikely ideas with a view toward injecting new life into thinking about strategy. The almost academic respectability of the name reassures me. I have been asked to put together a proposal for a project that will explore the relationship between poetry and strategic thinking.

The project will center around the production of a book. But what kind of a book? Something bristling with tables, graphs, and executive summaries? A "ten ways to" kind of approach? A short, sharp text adding poetry to the executive's tool kit doesn't seem the least bit appropriate. Quick-fix tool kits, however popular on the shelves of the business books section of Waterstone's or Barnes & Noble, are not necessarily the stuff out of which organizations can be built to last.

It seems to me the project as a whole will have a dual aim. There will need to be finite skills development to enhance executive thinking. There will need to be leverage at that point in executive existence where public meets private. The book will need to speak to the moment when the man or woman with the large window overlooking the Thames or Park Avenue or Sydney Harbour Bridge and the large expanse of shiny desk in front of them, transmutes into the person who unlocks the car in late evening and looks, hardly recognizing, at the eyes in the driving mirror; or shoulders a briefcase as the crowds come upwards, and steps down into the Underground.

I have thought of a title already. It comes from Percy Bysshe Shelley. The quote it comes from goes like this.

> It is impossible to read the productions of our most celebrated writers . . . without being startled with the electric life which is there in their words. . . . They are the priests of an unapprehended inspiration, the mirrors of gigantic forms which futurity casts upon the present.

Shelley wrote that in the first half of the nineteenth century as part of something he called *A Philosophical View of Reform*. Could this be one of the reasons why poets aren't as important as they used to be? We have no bards employed by presidents or prime ministers. Are poets these days dissident voices in a world that has no room for dissidence? Maybe it's just like Socrates thought, that they somehow set about prising the lid off things, offering a potentially unpalatable alternative view?

The title I mooted was *Electric Life*. It would do as a working title. It was neat. It was catchy. The idea of the poet as prophet, a seer and visionary who can help the rest of us get beyond our limited view of what's what, that had traction. But the quote itself was unlikely to grab the attention of my readers in the long run.

And yet. And yet. Those "gigantic forms which futurity casts upon the present," aren't *they* of extreme relevance to the strategist? Don't *they* impact with shocking force and significance on the smallest everyday decision an executive makes?

Movers and Shakers: Poetry, Advertising, and The Boston Consulting Group

The strategy fellow of the Said Business School in Oxford is sitting next to me. We are at one of those college dinners where the candles flicker down at the end of the evening and the wood paneling of the ancient room shadows into the dark. I tell him about *Electric Life* and the BCG connection.

Sounds intriguing, he says, a very intriguing connection. But how will the movers and shakers in any of the top organizations react?

I share his wonder. But more than that, the phrase "movers and shakers," the common epithet for the real go-getters in an organization, has tweaked something in my memory—in my auditory memory, in fact—that locked-up part of my brain accustomed by quite a few years of reading and thinking about poems to listen, without my being aware of it, for echoes and patterns and tiny hints in the way things sound.

I locate the lines quite far on in a book I received as a prize one year in high school.

> We are the music makers,
> And we are the dreamers of dreams,
> Wandering by lone sea-breakers,
> And sitting by desolate streams;
> World-losers and world-forsakers,
> On whom the pale moon gleams:
> Yet we are the movers and shakers
> Of the world for ever, it seems.

Arthur O'Shaughnessy published his much-anthologized "Ode" in 1874, and the "we" he was talking about were poets. I wondered how "movers and shakers" could have made the transfer from this relatively undistinguished poem to the heart of business jargon. I wondered what has made the phrase live on at the heart of business speak when the poem has been dead for more than a hundred years.

Why has BCG's Strategy Institute chosen poetry specifically? The strategy fellow has asked me. You know, bearing in mind how the combination of arts and business is often seen as a soft option.

A consultancy like BCG, he has said (he's involved in writing a history of business consultancies, and BCG is one of his subjects), isn't going to have much truck with soft options.

There's a belief, I have said in reply, that over the past decade or so the discipline of strategy has often been reduced to a narrow tool box. The SI wants to enrich strategic thinking in order to help BCG clients discover more options. The idea is that maybe poetry can play a role in that.

We're in agreement that to have a high-profile company with its eye, inevitably, on the bottom line thinking about poetry is surprising. For a company with a reputation for demanding convincing answers to the "so what?" question to contemplate launching off on what John Keats called the "viewless wings of Poesy" borders on the astounding.

I guess, the strategy fellow has said, your first task will be to establish relevance.

And challenge, I say, the idea of an unbridgeable gap between poetry and business, the whole idea that they inhabit separate spheres.

To this end I pose myself a question: in what core business activity does poetry already play a crucial part?

The answer I come up with is advertising. In particular, two highly successful advertising campaigns from the late twentieth century come to mind.

Wonderbra for the Way You Are
and
Have a Break: Have a Kit Kat

Both of these advertisements make crucial use of elements borrowed from poetry. What are they?

- Rhyme
- Sound pattern devices
- Rhythm

Case Study: How Poetry Sells

Rhyme: Wonder**bra** for the Way You **Are**

The logic of the phrase is simple, its message that here is a bra for your kind of lifestyle, the lifestyle of the modern women. The secondary message is, here's a bra that's adjustable to suit you. All pretty straightforward. But something else is happening, too, in the rhyming of *bra* and *are*. The product, *bra*, is mapped by its obvious rhyme onto the idea of *are*. We read the words and we hear the additional sound message that this bra is somehow fundamental to our sense of self, our "are-ness." How we choose to engineer our body shape is, in a flash, rendered inextricable from our identity.

This advertisement is communicating quite skillfully through what the poet T. S. Eliot called "the auditory imagination." It's using a (poetic) technique outside the logic of the words it employs to appeal to a part of the consumer that receives information beyond the logical or analytical realm. Echoes and suggestions of meanings are being set up that resonate with far greater meanings than what the words are (logically) saying. The beyond-logic message goes something like this: *if you don't buy this bra, before long you may find out you're a nonwoman.*

Sound Pattern Devices: Have a Break: Have a Kit Kat

This jingle thrives on the idea that relaxation and the chocolate biscuit are inextricable. On the surface, it's a suggestion: when you have a break, why not have a Kit Kat? It also plays on a pun: the break as time off and break this biscuit in two before you eat it. It has two main (poetry) ways of giving depth and resonance to its suggestion. The words *break* and *Kit Kat* use the device poets call alliteration. The explosive *k* and *t*, repeated close together, invite us to hear the biscuit breaking, so nice and fresh and appetizing. And our mouths water, just like Pavlov's dogs'.

Rhythm

But the rhythm of the Kit Kat jingle provides even more than alliterative emphasis: it provides a kind of closure to the suggestion, turning it into a statement, a fait accompli of a stolen moment in a crowded workday. The rhythm goes: da-da-**DA**; da-da-**DA-DA**. Have a ***break***: Have a ***Kit Kat***. The double emphasis—***Kit Kat***—capping, so to speak, the single emphasis at the end of the first phrase is what gives closure, in this case a satisfying inevitability which generates precisely the ethos the text of the advertisement is pointing to. Associating *break* and *Kit Kat* is (your auditory imagination tells you, far beyond the logic of the words) the right, the inevitable, the only thing to do.

What Has Poetry Added?

The power of poetry has been added to the words of the advertisements to reach beyond those words and elicit a response that does not depend on logic or fact. The poetry aspect has reached into the customer's decision-making process to access nonlogical but highly decisive responses that affect the purchasing patterns of whole sectors of society.

If aspects of poetry can have this kind of effect on consumers, is it not reasonable to suppose that producers (in this case, business executives) may be able profitably to harness these characteristics of poetic utterance? That the poem, in its fully developed complexity, can reach farther into their thinking processes than can the logic of analysis, the ordinary mechanisms of cause and effect?

Where Business Meets Poetry

So far, I have established theme and usage as nodal points of intersection between poetry and business. What I'm left with is the question of issues, the idea that poetry addresses areas of existence quite different from those that business addresses. I set out the question to be answered: where do the issues that poetry deals with intersect the issues vital to executives and business practitioners?

There were some clear candidates: taking risks, making decisions, being a leader, and—maybe less obvious but certainly an ultratopical connection—making ethical choices. I came up with a list of poems a yard long, from ancient Greek to contemporary American. The issues they address are laid out in table 2.

Just about all the important, human topics that poetry addresses are also vital, in one way or another, to the issues that twenty-first-century executives and organizations are, or should be, concerning themselves with. But, while most thinking, responsible executives would nod their heads about the desirability of overlap on questions of despoliation (green politics, sustainable economies), accede to the need for equal opportunities, and express approbation for loyalty and brotherhood, what would concern

TABLE 2

Capitalism (evils of)	Risk
Capitalism (benefits of)	Authority
Money—avarice/greed	Insularity
Money—benevolent use of	Calculation
Work—in different cultures	Perception
Discrimination—racial, gender, etc.	Oppression
Trade	Exploitation
Decision making	Despoliation
Power	Indirection
Loyalty	Desire
Greed	Ambition
Leadership	Sacrifice
Opportunity	Production
Opportunism	Consumption
Competition	Technology
Education	War
Brotherhood	Peace

them in their everyday lives as businesspeople in a competitive environment would be their responsibility to shareholders and the accompanying exigencies of the bottom line.

Bill Gates and the Business-Poetry Connection

So thematic relevance, while it would be part of the "contract" the book would offer the executive reader—an invitation to step on unfamiliar yet in some ways shared-issue ground—could only be a first step.

If I could show that more than just a handful of closet practitioners had bridged the perceived gap between poetry and the business world, that would also act as a significant lever of interest.

I discover from a survey carried out by the Academy of American Poets that more than one-eighth of their members are employed in areas that are business related. They are in manufacturing, financial services, science, technology, and just plain business. They belong to a brotherhood of whom nearly 70 percent are university graduates and over two-thirds are daily Internet users. This indicates that there is a core constituency of business-focused people for whom poetry is an important part of life if not yet of their business life. I also discover from Tree Swenson, the president and executive director of the academy, the heartening (and surprising?) news that Bill Gates was one of the star poetry readers at the academy's last annual convention in New York City.

I'm deep into figuring out how I can get an interview with Bill Gates on the role he believes poetry plays in business thinking when two calls come. The first is to clarify who spoke at the academy's convention. The news is disappointing. I have misheard during a moment of transatlantic crackle. It was not Bill Gates who read, it was Henry Louis Gates, the scholar and critic. Almost before that information has time to settle, the second call comes, the call that will tell me whether the project goes forward or not.

I've half wondered if the whole thing will die a natural death. Isn't it too unusual? Too unlikely? But no. The offer comes to me then and there. Would I like to firm up the intention and arrange to meet in Munich first and later in the United States? The director of publications for The Strategy Institute, who put forward the original notion of the linkage, is a keen poetry aficionado and very well versed in contemporary American poetry. He asks if I know much about the American poet laureate Robert Pinsky. I don't, but I take some small comfort in the fact that I've met the Nobel laureate, Seamus Heaney, at a party or two.

I put the phone down. *Electric Life* has taken on its own life. The Boston Consulting Group has pledged a portion of itself and its budget to the pursuit of poetry.

I get that curious, tremulous sensation that tells me this is the beginning of something interesting. It's hard to describe the nature of the feeling, exactly. Something like the fear a tennis player gets, stepping onto Centre Court at Wimbledon. Something like a trader gets when interesting numbers start to jump onto the screen. Or like the chair of a company feels when it hits number-one market position for the first time.

❧ *Dirge*

by KENNETH FEARING

1-2-3 was the number he played but today the number came
    3-2-1;
    bought his Carbide at 30 and it went to 29; had the favourite
    at Bowie but the track was slow—

O, executive type, would you like to drive a floating power, knee-
    action silk-upholstered ix? Wed a Hollywood star? Shoot
    the course in 58? Draw to the Ace, King, Jack?
    O, fellow with a will who won't take no, watch out for three
    cigarettes on the same single match; O, democratic voter
    born in August under Mars, beware of liquidated rails—

Denouement to denouement, he took a personal pride in the
    certain, certain way he lived his own private life,
But nevertheless, they shut off his gas; nevertheless, the bank
    foreclosed; nevertheless, the landlord called; nevertheless
    the radio broke,
And twelve o'clock arrived just once too often,
    just the same he wore one grey tweed suit, bought one straw
    hat, drank one straight Scotch, walked one short step, took
    one long look, drew one deep breath,
    just one too many.

And wow he died as wow he lived,
    going whop to the office and blooie home to sleep and biff got
    married and bam had children and oof got fired,
    zowie did he live and zowie did he die,

With who the hell are you at the corner of his casket, and where
    the
    hell we going on the right hand silver knob, and who the hell
    cares
    walking second from the end with an American Beauty wreath
    from
    why the hell not,

Very much missed by the circulation staff of the *New York
    Evening Post*; deeply, deeply mourned by the B.M.T.,

Wham, Mr Roosevelt; pow, Sears Roebuck; awk, big dipper;
    bop, summer rain;
        bong, Mr, bong, Mr, bong, Mr, bong.

Sharpeners versus Levelers

...He went home as bold as he could be
with the swinging rainbow on his shoulder.

Can Reading Poems Make You Think Differently?

It made intuitive sense that successful executives and highly regarded lead-
ers would have a full complement of the qualities that were eventually to
become the right-hand column of my list of abilities a poem develops. But
I needed a stronger link if I was going to stand a chance of winning over
my understandably skeptical future readership. I found the stronger link
focused around the role of ambiguity in people's thinking processes. If you
can tolerate ambiguity, you will tend to have in your armory of thinking
strategies the ability to recognize, and the willingness to take up and
sharpen, nuance and difference. If you are not trained to handle ambiguity,
you will tend to adopt a strategy whereby you minimize differences and
level out shades of nuance. These are known in psychology as the cogni-
tive strategies of sharpener versus leveler. Here are some points of com-
parison between the two.

The leveler:

- Is anxious to categorize sensations
- Is unwilling to give up a category once it has been established
- Levels (suppresses) differences and emphasizes similarities
- Seeks perceptual stability
- Finds the unique, unclassifiable sensation particularly offensive

The sharpener, on the other hand:

- Tolerates anomalies
- Is ready to think and perform symbolically
- May seek out ambiguity and variability of classification
- Keeps in mind, simultaneously, various aspects of a whole
- Abstracts common properties
- Plans ideationally
- Is ready to assume an attitude toward "the merely possible"

One version of the cognitive strategies of the sharpener was described by the poet John Keats more than 140 years ago as the quality

> which Shakespeare possessed so enormously. I mean *Negative Capability*, that is when man is capable of being in uncertainties, Mysteries, doubts, without any irritable reaching after fact & reason.

The idea of the poet being a sharpener rather than a leveler was one important link. But did any research suggest that poetry *readers* might fall into the sharpener rather than the leveler category? The irony of looking for "facts" to support a hypothesis about the need to think beyond them was not lost on me.

I found two small studies that were beginning to open up the avenues of connection that could create in my audience a context of relevance, a ground for applicability. The first is recounted by the cognitive and literary theorist Reuven Tsur, who describes some experiments he undertook in the course of developing his research in cognitive poetics. There were two basic questions. What difference does how you're *trained* to think make to whether you use sharpener or leveler strategies and does having been trained to work with poems enable you to use different thinking strategies than if you were not?

Working with groups of literary professionals and students, balanced by control groups of non-literary-trained participants, Tsur and his colleagues sought to determine variations in cognitive strategy when the subjects were confronted with different versions of a poetry text, altered to display subtle variations of emphasis and patterning. Participants had to evaluate the different versions considering various criteria on a seven-point scale, for example, open-closed, simple-complex, static-dynamic, emotional-unemotional, or interesting-boring. This experiment did not seek to evaluate personality. It sought to tease out the thinking strategies adopted *in this instance*.

While the responses from both groups generally fell within the same region of the scale, the differences perceived between the versions of the poems were markedly greater in the literary-trained participants.

These results indicated that the nonliterary participants tended to level out the differences between the versions that confronted them. Those with literary training were able to perceive subtle differences that amounted to a strong sense of the variations they were presented with.

We can say that the groups that had not been exposed to literary training lacked a set of skills those with literary training had access to or at least were less willing to use those skills when faced with a complex language entity whose meaning was not obvious. Those with literary training tended to exhibit sharpener characteristics when faced with the shifting ambiguities and complexities of the poems, whereas those without literary training exhibited leveler characteristics, apparently unwilling or unable to pick up nuance or work with ambiguity as fully or effectively. Rather than exploring the meanings of what confronted them, they appeared to want to contain their exploration to fit the kind of thinking space that was readily to hand in their existing repertoire of thinking skills.

More Questions, Different Hypotheses

The second piece of evidence came out of a study at Stanford University that focused on what kinds of thinking skills are utilized in approaching poems and stories. Does one make you think in a way that is different from the other? Do experienced readers respond differently from inexperienced ones?

In a series of monitored discussion groups, verbal responses were evaluated in terms of the variety and number of reasoning operations used. The study found that poems caused the reader to generate almost twice as many alternative meanings within a discussion than did stories (4.6 to 2.8 per communication unit). Poems also caused the readers to formulate considerably more alternative hypotheses about overall meaning than did stories (2.3 to 1.6).

Further aspects of the experiment compared freshmen (with little training in reading poems) to graduates (greater skill training in reading poems).

The results showed that the experienced readers made greater use of self-monitoring strategies to help guide and evaluate the efficacy of their thinking processes. Poetry generated twice as much self-monitoring as did stories (2.5 to 1.2).

While a small, single study can never be more than a pointer, all this seems to suggest that the more skills development you have in reading poems the more facility you will have in what could be termed expansive rather than contractive thinking, the open-ended or appositional approach of the sharpener rather than the quick closure, propositional, either/or strategy of the leveler.

What the Sharpener Sees That the Leveler Doesn't

I decided to try my own small experiment with an engineer who had been reading poems for a while and a lawyer who hadn't. They both had the ambition to become writers and were hoping to sign up for one of my undergraduate courses. The engineer was from South America, in his thirties, outgoing and very much the kind of man who takes up and engages with everything that comes his way. The lawyer was English, a few years older, and had struck me in an interview as wanting everything to be pretty definite and clear-cut. I gave them the following poem and asked them to tell me what they made of it.

Case Study: What the Lawyer and Engineer Saw

The Road Not Taken
by ROBERT FROST

Two roads diverged in a yellow wood
And sorry I could not travel both
And be one traveler, long I stood
And looked down one as far as I could
To where it bent in the undergrowth;
Then took the other, as just as fair,
And having perhaps the better claim
Because it was grassy and wanted wear;
Though as for that the passing there
Had worn them really about the same,
And both that morning equally lay
In leaves no step had trodden black.
Oh, I kept the first for another day!

Yet knowing how way leads on to way,
I doubted if I should ever come back.
I shall be telling this with a sigh
Somewhere ages and ages hence:
Two roads diverged in a wood, and I—
I took the one less travelled by,
And that has made all the difference.

Here are their responses.

The Lawyer

The poem is about a man who has been faced with a decision about which path to take and is remembering it and considering its implications some time afterward. He's a bit indecisive and seems unsure how things really were. He might even be a bit silly. First of all he says one path was less traveled than the other; then he says they were about the same. Then he says neither looks traveled at all—no one has trodden them.

He's also confused about the possibilities open to him. He talks about taking the one path later but follows it up by saying he doubted he would. He's a bit of a woolly thinker all in all.

The poem seems to go on rather a long time about something that's fairly straightforward. He took the road he thought was less traveled; it was a difficult decision at the time, but now he sees that it's made a decisive and positive difference in his life.

The Engineer

I thought this was a straightforward poem, but the more I read it the less I thought it could be. This guy is in a mess. His thinking is all over the place. Was the path less trodden or wasn't it? He doesn't know. He didn't know then, but he had to take one. He thought the evidence of his eyes meant one thing, then he thought it meant another. His perception of the facts was variable. There wasn't enough data to go on. That's a central thing the poem is about.

And the poem isn't only about making a decision. It's about the effect decisions have on you. They change you. He's a different man after taking the second path. He can never be the man that taking the first path would have made him. It's an important decision in two ways: (1) it decided an important life direction, set up a chain of events; and (2) it is part of what divides what he is from what he might have been.

I feel sorry for the man. Although he is a bit sorry for himself, a bit self-dramatizing, with that "I—I" business, I can feel his dilemma. There's something about youth and age here. The poem seems to be divided into two halves.

In the first half, the part that concentrates on the original decision moment, the lines mostly end with strong, active words: *stood, growth, claim*. It's like back then he had a strong drive to things and looked to their possibilities. He seems pretty optimistic really. I get that from the word *fair*, how it makes me think of light, justice, and good fortune all rolled into one. The second half is different. It's more passive. The word *lay* is the first of a lot of nonactive words (*day, way, by, I*), and then *sigh*, although it's a doing word, is about doing of the most unvibrant kind. A sigh. That's a really passive thing to utter.

There's a kind of off-keyness, too, about the way the poem makes me feel. It goes along in a jingly kind of way, di-dah, di-dah, di-dah, di-dah. But then there are all kinds of undercurrents. I didn't get them when I first read it. But then I read it out loud, and I could hear how the middle sounds were hissing, the *s* sounds of *grass* and *pass*, but then you get *black* and *back*, they're really hard, they interrupt, those *k*s especially. And they echo each other, *black* is just *back* repeated, but with an extra *l*. It's all about stopping and regressing, that bit. What you see at the beginning is *yellow*, the autumn gold kind of color; but then black is a stage of decay much further on than the yellow; and *back*, OK, it's about returning, but it also makes you think of retreating or giving up.

So I think a lot of complicated things are going on here. It's like you have to think out in ever increasing circles. It's not about one thing; it's about lots of things. And they're all there, depending on each other. It's like balancing plates in the air.

Strategy, Theory, and Factual Information

What do these implications that reading poetry encourages more expansive ways of thinking amount to?

It seemed that the hub of the matter lay in what the business executive or strategic thinker or policy maker has to do in turning "facts" into usable material out of which decisions arise that contribute to economic and organizational success. I came up with the following formulation.

> Strategic thinking depends on the generation of a provisional theory of movement from somewhere to somewhere that accommodates the various

complex elements of a given but generally opaque and unstable (strategic) situation. Many of these elements come in the form of fact or a distillation of fact into factual analysis. The facts need to be tested against a shifting set of hypotheses that themselves have to be generated from the perceived relationship between fact and situation and between situation and the wider context or constituency within which the strategy is being formulated. The operation is happening on two distinct levels: the level of data (facts) and the level of theory (strategy).

In my research I picked up a quote from J. J. C. Smart about the kinetic theory of gases.

> Roughly speaking, we may say that within a theory or within the *description* of fact we are on one level of language; but when we step from the level of theory to the level of fact or vice versa, we are in a region where . . . the *logical* relations of implication and contradiction do not strictly apply.[1]

The implication here is that facts belong to one order of thinking, conceptualization into something usable requires entry to another order of thinking that exists above and beyond the facts being utilized.

I located two statements from recent articles in the *Harvard Business Review* that had a direct bearing on the distinctions I was developing.

1. [Recent research has shown that] "The effective way to improve the performance of a company is to invest in *how leaders shape their interpretive outlooks.*"
2. "While factual rigor, up to a point, is extremely important, there comes a moment where the leader's task is, arguably, more about managing ambiguity than honing the accuracy of his knowledge about the business environment."

The matter of what is selected, how it is viewed in relation to both what is and is not selected, and how selected and unselected material is viewed in terms of itself and relevant factors outside itself in past, present, and future—in short, the power to originate alternative hypotheses and provisionally reconcile potentially conflicting goals and responsibilities—is centrally instrumental in the interpretive process that transmutes fact into theory and data into a viable statement of strategic intent.

But how effective in all this is the person who relies, more or less, on "factualist" thinking strategies? How much *more* effective would the person be who has, at her or his disposal, as part of the ordinary recourse with which s/he meets the world, that very "negative capability"—the distinguishing feature of sharpeners—of which John Keats spoke?

We are still the inheritors of F. W. Taylor's theories of scientific management, which were carried forward into the widespread time-and-motion approaches of the 1940s and 1950s. These approaches were based on strictly applied conceptions of rationality, and their influence extended late into the twentieth century when texts such as Charles Kepner and Benjamin Tregoe's *The New Rational Manager* were still arguing that a refinement of cause and effect thinking is the main differentiater in a successful strategy.

Isn't it the case that the people who reached the top were often those who were best at deploying factualist cognitive devices? Did people who had nonfactualist inclinations or tendencies perhaps do their best to conceal them?

An anecdote from one of the most powerful men in the arts in the United States will serve as an exemplar.

Dana Gioia and the Jell-O Success Story

Dana Gioia, chair of the National Endowment for the Arts, has been talking to me for nearly an hour in his high-ceilinged office in Washington, DC, about poetry and business. Gioia has a highly successful business career behind him and has written one of the most influential books on poetry to be published in recent years. His *Can Poetry Matter?* has a section titled "Poetry and Business." It focuses on how many poets have had business careers and what kind of pay-off there might be. Wallace Stevens, T. S. Eliot, the list is extensive. His own experience as a poet in business is important. He attributes his success as the marketing director of General Foods largely to the thinking abilities he brought to the situation. He believes his approach, back in the 1980s, was radically different from the more common approach of the factualists. "I turned around Jell-O from a seven-million-dollar loss," he says, "to a climbing twenty-million-dollar profit venture. How did it happen? I looked at things differently. I made associative connections. I thought around and beyond and through the data that confronted me."

More precisely, Gioia helped turn Jell-O making from a rather lengthy chore to a fun activity, making appealing shapes, that any mother could undertake with her children. In his team's introduction of Jell-O Jigglers,

Gioia also increased usage of the Jell-O product by introducing a swifter setting time. He credits this imaginative engagement with the world of the modern mother to his ability to think creatively. It is perhaps no coincidence that during the development of this strategy for rescuing Jell-O his evenings were devoted to poetry.

It's hot and steamy in Washington and the fan on the ceiling goes round and round, casting a moving shadow on the book-lined walls, the quiet amplitude of the chairs and tables.

"But you know what?" he says. "I kept it secret for a long time, my writing poetry. And then a piece came out in the *New Yorker*. I'd won a prize for a poem, and the news got around. My boss, who was the CEO of General Foods, called me into his office. He was one of the old style CEOs, a real tough guy. I went into this office, and he was smoking a cheroot like always. He kept me standing for a minute then signaled me to sit down.

"What's this I hear?" he said. "What's this I've been hearing? I read about it, Dana. Tell me. Is it true? Is it true you're a poet?"

"I'm afraid it is, sir," I said.

I tell you, he gave me that look he was famous for and spat the cheroot out there on the ashtray and said, "*Shit!*"

Dana Gioia's CEO would not have taken kindly to a situation where "the logical relations of implication and contradiction do not strictly apply." He might well have spat out his cheroot and uttered the familiar expletive. But for the twenty-first-century business executive faced with the arduous task of turning a mass of data into a theory or strategy that will differentiate his or her company from all the others trying to do likewise, the ability to "assume an attitude toward 'the merely possible,'" is vitally relevant. It's a part of being able to envision "what is not—*yet*."

✑ *Legend*

by JUDITH WRIGHT

The blacksmith's boy went out with a rifle
and a black dog running behind.
Cobwebs snatched at his feet,
rivers hindered him,
thorn-branches caught at his eyes to make him blind
and the sky turned into an unlucky opal,
but he didn't mind,
I can break branches, I can swim rivers, I can stare out any
    spider I meet,
said he to his dog and his rifle.

The blacksmith's boy went over the paddocks
with his old black hat on his head.
Mountains jumped in his way,
rocks rolled down on him,
and the old crow cried, "You'll soon be dead."
And the rain came down like mattocks.
But he only said
I can climb mountains, I can dodge rocks, I can shoot an old
    crow any day,
and he went on over the paddocks.

When he came to the end of the day the sun began falling.
Up came the night ready to swallow him,
like the barrel of a gun,
like an old black hat
like a black dog hungry to follow him.
Then the pigeon, the magpie and the dove began wailing
and the grass lay down to pillow him.
His rifle broke, his hat blew away and his dog was gone
and the sun was falling.

But in front of the night the rainbow stood on the mountain,
just as his heart foretold.
He ran like a hare,
he climbed like a fox:
he caught it in his hands, the colours and the cold—
like a bar of ice, like the column of a fountain,

like a ring of gold.
The pigeon, the magpie and the dove flew up to stare,
and the grass stood up again on the mountain.

The blacksmith's boy hung the rainbow on his shoulder
instead of his broken gun.
Lizards ran out to see,
snakes made way for him,
and the rainbow shone as brightly as the sun.
All the world said, Nobody is braver, nobody is bolder,
nobody else has done
anything equal to it. He went home as bold as he could be
with the swinging rainbow on his shoulder.

The Case of the Strange-Looking Bird That Landed on My Windowsill

Nothing has changed since I began.
My eye has permitted no change.
I am going to keep things like this.

Rational Thinking and Wrong Decisions

There's an old Sufi tale about the bird that landed on the windowsill. It's common currency among certain practitioners of complexity theory, and I've just read it again.

The Sufi tells how a man is looking out of his window and a vulture that's been circling around comes down and lands on it. They look at each other, and the man says to himself, "That's a strange-looking bird. I wonder what it's doing here?"

And then he determines that it looks so strange he'd better make it look more like a real bird. All those raggedy feathers! They can't be necessary. And that great hump at the back, it's just so much baggage. And no bird could really need the excess weight of that enormous beak.

So he clips and tidies, and the bird looks, in many respects, more "birdlike."

The only trouble, of course, is that it can no longer fly.

It's in the Sufi's tale that I find one of the points of applicability that I'm looking for. Thinking in a straight line—or not. Thinking rationally, logically, deductively—or thinking some other way. How to apply the difference? What are the effects of it?

The Sufi hasn't done anything wrong, at least not according to the laws of logic. He "knows" that a bird needs certain attributes to do certain things, and his take is that the vulture doesn't have those attributes. So he sets out to impart to the vulture the attributes experience tells him will lead to the achievement of the well-known bird-goals of flight and so on. Here is the leveler strategy put into action. Here the results of its inappropriate use start to become clear.

This tale is used in training sessions by complexity consultants and a whole raft of people bent on trying to encourage diversity and flexibility in the way businesspeople think. You've got to think through things not around things or around things not through things, one or the other. If the Sufi's tale is widely used and accepted, what does it do to jog, or nudge, or free up, or improve "business thinking"?

The Sufi's tale is a parable that says, "Is the way you look at things too uncomplicated? Are you blinkered? Are you stuck in a thought rut?" You can take the lesson and run with it, relatively pleased that you're not (usually) as stupid as the Sufi's man. The unequivocal nature of the message is consoling. The man is a narrow-minded bigot. Or if he's not that then he's seriously deluded. You're not a bit like that, are you? Oh no, certainly not. You've heard the warning, and you'll heed it. You'll take care in the future not to be one bit like that Sufi's man, thank-you.

But how? Once you've nodded sagely and gone on your way, what then? The Sufi's tale has planted an idea, issued a warning. But what has it done to give you a skill that can make you do things differently from the man in the tale?

Hawk versus Vulture: How Poems Make You Think

I decided to investigate how a poet thinks about birdness. I couldn't find any poems about vultures; the nearest I could come up with was this one by Ted Hughes.

Hawk Roosting
by TED HUGHES

I sit in the top of the wood, my eyes closed.
Inaction, no falsifying dream
Between my hooked head and hooked feet:
Or in sleep rehearse perfect kills and eat.

The convenience of the high trees!
The air's buoyancy and the sun's ray
Are of advantage to me;
And the earth's face upward for my inspection.

My feet are locked upon the rough bark.
It took the whole of Creation
To produce my foot, my each feather:
Now I hold Creation in my foot

Or fly up, and revolve it all slowly—
I kill where I please because it is all mine.
There is no sophistry in my body:
My manners are tearing off heads—

The allotment of death.
For the one path of my flight is direct
Through the bones of the living.
No arguments assert my right:

The sun is behind me.
Nothing has changed since I began.
My eye has permitted no change.
I am going to keep things like this.

How does the poem do things differently—and more—than the Sufi's tale in developing and encouraging new ways to think? It's quite a complicated poem; I always read it twice. I read it out loud, too, or get someone else to read it to me. That way how it sounds gets into my head. It's not just words on a page; it takes on a kind of resonance, and I can see the hawk up there with the world laid out before him. More than that, I *am* the hawk for the space of these lines. It's quite an experience.

In what ways, though, might that experience encourage those shifts in thinking capacity that I've suggested? How might the poem bring about, more completely than the Sufi's tale, a questioning of givens, a raised awareness of complexity, an expanded context for the consideration of issues?

There are four main areas where I found the reading of "Hawk Roosting" had significantly more impact on thinking capacity than did the Sufi's tale.

1. Testing viewpoints

   - In the Sufi's tale the man meets the bird on his own home ground, not the bird's. "How do I think a bird should be, for the things I believe a bird should do?" is the question.

- The poem says "How does a bird feel? Look at things? What's it like to be in the bird's territory? Is it like that? I hadn't thought about it that way." So I have to enter, not just hear about, the complexity of the situation. I have to apprehend fully, rather than just contemplate, the other, potentially alien view.

2. Seeing power as relative

  - In the Sufi's tale the man takes his own power for granted and exercises it. Looks wrong? I'll clip it. This is my jurisdiction. It's as simple as that.
  - The poem looks at the power of the bird in its terms: "I kill where I please because it is all mine." Questions of jurisdiction, territory, and legitimacy jump out at you. Is that how I act? How my boss acts? How my government acts? Is it how people *should* act?

3. Questioning validity

  - The message of the Sufi's tale is a statement, unequivocal. We can take it more or less passively and sit back. OK, aha, yes, I won't be that stupid in the future—if I ever have been in the past.
  - The poem tries out, makes suggestions, compares things. There's no single statement in it: bird-power—yes; but how valid? "Nothing has changed since I began"—not in nature, maybe, but the balance of power between man and nature has changed radically. "My eye has permitted no change. / I am going to keep things like this." The statement pulls you up in its monumental arrogance, its grandiose assertion. *Who is this bird kidding?* might be a reaction. But hang on. Haven't we heard that before? What's that an echo of? The voice of the dictator? The power-freak? The megalomaniac? The out-of-control CEO? The world leader? The fundamentalist? "For the one path of my flight is direct / Through the bones of the living." It is the proud (or mad?) assertion of the predator/hunter—but doomed? Doomed, surely? The bird voice says "no falsifying dream," but the dream of absolute power itself is false? What is the fate—past and present—of dictators, madmen, visionaries—or just plain leaders—who thought this way?

4. Making complex comparisons

  - The Sufi's tale—a kind of parable—presents us with an easy choice. It makes us think, but the thought is single, uncomplicated. It says "think before you act" and "don't get stuck in a rut of usual thinking." But it doesn't say how to think or what to think about.
  - The poem says stop and think. This power thing is pretty complicated. Look at it from one view. Look at it from another. Think about the dif-

ferent elements that make up power in a given moment, a given situation. Think about how we kid ourselves about power. Think about how the high and mighty don't see that the fall from grace is imminent. Think about how the unbridled exercise of power falls like a shadow ("with the sun behind it") over us all.

Negative Capability: How the Good Leader Makes Decisions

The Kit Kat and Wonderbra formats show that advertising recognizes the power of a "beyond realm" in how consumers make the choices they do. I decide to explore the role this beyond realm can have in how executives make decisions.

Good leaders, my research tells me, are those who make consistently good decisions. They can make them even in the face of unreliable facts.

This was where a significant payoff for my readers was lurking. I found it laid out and elucidated in the influential material of the neuroscientist Antonio Damasio.

Damasio describes in his book *Descartes' Error* how his patient, a man named Elliot, suffered brain damage to an upper right (emotion-holding) section of his skull. He could still function with a high degree of normality, scoring well in activities that tested his ability to make estimates on the basis of incomplete knowledge, his facility for changing his mental set, in short, the standard tests of "rationality." Even his personality tests proved within the normal range. And yet Elliot was unable to perform one function crucial to human life: he was unable to make decisions. On the occasions when he *did* choose between the options confronting him, his choices were, by any standard, wildly inappropriate and counterproductive to the task at hand.

When Elliot drove on an icy road, for example, the emotions associated with "risk" and all the nuances of response, the myriad tiny adjustments you would usually make to accommodate your judgment of conditions, possibilities, and reactions, were absent. So Elliot was unable to formulate a way of handling himself and his car that took into account ideas of: "skid," "accident," "death," or "mortal danger." With a large part of his emotional component nullified by the accident, Elliot was unable to function effectively in the world.

This is how Damasio sums it up.

There appears to be a collection of systems in the human brain consistently dedicated to the goal-oriented process we call reasoning and to the response selection we call decision making. . . . *This same collection of systems is also involved in emotion and feeling.*

Making decisions is logical *and* illogical. Those "golden guts" executives who pick up the weak signals, they have cornered the market in harnessing the two.

But this took me back right to the beginning. What Socrates was worried about in the poets is now seen as indispensable to effective decision making.

> [T]he lyric poets are not in their right mind when they are composing their beautiful strains: but when falling under the power of music and metre they are inspired and possessed. . . . [T]here is no invention in [the poet] until he has been inspired and is out of his senses, and the mind is no longer in him.[1]

I could just see the headline: "Damasio Rehabilitates the Poets: Socrates Only Got Half the Picture, Big News for the Business Executive."

Maybe. How it would work in practice was another thing.

Where Poems Take You: Out of Sight, Not Out of Mind

"The place Damasio identifies as being vital in making decisions is the place reading a poem causes you to enter" or—I needed to qualify this—"the place reading a poem causes you to go *when you really come to grips with it.*"

There is, at least, an equivalent in psychology to the place Elliot, with his emotional capacity disabled, couldn't reach: the place that had been destroyed in his head, that lies beyond yet is a vital complement to, rational analysis. This realm is broadly comparable to the realm sometimes known in psychology as the *precategorical*.[2] This realm informs our ability to appraise, adapt, filter, and orient ourselves in the complexities of the world with which we find ourselves surrounded at every instant. This precategorical realm isn't one we can get to by will. It's diffuse, and, by definition, if its contents haven't been categorized it isn't susceptible to being tied down by language.

The categorical realm, on the other hand, is where much of our everyday thinking—the thinking we *know* we do—operates. Within it we deduce, we rationalize, we propose, we decide how long it will take us to get to the train station and which is the best route at rush hour. You can get at the categorical part of your brain by willing yourself into it. I *must* make this decision. What are the facts I have at my fingertips and how can I analyze them? What do I think will be the outcomes of actions (a) or (b)?

In the precategorical realm things work differently. If you're dealing with a knotty problem that you can't seem to solve and you go to bed and wake up the next morning and think, I've got it! then chances are that rest from what Keats called the "irritable reaching after fact & reason" has allowed you into the diffuse yet vital space of the precategorical. And that was where you found your answer: in what you "felt" about things but didn't know, and had to wait for, and couldn't just make a decision to access it.

Ideas, as far as most business thinkers are concerned, find expression through language. If charts and graphs and tables are used, they still have to be augmented by language explanation. The precategorical, the realm beyond logic, is also beyond language; *logos*—the Greek for "word"—does not apply here. Something else does, a something that hovers behind or outside or beyond the outer edges of what language does for you. Reading a poem can move you toward that realm, because a poem is a vehicle that uses language to get beyond language. It's a meaning in motion that inhabits both logical and nonlogical realms.

ᐱᕈ *Ars Poetica*

by ARCHIBALD MACLEISH

A poem should be palpable and mute
As a globed fruit

Dumb
As old medallions to the thumb

Silent as the sleeve-worn stone
Of casement ledges where the moss has grown—

A poem should be wordless
As the flight of birds

A poem should be motionless in time
As the moon climbs

Leaving, as the moon releases
Twig by twig the night-entangled trees,

Leaving, as the moon behind the winter leaves,
Memory by memory the mind—

A poem should be motionless in time
As the moon climbs

A poem should be equal to:
Not true

For all the history of grief
An empty doorway and a maple leaf

For love
The leaning grasses and two lights above the sea—

A poem should not mean
But be

Traveling through the Dark

You are neither here nor there,
A hurry through which known and strange things pass

Where Decisions Happen

I've got this far and set out a formal statement of my hypothesis: *poems bridge the gap between knowing and perceiving because they use the highly differentiated, logic-driven structures of language to point to the undifferentiated arena where emotion holds sway. Poems put down their roots in the no-man's-land between thinking and feeling, the borderland where logic shades into the nonlogical, where a world defined and delineated by language gives way to the more diffuse territory of what psychologists sometimes call "the feeling state."*

Three strands make up this bold, if unpalatably dull, theoretical statement.

1. Thinking is a more complex process than we give it credit for.
2. Thinking contains rational and nonrational elements. Making effective decisions depends on accessing both.
3. Poetry brings together these rational and nonrational elements more clearly and intensely than other modes of expression.

There are two further elements specific to establishing the poetry-business connection.

4. Reading poetry can encourage the play between the rational and nonrational processes.

5. This improved confluence enhances your decision-making abilities and therefore enables you to operate more fully and effectively in a complex, decision-led world.

To see how all this works, I went to a poem that casts light on my hypothesis: Seamus Heaney's "Postscript." I also went back to what the ancient world feared: the idea that a poem represents much more than it narrates.

Postscript

by SEAMUS HEANEY

And some time make the time to drive out west
Into County Clare, along the flaggy shore,
In September or October when the wind
And the light are working off each other
So that the ocean on one side is wild
With foam and glitter, and inland among stones
The surface of a slate-grey lake is lit
By the earthed lightning of a flock of swans,
Their feathers roughed and ruffling, white on white,
Their fully grown headstrong-looking heads
Tucked or cresting or busy underwater.
Useless to think you'll park and capture it
More thoroughly. You are neither here nor there,
A hurry through which known and strange things pass
As big soft buffetings come at the car sideways
And catch the heart off guard and blow it open.

I discussed with myself how reading the poem might cause you to have to move between different realms of the thinking process.

What's the paraphrase of this, that is, the "story"? What's there, logically, in everyday language?

If I were you, I'd drive out to the coast sometime. Why not try autumn? You'll see some amazing sights there, it's pretty magical, and sometimes it can really have an effect on you.

Is the effect of the journey positive or negative?

Negative—according to the story. If you take that journey, you end up severely dislocated, "neither here nor there," reduced from the logical, in-control human who can "make the time to drive out west" to the mere abstract quality of "a hurry." It's a journey from active to passive. Those "buffetings" bring about the final destruction of the in-control human being; they "catch the heart off guard and blow it open."

But is that what the poem really says?

No. Instead of negativity and fear, the poem creates a strong feeling of excitement, anticipation, or joy.

How does this happen?

The story told by the logic of language is only part of the poem. There's a kind of heat being generated by the friction between what the poem *says* (language) and what it *means* (something beyond the language).

But what's in it beyond language?

The poem isn't a story; it's more like a song or an incantation. This is because it relies on something other than logic to make its meanings.

What does it rely on?

Things called its formal qualities.

What are they?

Rhythm (meter or measure are other ways of putting it)

Images, metaphors

Rhyme, sound patterns

Shape, layout, emphasis

What combination of these falls where

How do you tune in to these formal qualities?

By listening, looking, feeling, imagining. And by reading poems.

Why reading poems?

Because (tautological argument) reading poetry improves the play between the rational and nonrational parts of your thinking mind.

Thinking through Your Ears

How does what we hear have a different meaning from what we see? How is dislocation and destruction (in the logic) turned into excitement, energy, and "renewal" in the poem overall? The poem employs language, in some way, to speak beyond itself and patterns sound so that we turn it into meaning through that part of our thinking that we might loosely call the feeling state.

Rhythm, meter, or measure is central to how this happens. Here is how the rhythms work in "Postscript" (what's referred to technically as how it scans).

There's a leisurely start, a kind of base rhythm, of five beats to the line.

And *some* time *make* the *time* to *drive* out *west*
Into *Coun*ty *Clare*, a*long* the *flag*gy *shore*,
In Sep*tem*ber *or* Oc*to*ber *when* the *wind*

Then the poem accelerates into an eleven-line sentence in which words and pictures seem to stumble over each other, clauses are heaped up, and images jostle for our attention. No emotion is named. "Wild" suggests, but doesn't pin down, a state of generalized unrest or excitement that starts to take over. The regularity is taken up again in "Their *fea*thers *roughed* and *ruff*ling, *white* on *white*," whereas all the other lines set out to wrong-foot you in some way, playing about with the five-beat rhythm, pretending this is the rhythm they have in mind but veering away from it at the last minute.

There's a kind of lilt in the last part of line 6 ("*in-land* a*mong stones*") that operates as a minicrescendo, the crest of a sound wave carrying us over into the next wavelike line ("The *sur*face of a *slate-grey lake* is *lit*"), which in turn deposits us foursquare on "By the earthed lightning of a flock of swans," smack in the spatial center of the poem (line 8 of 16).

That central line scans "*By* the *earthed light*ning of a *flock* of *swans*." It's a powerful metaphor that capitalizes on the conjunction of two concepts, expressed as an image, that we'd usually see as being quite separate. In terms of the logic of the poem, that center is a disintegrative one. Lightning splits apart, destroys, annihilates. But the *feeling* of the poem, which the image plays a central part in creating, points you toward the other aspect of lightning, the power surge of sheer energy that unites earth and heaven in a single, reconciliatory spasm of illumination. And these two paradoxical possibilities are bound up with the beautiful, evocative zigzag shape of swans flying, which draws together the acute angle of lightning and the peace and order of the ascending birds.

The rhythm generates unrest just out of sight through the auditory imagination that T. S. Eliot referred to. Meaning is coming to you here through your ears. Just as surely as drumbeats in the jungle pass news between remote communities, so the pattern of emphasis, the rise and fall, the stress and unstress of the sounds of the poem, make up a meaning that exists alongside the categorizing function of the words that compose it.

The poem is requiring you to modify, quite drastically, how you work out what something means. By its very nature, the poem is throwing things up that delay the pinning down you'd usually do quite swiftly. It's causing you to consult things you can't get at by rational deduction. It's encouraging you to access what lies outside logic and words in the realm of response by feeling. To come to grips with what the poem is doing, you have to be able to move readily between logic and nonlogic, abandoning neither, utilizing both. This ability is the essence of "poetic competence."

Cambridge Again: The Power of Poetic Competence

Back in Cambridge, three years after the launch of the project, which is where this tale started.

The Scene: Downing College, a high-ceilinged room with full-length windows all along one wall. The windows look west, out over stone steps that lead down to a well-manicured lawn with a small fountain just in the middle of it. The sun isn't setting yet, but the light tells you it's evening, the beginning of one of those long, pale evenings you get in the middle of English summers. In the center of the lawn, the fountain plays so delicately that you'd think time wasn't an issue. In the room, a large clock sits over a whiteboard.

It's hot, and the windows are open. You can hear the bells in the town beginning to signal 6:30. On the whiteboard are headings like "No Asia presence?" "Educating continental Europe," and "Rigorous control of pilots." At a conference table, four men and two women sit, each holding a single typed sheet of paper. This is what is on the paper.

Traveling through the Dark
by WILLIAM STAFFORD

Traveling through the dark I found a deer
dead on the edge of the Wilson River road.
It is usually best to roll them into the canyon:
that road is narrow; to swerve might make more dead.

By glow of the tail-light I stumbled back of the car
and stood by the heap, a doe, a recent killing;
she had stiffened already, almost cold.
I dragged her off; she was large in the belly.

My fingers touching her side brought me the reason—
her side was warm; her fawn lay there waiting,
alive, still, never to be born.
Beside that mountain road I hesitated.

The car aimed ahead its lowered parking lights;
under the hood purred the steady engine.
I stood in the glare of the warm exhaust turning red;
around our group I could hear the wilderness listen.

I thought hard for us all—my only swerving—,
then pushed her over the edge into the river.

The joint CEO of the company, Stuart, stands up and reads the poem. He is Irish, in his midforties, a graduate of Queen's University, Belfast. He reads with strength and sincerity and no hint of embarrassment. His executive team listens intently. Acting as facilitator, I get up and move to the front of the table. There's a short silence. The investigation of meaning is about to begin.

The Discussion (an Extract)

C. M. *(facilitator):* So, what does anyone make of the poem?

STEVE *(joint CEO):* He's talking about making a difficult decision.

C. M.: What sort of decision? Anyone like to expand on it?

MARIE-ROSE: Where you've got two things conflicting. What's in front of you and what might happen as a result of it.

C. M.: That's right, isn't it? [*Nods all around.*] Anything else?

TREVOR: Whatever he does will be wrong in a way. There's no way round it.

GEORGE: Well, there is. It's perfectly clear. He has to get rid of the deer or it'll cause an accident.

C. M.: Is it as simple as that? What do people think?

JESSIE: It's not simple. It's not simple at all. There's life right there, under his hands. We can see the fawn—

MARIE-ROSE: It's that word *waiting;* that's the one that does it.

GEORGE: But what is he supposed to do? He's got no tools, or knives, or anything—

C. M.: Is it just the immediate problem the poem is confronting us with?

JESSIE: No, it's the way it's set, out there in the middle of nowhere, no towns or anything, in the dark, on your own.

C. M.: So what's the point of setting it there? Anything important?

STEVE: Yeah, there are two kinds of darkness in the poem. The darkness of not knowing what to do and that darkness you get right out there, in the wilderness, when nature's very big and you're very small.

GEORGE: Oh-oh. I feel "ecology" coming on. Don't tell me: part of the problem here is that in our technological age we've cut ourselves off from "nature" and—

MARIE-ROSE: But that *is* part of the problem; look at how he lines up the car and the dark against each other. Look how he makes the exhaust like a . . . like a . . . channel for birth, or miscarriage—

STEVE: On the other hand, the car is a good thing: it's the motor that keeps on running. And the headlights—

JESSIE: But they're giving a narrow view, just straight down the road, no context.

C. M.: So it's not clear-cut?

JESSIE: No, it's not, there are so many issues . . .

STUART (*joint CEO*): In a way, it's like, when's the right time to kill a project? What's the result in the short and the long term? Who's going to benefit, who or what may get hurt?

C. M.: What about the traveler? What do we think about him?

GEORGE: A good decision maker. A decisive guy.

TREVOR: I don't know. He's a bit of a cold fish. What's that "my only swerving" bit? He's a hunter, isn't he? Sounds like he doesn't usually think much about things.

JESSIE: That's right, look at the deadpan way he tells it. And words like "dragged her off." Off what? The road? Or off the bonnet? Did he maybe hit her and he's trying not to admit it?

STUART: I don't know. But it is ambiguous. That "thought for us all": who's there besides him? Does he mean himself, the doe, the fawn? Or other drivers who might come along?

C. M.: Or does he maybe mean "us" as in all human beings who are faced with a tough decision? Is there anything like an ethical dimension here?

TREVOR: It's hard to put your finger on. It's something to do with—

MARIE-ROSE: I know what it is. It's like Everyman, and how do we make a decision when there's nothing obvious to guide us? He's caught between value systems—

STUART: That's right, but it's more than that. It's the feeling of the whole poem. Like it's just one event, but it stands for a whole lot of issues. It's a . . . in a way it's a tragedy.

C. M.: So there's all sorts of layers there? It doesn't just mean one thing but a lot of things?

STUART: Yes, that's right. It's tricksy. Like "the fawn, alive, still, about to be born." It mixes up all kinds of things: still alive, alive but lying still, stillborn—all those things point you in different directions—

GEORGE: [*looking at his watch*]: Meaning is meaning, isn't it?

TREVOR: Not here. Not here, it isn't. Something else is going on.

C. M.: Would it be different, d'you think, if a woman was telling it?

GEORGE: Oh, don't tell me—it's political correctness time.

JESSIE: Yeah, that pushing over, it's like a shock, like it's in the middle of the poem and goes all through it—

TREVOR: Not that that makes sense really, not logical sense. You just *feel* it does.

MARIE-ROSE: It's the way it sounds, too. What he does is all clipped, the actions. The wilderness stuff is softer and comes out less jerky. "Around our group I could hear the wilderness listen." It's like a heartbeat.

C. M.: So part of the meaning is what you hear, not just what the words say?

JESSIE: I think so. [*She looks around at the others. They all nod, except George, who is putting his papers away.*]

Postscript: How Did It Go?

A week later, I get a letter from Stuart, the joint CEO. This is how it goes.

Thank you for the poetry workshop. I think it went well, particularly for such an unusual subject. We've had good feedback, the vibes in general have been good, as you probably gathered they would be from discussions at the dinner afterwards.

These are the main points that have come across; they include Steve's and my observations.

It was a very interesting exercise. Difficult at first, because that's not the way we usually approach things in IT.

It was hard to resist trying to put everything in order so it made logical sense. Once you got over that, you could see the sense it made was different. The difference stretched the group, and that was good.

It made everyone (or nearly everyone!) think again about how you decide what to do about tricky problems. Just how big they are. And the lack of clear-cut answers.

I would use this method again. I think it could be useful in bringing different views and approaches out into the open. It could be useful in ironing things out with our U.S. and Asia-Pacific operations, particularly as they grow.

I guess the downside was that it raised lots of questions but didn't say how to answer them.

Please keep us posted on how things go with your project. We need more initiatives like this.

With best wishes,
Stuart

Rough Country

by DANA GIOIA

Give me a landscape made of obstacles,
of steep hills and jutting glacial rock,
where the low-running streams are quick to flood
the grassy fields and bottomlands.
                                    A place
no engineers can master—where the roads
must twist like tendrils up the mountainside
on narrow cliffs where boulders block the way.
Where tall black trunks of lightning-scalded pine
push through the tangled woods to make a roost
for hawks and swarming crows.
                                    And sharp inclines
where twisting through the thorn-thick underbrush,
scratched and exhausted, one turns suddenly
to find an unexpected waterfall,
not half a mile from the nearest road,
a spot so hard to reach that no one comes—
a hiding place, a shrine for dragonflies
and nesting jays, a sign that there is still
one piece of property that won't be owned.

Traveling Further:
The Lawyer and the Engineer

But now and then I drive out to the woods
and park the car: the headlamps fill with moths;
the woods tune in; I listen to the night

Retaking The Road Not Taken

The lawyer and the engineer were just starting out on their journey of exploration into how poems can make you think. The way they wrote and the conclusions they came to showed where each was in the development of his thinking abilities when it comes to using and capitalizing on the uncertainties and ambiguities that you take on when you confront the complex entity of a poem. They have come a long way since they wrote the responses you've seen. I've worked with them in the time since, and their thinking and exploring capabilities have developed markedly. They've sat Oxford University examinations in something called "Reading for Writers," which tests, among other things, the breadth and flexibility of the thinking skills they bring to reading poetry.

Over time, they could get to the kind of response this case study focuses on. What's set out below is not a definitive "answer" to the poem. But it shows how having the flexibility to pick up nuance and postpone closure enables you to draw out all sorts of meanings and inflections that wouldn't be visible to the thinker whose overarching aim is to "cut to the chase."

Case Study: Thinking beyond the Lawyer and the Engineer

The Road Not Taken
by ROBERT FROST

Two roads diverged in a yellow wood
And sorry I could not travel both
And be one traveler, long I stood
And looked down one as far as I could
To where it bent in the undergrowth;
Then took the other, as just as fair,
And having perhaps the better claim
Because it was grassy and wanted wear;
Though as for that the passing there
Had worn them really about the same,
And both that morning equally lay
In leaves no step had trodden black.
Oh, I kept the first for another day!
Yet knowing how way leads on to way,
I doubted if I should ever come back.
I shall be telling this with a sigh
Somewhere ages and ages hence:
Two roads diverged in a wood, and I—
I took the one less traveled by,
And that has made all the difference.

Strategy: Foresight or Retrospect?

Frost's poem is about a decision that becomes strategic in retrospect. Taking the second rather than the first way "has made all the difference." Something pretty vital and lasting has come from that apparently straightforward binary choice: the high road or the low road? Left or right? Expansion of R&D, or refocusing funding into global marketing initiatives? It's the kind of choice that strategy theorists might categorize under the label of "dualism." They might also advocate moving away from such an "either/or" approach toward the "either/and" of what has been called "committed relativism."

The traveler, though, is evidently a poor candidate for the relativist approach. He doesn't consider other options such as retracing his steps; he isn't concerned with looking around for different paths. If he were around in the twenty-first century, he could use his cell phone to collect additional information: what are the possibilities of beating through the undergrowth? But he doesn't seem the type. We can readily sympathize with his situation. Should we or should we not fire the vice president for marketing? We "must" expand our operational base. There are two possibilities only: Kentucky or Chong Qing?

The insidious little interconnections between the myriad decisions we take in the course of a day make up the fabric of our lives and the lives of others. Apparently small decisions can have unprecedentedly large implications we are quite unaware of. So any decision we make is part of a whole set of other decisions that we've made and will make in the future. It's part, too, of a matrix of outside interconnections so vast that no amount of rational application could ever unravel in advance all the complexities of their ethical and moral, never mind practical, implications. And it follows that any decision can be "strategic," that is, can attract to itself a high degree of influence over shaping the future, albeit in retrospect.

Interpreting Data: "Facts" and Variable Perception

Frost's traveler, unencumbered by any obvious responsibility and apparently not predisposed to seeking divine guidance, does what most of us do and tries to assess the "facts" that confront him. But he can only "see" a certain distance ahead. The road "bends in the undergrowth" of time, of imprecision, of jostling possible outcomes. Like the rest of us, the traveler's desire to predict the consequences of choosing one option over another is inevitably thwarted. His attempt at clairvoyance about which is *really* the "right" decision can only go so far.

With the benefit of hindsight, it's clear to the traveler that the distinction he drew between the states of the two paths was erroneous. We can see just how movable a feast "data" or "facts" really are. But they aren't just movable with the benefit of time and greater experience. Having acknowledged that there wasn't much to choose from between the two paths, the traveler goes back on himself and reasserts in the penultimate line the "less traveled" aspect of the path he chose. Is it, then, a question of the subjective impression the paths made on him? Is it the "duck and rabbit" syndrome, perception shifting minute by minute, the assessment of what "is" making and remaking itself in our consciousness over time?

The "truth" of the situation is no more accessible to the traveler now than it was when he first addressed it. Judgment of the "facts" of the case remains complicated. The mutability of perception means a definitive answer is something he may never have.

Counterfactual Thinking

The traveler is faced with making a pressured decision in an under-researched environment. Isn't this what entrepreneurs habitually do? Research shows that this pressure brings about mechanisms referred to as "counterfactual thinking" and "self-justification." It looks as though there could be some wishful (counterfactual) thinking going on in the case of Frost's traveler. Maybe, at the moment of that original choice, the traveler knows instinctively that he should take one path rather than the other. But, being schooled in the ideas of rationality (evidence, proof, logic), he feels he needs hard data to back him up. The one path, surely, has the "better claim" because it's "grassy" and less worn than the other. Or is it? If there's a difference between the two, it's marginal. But he *needs* some kind of difference, so as he looks some slight dissimilarity begins to be "revealed" to him.

Can Decisions Be Remade?

One of the ways the traveler justifies his decision is to "kid himself" about the possibility of taking both paths. There's that rather strange addition: "sorry I could not travel both / *And be one traveler*": what can that mean?

The traveler, at the decision point, regrets that he can't take both paths; that's straightforward enough. We recognize the impulse: wouldn't it be nice to be able to hike salaries *and* invest in R&D? But Frost opens up another aspect of the dilemma: "And be one traveler." Decisions don't just affect situations or other people; they profoundly constitute the decision maker. Living inside one skin, as we do, is the final limiting factor of our experience. Many of us, like the traveler, may have longed to be two people at once. Wouldn't it be good to be able to be the nice guy and keep on the marketing VP *and* at the same time make the "hardnosed" business decision of replacing him?

Wanting to be two distinct kinds of people leads Frost's traveler to kid himself about the possibility of return, the possibility, in other words, of remaking his decision at a future time.

The Greek philosopher Heraclitus believed that it's impossible to "bathe in the same stream twice." Time has passed, be it an hour, a day, or a decade. We, and the constituent elements of the decision facing us, *must* have changed, however marginally. In other words, even if we go back and reconsider, we cannot possibly be reconsidering precisely the same thing. Our decision, therefore, however much it may resemble the decision that confronted us previously, is different, a new decision. There's no such thing, according to this way of thinking, as a second chance.

There's one place, of course, where you *could* choose to keep remaking the decision: in your mind. Like Frost's traveler, you could revisit the choice again and again, see the look on the VP's face when you tell him he's out of a job, decide, after a while, that this was *the* crux decision in all the things that went wrong for you. Firing your VP is the thing that shaped your future. But what would be the point of torturing yourself like that?

Risk and the Entrepreneurial Spirit

After studying one path for a long time, the traveler precipitately "took the other." Why, if there's really not much difference between the two ways, does he take the second? He does so because at the time he *thinks no one else has traveled it.* It "wanted" (lacked) wear and "wanted" (seemed to demand) wear. So the path stands out to the traveler as a kind of challenge, the mysterious, unmapped territory, the equivalent, perhaps, of that large, lake-strewn area of Canada marked "wilderness."

It's an impulsive and risky decision. Whether or not it's foolhardy depends on the context in which we judge it. The traveler, looking back, judges it negatively, but do we trust him? Doesn't he have a bit of a "poor me" tendency? The way Frost makes the "I" rhyme with "sigh," importantly placed at the end of the line, makes us think he might. And the rather melodramatic "and I— / I took" sits incongruously with the rum-ti-tum rhythm in which the tale is recounted. "Two **roads** div**er**ged in a yel**low wood** / And **sorry I could** not tr**av**el **both**"—the four-beat rhythm is virtually uninterrupted; nothing unexpected happens. Indeed, we might wonder if such a prosaic character as the older traveler could ever have been capable of the impulsive action he attributes to his younger self.

The rhymes, too, in their five-line sections, contribute to our growing impression of a cautious older character. *Wood, both, stood, could, growth:* this a-b-a-a-b pattern, repeated throughout the poem, works up in the reader an unconscious sense of one step forward and two steps back, a sense of *no progress being made.*

Frost's choice of words to end his lines seems to back up the negative view of the older traveler. In the first half of the poem, the part that concentrates on the original decision moment, the lines mostly end with strong, active words: *stood, growth, claim.* The emphasis is on will and possibility. Optimism and a feeling of outwardness is carried through by *fair* with its connotations of light, justice, and good fortune.

Contrast this with the line endings of the second half. The passive implications of *lay* foreshadows a series of strikingly nonactive words (*day, way, by, I*). *Sigh* is the only active word and a word of the most unenergetic kind. *Black* and *back*, striking for producing a hard, clicking, interruptive aspect among the great mass of softer sounds, both highlight the idea of regression. *Black* describes a stage of decay much more advanced than autumnal yellow; and *back*, while signifying return, also contains more than a hint of the notion of retreat (turning back or away from what confronts you). So the second half of the poem, where the focus is on the older traveler, is a place of stasis. The vigor and boldness of the original choice is where the energy and spirit of the venture seem to reside.

Does this mean our sympathy is directed toward the younger traveler's desire to defy convention, his wish to embrace the mystery of the untrodden way? The desire for adventure is, after all, a charismatic quality, and the notion of discovery is a motive force underlying the whole of existence. What would the world have been like if there had been no Captain Cook to sail out over the edge of the known? No Marconi to conceptualize the unlikely possibility of words traveling soundlessly through ether? No J. L. Baird to "see" how pictures could be compressed in a tube?

The Poem as a Strategic Unit

The poem opens up a space for contemplation around the universal human dilemma of how we decide between alternatives on the basis of incomplete or insufficient information. What role do experience, knowledge, faith, judgment, and inclination play? Is there an element of mystery in how decisions come about?

The poem is not only about uncertainty, but generates multiple uncertainties on the part of the reader. Just what value *do* we place on youthful rashness? Frost isn't going to allow *us* any simple, binary decision of preference between the older and younger view. There's a way in which the younger traveler, keeping "the first for another day" even while "knowing how way leads on to way" and therefore *rightly* doubting he'll "ever come back," is indulging in a degree of counterfactual thinking that borders on careless arrogance.

Frost uses the uncertainty of decision making as a strategic tool in the structuring of his poem. That "difference" the traveler's choice made—

how can we tell if it's positive or negative given, as we've seen, that the *poem* (if not the traveler looking back) leaves the question open? How *are* we to value the audacity of the young traveler's choice?

The conclusion you come to on that depends very much on how you interpret the "data" of the poem: the words and how they are arranged, ordered, and presented; the "music" of the piece, how sounds clash or agree; the speed and weight (rhythm) of different sections and how that affects you; and the subtle variations and balances of tone.

The poem, in other words, is not a logical or discursive statement. It is a dynamic entity working on us in a variety of ways. It demands that you make if not outright "choices" (because there is no ultimately right or wrong way to interpret a poem) then at least a series of evaluations about the merits of various possible "meanings." The data or facts of the poem are slippery and open to multiple interpretations. You can no more exhaust the ramifications of a (successful) poem than you can tie down the multiple complexities of making a choice.

ᏍᎰ 8 ᏍᎰ

Taking It Further: Trying It Out

Down the lines
that had never met and never would now, it came,

the hum of the barely discernible

So far the terms of the discussion have been, as they must inevitably be in a book, more or less rational, following the accepted forms of a logical discourse, moving, albeit with sideslips and a degree of circumlocution, from (a) to (b). There have been suggestions, definitions, extrapolations, juxtapositions, and perhaps occasionally expostulations. The terms of the argument have been set and broadly followed. My reader has, I hope, had the sense of an exploration, of the potential for an ultimate convergence, a mutual growth of understanding of the issues between us. And so at this point I invite my reader to plunge in, to begin in a small way to test the hypothesis, to take on and wrestle with some poems for him- or herself.

There are five poems for consideration, each with a small amount of information about the poet and some of the issues in interpreting the poem that have surfaced in the past. These can act as preliminary pointers to finding a path through the poem. They can certainly act as a sounding board for any reader's new or emerging thoughts.

How should a poem—the physical entity on the page—be approached? By stealth, I would suggest, and with a degree, however preliminary, of respect and affection. The first acquaintance can occur in any way that suits the individual reader. Some people read poems silently, several times over, and then read them aloud. This is what I do, and I like to have other people read the poem to me as well. That way I can hear a variety of takes on the overall "attitude" or tone of the poem. Some I'll agree with; some I may instinctively recoil from. It doesn't mean I won't end up hearing the poem in several ways and enjoying and exploring the validity of all of them.

∾ *Penitence*

by JOHN BURNSIDE

I was driving into the wind
on a northern road,
the redwoods swaying round me like a black
ocean.
   I'd drifted off: I didn't see the deer
till it bounced away,
the back legs swinging outwards as I braked
and swerved into the tinder
of the verge.
   Soon as I stopped
the headlamps filled with moths
and something beyond the trees was tuning in,
a hard attention
boring through my flesh
to stroke the bone.
   I left the engine running; stepped outside;
away, at the edge of the light, a body
shifted amongst the leaves
and I wanted to go, to help, to make it well,
but every step I took
pushed it away.
   Or—no; that's not the truth,
or all the truth:
now I admit my own fear held me back,
not fear of the dark, or that presence
bending the trees;
not even fear, exactly, but the dread
of touching, of colliding with that pain.
I stood there, in the river of the wind,
for minutes; then I walked back to the car
and drove away.
   I want to think that deer
survived; or, if it died,
it slipped into the blackness unawares.
But now and then I drive out to the woods
and park the car: the headlamps fill with moths;
the woods tune in; I listen to the night
and hear an echo, fading through the trees,
my own flesh in the body of the deer
still resonant, remembered through the fender.

About "Penitence" and John Burnside

"Penitence" is the last poem in John Burnside's collection *A Normal Skin* (1997). In many respects it seems quite similar to William Stafford's "Traveling through the Dark." But is it really? Both poems deal with the death by collision of a deer on an isolated road and the reactions of a driver to this sudden event. Many critics, though, have pointed to just how different those reactions are, in particular how Burnside's poem focuses, in contrast to Stafford's, on guilt and regret. In that respect, does "Penitence" perhaps overdramatize its speaker? Is "Traveling through the Dark" an exposition of a macho, hunter-oriented world?

John Burnside is a British writer who lives on the coast of Scotland. His memoir, *A Lie About My Father,* was published in 2006 and his latest book of fiction, *The Devil's Footprints,* in 2007 along with his eleventh collection of verse, *Gift Songs.* Burnside is a committed environmentalist and former horticulturalist, and in his isolated home, with hardly another house in sight, he can see the stars at night very clearly. "You have to go out into the wilderness to establish your reconnection to the universe," he has said.

ॐ *In Memory of Henry West*

who lost his life in a whirlwind at the Great Western
Railway Station, Reading, March 1940, aged 24 years

by JANE DRAYCOTT

Not expecting the future in so soon, he turned
and looked for the swarm of bees. Down the lines
that had never met and never would now, it came,

the hum of the barely discernible: ribbons of flies
in a sheep down a culvert, the crack of the ice-plate
under a boot, himself in the fog.

The iron work announced his name, then the flat
hand of the storm pushed him towards the gap.
In the eye of the wind he saw himself, halted forever

in the freezing cattle-wagon of the third class waiting room,
stopped on the table top of a Siberian winter, surrounded
by bears and the icy stares of commuters, and round him

further and further, the dopplers of a thousand 125s,
the high speed sleeper and all the other sleepers going west.

About "In Memory of Henry West" and Jane Draycott

Jane Draycott has referred to writing poetry as a "dark and slippery art," and
her concern with embedding large themes in the concrete environs of a par-
ticular incident are at play in this poem. The highly atmospheric reference to
Siberia and the combined feeling of vast movement through time and space
give the poem a particular visceral resonance. The image of the "whirlwind"
is factual but seems also to be standing for something much bigger, to which
the "cattle-wagon" and the 1940 date of the incident give, perhaps, a clue.

Jane Draycott's most recent collections are *Prince Rupert's Drop* and *The
Night Tree,* both of which were UK Poetry Society recommendations, and
Over, published in 2009. She lives in the quintessentially English town of
Henley on Thames, Oxfordshire, and has received critical acclaim for the
wit, precision, and intelligence of her work. She has a particular interest in
cross-genre and collaborative work and has recently been creating sound
montages and audio archives with London's working watermen.

❧ The Door: Anticipation of Wisdom
by KAPKA KASSABOVA

One day you will see clearly:
you've been knocking on a door without a house.
You've been waiting, shivering, yelling
words of badly concealed and excessive hope.
Where you saw a house, there'll be just another side.

One day you will see clearly:
there is no one on the other side,
except—as ever—the jubilant ocean
which won't shatter
ceramically like a dream
when you and I shatter.

But not yet. Now
you wait outside, watching
the blue arches of mornings
that will break but are now perfect.
Underneath on tiptoe
pass the faces, speaking to you,
saying "you", "you", "you",
smiling, waving, arriving
in unfailing chronology.

One day, you will doubt the exactness
of your movements,
the accuracy of your sudden age.
You will ache for slow beauty
to save you from the quick, quick, life.

But not yet. Now
you say "you", there is always "you",
"you" fills the yawn of time and surrounds you, until
you knock the door down, one day,
and walk over to the other side
where
nothing will be revealed.

But not yet. Now let's say
you see a door, and knock,
and wait for your knocks to be heard.

About "The door: anticipation of wisdom" and Kapka Kassabova

The deceptively simple language of this poem could make it appear rather abstract and philosophical, a series of statements on the theme of existence perhaps. From its intense emotional coloring and tight patterning emerges, however, something that is finely balanced between a lament and an affirmation of joy and hope. Kassabova is praised for the lyricism and humanity of her work, which has been referred to as "sustained thinking in a musical framework: the various melodies of intelligence."

Kapka Kassabova was born in Bulgaria and has lived in Britain and New Zealand. A background of geographical and cultural displacement informs her strongly felt themes and underpins a yearning quality that critics have commented on. She has been characterized by Mark Strand, former U.S. poet laureate, as a writer of perpetual exile. She has written novels as well as poems, and her first novel, *Reconnaissance* (1999) won a Commonwealth writers' prize.

৩ৈ *Snow*

by LOUIS MACNEICE

The room was suddenly rich and the great bay-window was
Spawning snow and pink roses against it
Soundlessly collateral and incompatible:
World is suddener than we fancy it.

World is crazier and more of it than we think,
Incorrigibly plural. I peel and portion
A tangerine and spit the pips and feel
The drunkenness of things being various.

And the fire flames with a bubbling sound for world
Is more spiteful and gay than one supposes—
On the tongue on the eyes on the ears in the palms of one's hands—
There is more than glass between the snow and the huge roses.

About "Snow" and Louis MacNeice

"Snow" seems at first to have the cosy feel of a drawing room, the "great bay-window" and the roses and the fire and the tangerine giving hints, perhaps, of a celebration. But the famous phrase "the drunkenness of things being various" opens a more complicated and potentially disturbing world. The enigmatic last line has been seen by some commentators as an evasion, by others as the heart of the poem's short meditation on intensity and ordinariness.

Louis MacNeice was associated in the 1930s and 1940s with the political Left, but, as he put it, "My sympathies are Left. . . . But not in my heart or my guts." He was born in Belfast and studied classics and philosophy at Oxford University. He lived in London for most of his life but took great pride in his Irish heritage and frequently returned to the country where he was brought up. He has been acknowledged in recent years as a strong influence on contemporary Northern Irish poetry. MacNeice wrote radio drama as well as poetry, and his most famous radio piece is the parable play *The Dark Tower*. He died in 1963.

୬ *Mending Wall*

by ROBERT FROST

Something there is that doesn't love a wall,
That sends the frozen-ground-swell under it,
And spills the upper boulders in the sun,
And make gaps even two can pass abreast.
The work of hunters is another thing:
I have come after them and made repair
Where they have left not one stone on a stone,
But they would have the rabbit out of hiding,
To please the yelping dogs. The gaps I mean,
No one has seen them made or heard them made,
But at spring mending-time we find them there,
I let my neighbor know beyond the hill;
And on a day we meet to walk the line
And set the wall between us once again.
We keep the wall between us as we go.
To each the boulders that have fallen to each.
And some are loaves and some so nearly balls
We have to use a spell to make them balance:
"Stay where you are until our backs are turned!"
We wear our fingers rough with handling them.
Oh, just another kind of outdoor game,
One on a side. It comes to little more:
There where it is we do not need the wall:
He is all pine and I am apple orchard.
My apple trees will never get across
And eat the cones under his pines, I tell him.
He only says, "Good fences make good neighbors."
Spring is the mischief in me, and I wonder
If I could put a notion in his head:
"Why do they make good neighbors? Isn't it
Where there are cows? But here there are no cows.
Before I built a wall I'd ask to know
What I was walling in or walling out,
And to whom I was like to give offense.
Something there is that doesn't love a wall,
That wants it down." I could say "Elves" to him,

But it's not elves exactly, and I'd rather
He said it for himself. I see him there,
Bringing a stone grasped firmly by the top
In each hand, like an old-stone savage armed.
He moves in darkness as it seems to me,
Not of woods only and the shade of trees.
He will not go behind his father's saying,
And he likes having thought of it so well
He says again, "Good fences make good neighbors."

About "Mending Wall" and Robert Frost

The simple act of building a wall with a neighbour opens up questions of boundary and territory in this poem, but also exposes the difference between tradition and modernity. Is Frost's speaker patronizing his country-bred neighbor, who "moves in darkness"? Are the forces that mysteriously bring down all walls better understood, in fact, by the neighbour than the apparently more sophisticated speaker? The poem is marked as being written "North of Boston.1915" and is often seen as addressing, however obliquely, the horrors of World War I.

Robert Frost, one of America's best-known and best-loved poets, has exercised a considerable influence on contemporary poetry. His contemplation of large existential and political issues through the homely and the everyday finds echoes in, for example, Jane Draycott's "In Memory of Henry West." Although he is strongly associated with New England, where he spent much of his life, his three-year period of residence in the United Kingdom, from 1912 to 1915, had a profound impact on his poetic voice. President John F. Kennedy said of Frost, "He has bequeathed his nation a body of imperishable verse from which Americans will forever gain joy and understanding." He died in Boston on January 29, 1963.

ᴕ *The Door*
by MIROSLAV HOLUB
(translated from the Czech by Ian Milner)

Go and open the door.
      Maybe outside there's
      a tree, or a wood,
      a garden,
      or a magic city.

Go and open the door.
      Maybe a dog's rummaging.
      Maybe you'll see a face,
or an eye,
or the picture
            of a picture.

Go and open the door.
      If there's a fog
      it will clear.

Go and open the door.
      Even if there's only
      the darkness ticking,
      even if there's only
      the hollow wind,
      even if
            nothing
                is there,
go and open the door.

At least
there'll be
a draught.

<hr />

About "The Door" and Miroslav Holub

Miroslav Holub's 1962 poem has been seen as an invitation to enter life, to
burst out of a condition of stasis into the world of experience. Whether or
not there is something beyond where you are that is worth getting to isn't,

perhaps, the issue. The action itself, the opening up of the possibility of change, is the focus. Critics have pointed to the poem's implicit rejection of the totalitarian political structures Holub was working within, and despite the elements of surrealism and humor in "The Door" a terse mood of anger or defiance characterizes its short lines and angular sentences.

As well as being one of the Czech Republic's most important poets, Miroslav Holub was also one of its leading scientists. His poetic method was formulated in direct opposition to the abstract and ideological emphasis of the Stalinist era, and he brought new subjects to Czech poetry, focusing on ordinary human beings, the "pawns of history," who he believed move things forward. Holub sought to write in a direct and unadorned way that could communicate widely. "I prefer to write for people untouched by poetry" he said, "I would like them to read poems in such a matter-of-fact manner as when they are reading the newspaper or go to football matches." He died in Prague in 1998.

Poetry and Creativity

You cannot, the voice down the phone line says to me, quote Wittgenstein in a business book.

Reading between the Lines

*Monstrous alliances never dreamed of before
began.*

Wittgenstein versus the Business Reader

You cannot, the voice down the phone line says to me, quote Ludwig
Wittgenstein in a business book.

Because, it says, the business reader simply will not take it.

Relevance, it says. Applicability. Where is the product? What has
Wittgenstein got to do with the bottom line?

The voice belongs to an editor I've turned to for advice about what
might be an appropriate market for the projected book. It's a crossover
book, we've told him. Not exactly business. Not exactly literature. The
idea is to open up what's been, up to now, a closed line of communication.

How would anyone sell it? he says. What shelf would it go on in the
bookshop?

Can't they just put it right at the front? I say. In the space for new ideas
that nobody's thought of?

Apparently that kind of thing just isn't possible. Publishing is big
business. Books fit into defined marketing slots. There's big head shak-
ing if there's a hint that a book might straddle a slot. That would make it
very difficult to market. The reps would get dispirited. Clarity is all
when it comes to your commissioning editor selling a book into her
organization.

Who's going to read it? he says. If it were academics, that would be easy. You wouldn't sell very many, maybe a few hundred at most, but at least there'd be a defined market.

There isn't, apparently, a market for books that cross boundaries.

Unless you're a big name already, he says. Unless you're on the circuit.

Oxford? I say. Wouldn't that be a bit of a pull? The Boston Consulting Group? Aren't those a couple of names that might make people take notice?

Business readers, he says, go for things they can use, tools, solutions.

What Poetry Brings to Business isn't really about quick solutions, I say. It's more to do with a cumulative process.

I can feel him shaking his head on the other end of the line.

I could see it, he says, packaged, for example, as one of *Six Ways to Creativity*. Or maybe as a New Wave take on aspects of leadership.

I kind of thought it might link into the notion of intellectual capital, I say.

Intellectual capital? That's yesterday's notion. Intellectual capital has been done to death. Take my advice. A nice, neat, tools-oriented package. Keep it short. Keep it simple. Put in the kind of headings business readers go for.

Such as? I say.

Oh, I don't know. "Emotional Intelligence: Doing It Now; Doing It Better."

You think that would pull in the punters?

Sure I do. Take it slow. Take it easy. Small bites. Obvious progressions. Let me know if I can be of any more help to you. Just hang on in there. You'll be fine.

Tangling with Wittgenstein

Wittgenstein, I write. Wittgenstein. Wittgenstein. Wittgenstein. I make a list of the reasons Wittgenstein must feature:

- He believes the most important aspects of things can be hidden from us because they are simple and familiar.
- He believes language is the chief culprit in hiding things from us.
- Why? Because language brings with it a whole package of associations that we can't easily get free from.[1]

"Philosophy," he says, ought really to be written only as a *form of poetry*." Human beings, he says, are profoundly enmeshed in philosophical—i.e., grammatical—confusions. They cannot be freed without first being extricated from the extraordinary variety of associations which hold them prisoner.

How does he think language holds us prisoner?

- We falsely believe that words have simple and singular meanings.
- These false perceptions of meaning lead us to ingrained ways of thinking.
- These ingrained ways of thinking are related to our sense that there's a way things "should be," an ideal or inevitable state we strive toward.

What's one of the key ways he thinks we can be set free from this tyranny of language?

- By reading poetry

Playing the Game: Talking the Talk

How can I convince my reader there's a problem with language?

How can I show that the way we make sense of things (and therefore the "meanings" we look for and find) depends partly on the language scheme (or discourse) in which we operate?

A discourse, I write, *is a kind of thinking room, constructed out of language, whose size, shape, disposition—and place in relation to other thinking rooms—constrains or allows:*

- *Expression*
- *Perception*
- *How you decide what things mean*

I shall have to investigate the potentially negative effects of (business) discourse on some of the things that matter to my readership. In particular I shall home in on:

- Communication
- Creativity

I decide first of all to take a look at the ways discourse works, how it operates in practice.

Case Study on how Discourse Works: Da Vinci and Daughter

Take a family bakery in a small town—England or Ohio, the precise loca-
tion doesn't matter. The father's been running it for years, he took over
from *his* father; and his daughter, now grown up, is joining him. In fact he's
taken great pleasure in adding "& Daughter" to the sign that's hung over
the door since 1870. Despite his pleasure, he's been troubled recently by a
downturn in his profits. He knows what the problem is: the in-house bak-
ing operation (he employs four men and two women in a barnlike building
out back and the taxes are crippling) is draining his revenue. He knows he
can bake his breads and cakes at a fraction of the cost in an out-of-town lo-
cation, and he's all set to do it. The evidence, in terms of concrete facts and
figures, is beyond dispute. But along comes his daughter with an MBA from
some fancy college, and she starts going on about research having shown
that customer perception of the move would be strongly negative. It might
even jeopardize the bakery's future, that's her belief, cutting turnover by
more than 40 percent. Their on-site baking in terms of image and customer
confidence is incalculable. Off-site production removes the differentiating
factor their existence is based on. Why, it would be like Ghirardelli out-
sourcing its chocolate manufacturing. How does she know? The survey she
conducted as part of her master's portfolio provided the evidence.

Evidence here means different things to the father and the daughter.
Both operate within the discourse of business but the daughter within a
language game, marketing, that constructs itself in terms of a kind of sci-
entific research. The father's language game of "production" is based not
on theory but on the empirical realm of practical application and result.
Whose approach, though, is more likely to come out on top?

Far into the twentieth century, the baker's experience and gut feeling
would probably have triumphed. In a culture less driven by consumer de-
mand and more by available raw materials, the past and extrapolating from
it might understandably hold sway. At the beginning of the twenty-first
century, the MBA theorist is more likely to have her way.

Digging Deep: Thinking about Talking

Where did that term *language game* come from? my reader asks. I'm not
aware of playing any games with language.

The game of language, I say, has to do with the aim of what's said, the field of meaning we operate in.

You mean language means different things according to the situation?

That's pretty much it, I say.

So give me an example.

Take science, I say. Its language game is about truth and falsehood, how to differentiate them, how to make something called "progress" maybe. But something else, religion for example, is aiming at something quite different. A believer will pray to God for an answer, and may receive one, but it will not be the kind of answer the scientist seeks or recognizes. Or take love: someone engaged in a love affair will not seek scientific evidence that he or she is loved. The "knowledge" that you're loved results from an "aim" based in the emotional/experiential rather than the rational/deductive realm.

He or she ponders for a minute, sips a coffee, makes a note on a page.

So it's more or less the spirit we act in? The aims of the language situation?

Pretty much so.

That's quite far reaching in its implications when you think about it. Things aren't transparent, the way we like to think of them. A lot of the ways we think about things in corporations are based on factual information being transparent and accurate. We have to trust the information that's in front of us.

What's being suggested here, I say, is the necessity of questioning givens.

I think most of us are taking that onboard, he says. Certain high-profile cases have made that a necessity.

One of the things this book is aiming for, I say, is raising awareness of the provisionality and interpretability of data and the role an acute awareness of language can play in that.

My reader looks at me tolerantly. It sounds like one of those games you play with the blotches, he says. You know: a crone or a maiden? A duck or a rabbit? A cowboy riding into the sunset? It's the frame, the things you can bring to bear on how you look at it. That's what makes what you see.

Surfing the Wordscape

I write this.

Wittgenstein thought you have to get right down into things to be able to resist the unseen forces of language. Poetry, he thought, opened up a new conception of the terrain you were traveling. Gave new, important views of the inclines and obstacles. "Do not forget that a poem," he said, "although it is composed in the language of information, is not used in the language game of giving information."

Then I exchange my writer's hat for my editor's hat and ask the following question.

Why would the executive/reader read that sentence?

I ask the further, related questions.

Does it appeal to a perceived need in the reader?

Does it appeal to an interest?

Answer: *none of these things.*

So I begin again.

Imagine you're riding through a land populated by words. They're moving around between rooms, houses, situations, towns, cities, or countryscapes just like people do. Everywhere they move they set up different relationships. They act differently, they even begin to look different.

You step off the pavement; you're trying to locate the residence where Thought lives. You've been told it's a big house, maybe even a mansion. But then there are a lot of houses, big, small, converted factories, condominiums. Right by you is a signpost reading "Thought." You see it and breathe a sigh of relief. But then you see it's not one signpost, it's pointing in multiple directions. There are eleven different ways to go. You can go to:

speak thoughtfully
speak without thought
think before speaking
speak before thinking
think while speaking
speak to ourselves in imagination
think of someone
think of a solution to a puzzle
let a thought cross our minds
whistle a tune thoughtfully and then without thought
just be thoughtful

How do you choose which direction to go in? Which are the blind alleys (for your purpose)? Which are the fruitful paths?

But then, on another trip, you land in a different part of the country. A designated terrain, maybe a bit like a national park. This is the Poem. It's a microcosm of the wider landscape; it has everything that has, but magnified, redoubled, and intensified. So it's as though you're experiencing the world but refined and intensified. At the corner of each word pathway there are many signposts. Some you can understand. Some you have to get to know better before you can decipher them. Maybe you need a guide at first; there are plenty on offer. But it comes to you gradually. So you're finding out new ways of navigation, back roads and shortcuts, the scenic route and the straight route.

When you return from the poem terrain you're empowered. You welcome the eleven-part signpost. You even get to thinking that eleven isn't enough. There should be fourteen at least.

When you get back to your home territory you can drop a word anywhere in the world and watch it ripple. All that stuff, depth and surface, surging out from it. You've been there. You know what's going on in the language landscape. Yours. Other peoples'. You've got a trick or two up your sleeve that aren't available to people who haven't been where you've been.

A Cautionary Tale

It's Chicago, eighteen months later, when I get a suggestion about how to make this general Wittgensteinian proposition about the role of language more value specific.

We're on a circuit of meetings that will take in, as well as Chicago, Washington, Los Angeles, San Francisco, and New York. We're in the process of forming a "friends of poetry" group within the wider BCG organization, people who are interested in the project and generally supportive of its ideas. The Chicago partner, Pete Lawyer, has read our summary and likes the ideas. In some ways he approximates my ideal reader. He's been in China for a while, and he's written a novel. He's one of those wide-thinking all-rounders who's a joy to meet in a successful company.

One way it's relevant, he says, is in refining communication. Some people who are great at analysis and quantification may not be so great at communication and the facilitation process. The kind of stuff you're talking about could come in here.

Then he tells us a tale about how a former regional president of one of BCG's star clients always traveled with an entourage of people whose job was interpreting whatever wishes or directives he expressed during his travels through the countries in his region.

Four guys, he says. He hired them specifically for that purpose. It was like this. Everything he said, the people all the way down the hierarchy would spend their time working out what he meant by it. Half the time they would get it wrong, and if they didn't they'd have spent an awful lot of time on it. So, he thought: It would be better to have my own interpreters out there. They'll get my thoughts across the way I want. And it'll be quicker. So that's what he did.

And how d'you think poetry can help with that? I say. How, as you see it, would reading poetry fit in?

Well, he says, it really makes you think about language. It makes you pay more attention to what each word means.

And then, he goes on, there's the question of tone and nuance. An awful lot of people these days think the facts speak for themselves, but I don't agree with them. One of the things that will differentiate us is getting that better. Picking up what isn't said, as well as what is said. Reading between the lines.

An Excuse and a Confession

I have a confession to make. My excuse is that I was brought up in Britain, and in the country rather than the city. New deals, new approaches— maybe they just weren't filtering through in my childhood. That, anyway, is my preconfession excuse.

What I have to confess is this: whenever I'm flying and the captain comes on to make his announcement and she's a woman, I do a double take. It doesn't worry me. It doesn't alarm me. But it *does disconcert me for a moment until I adjust.*

How can this be?

"Knowledge" about, for example, the relative strength and capability of men and women decisively affected how the job market was organized for much of the twentieth century. Women were effectively debarred until fairly recently from all kinds of "unsuitable" positions from the boardroom to the bus driver's seat to the captain's chair in the cockpit of a transatlantic jet.

But now? Things are different. Knowledge has been reconstructed, power hierarchies have shifted, and women are "naturally" accepted as capable of doing all these things.

My reaction belongs to an assumption about what's natural and possible that is now outmoded. But it's still there like the shadow of a habit, lurking at unguarded moments in the back of my mind.

Poetry Challenges Assumptions

Is there any proof that reading poetry can have an impact on the way we think? I turn to some evidence that poetry reading can at least impede the easy reliance that turns facts into assumptions and so closes down the different ways we might look at things.

Case Study: Poetry and the Unexpected

The linguist Yury Lotman identified the efficacy of poetry in preventing what he called "automatic perception" (making assumptions about what things mean or are going to mean).[2] Lotman describes an experiment that asked volunteers to interpret a newspaper article, a conversation between two young girls, and a poem. The point of the experiment was that the interpreters were given only one phoneme (sound unit) at a time and had to predict what would come next. For the young girls' conversation there was a 71 percent success rate in prediction; for the newspaper article 67 percent. But for the poem the success rate of the volunteers fell to 40 percent.

I ponder the "so what" factor for my reader, the executive. What it amounts to is: you've got to be on the alert with poetry in a way you don't have to with other forms.

What does this alertness do?

It gets you to question assumptions.

Why does poetry operate this way?

Because the aims of poetry discourse are generally significantly different from the aims of other discourses we usually operate in.

Getting Rid of the Regional President's Interpreters

T. S. Eliot, I say, said that a man who couldn't understand poetry couldn't tell the difference between order and chaos.

You know what they'll say to that? she says, "They'll say he was a poet, and poets *would* say things like that."

We're sitting in a bar in Dublin, she's a brilliant poet, and she's offered to look over what I'm writing from a poet's-eye view.

Wittgenstein, I say, holds that anyone who can't understand poetry is "meaning blind."

That's not going to cut much ice, now, is it? she says. Why don't you tell them you can help them get rid of the regional president's interpreters?

I trust her judgment. She's a highly respected writer and scholar in Dublin. She's on friendly terms with Seamus Heaney, the Nobel laureate, and he loves her work. She holds in her hand a paragraph of the draft I've given her. She reads this from it.

The way to cure "meaning blindness," and so get round some of the barriers language creates, is to assemble "reminders" rather than arguments. Poetry, Wittgenstein believes, is the best means of assembling these reminders. The logic of argument or explanation won't help us get rid of the language-blindness that corrals us into false meanings and missed opportunities. That, after all, would be too close to the formulations that entrap us in the first place. He wants instead to show us, to be a kind of guide, leading us over the taken-for-granted forms of everyday language, causing us to look at the actual "landscape" we are walking over, rather than having our heads buried in a map. He wants to fracture the artificial associations and inevitabilities we construct with our minds, through over-habituation with language. He wants to teach a skill that is critical and destabilizing.

For God's sake, don't go offering that to them, she says. It's dry as dust.

How These Words Happened
by WILLIAM STAFFORD

In winter, in the dark hours, when others
were asleep, I found these words and put them
together by their appetites and respect for
each other. In stillness, they jostled. They traded
meanings while pretending to have only one.

Monstrous alliances never dreamed of before
began. Sometimes they last. Never again
do they separate in this world. They die
together. They have a fidelity that no
purpose or pretense can ever break.

And all this happens like magic to the words
in those dark hours when others sleep.

Breaking the Word Barrier

. . . we knew which way to steer
beyond marked charts, and saw the island, as
first islanders first saw it

The Creativity Economy

Four o'clock on a hot June afternoon. The punts are moving lazily along
the surface of the Cam, and there's hardly a ripple. At Cherry Hinton, in
the deliberately utilitarian office of the CEO of ARM Holdings, PLC, a fly
is buzzing. I click to the next image in my PowerPoint presentation.

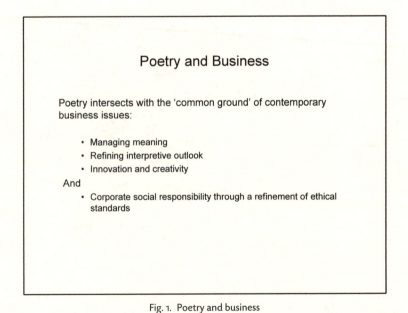

Fig. 1. Poetry and business

In relation to the third bullet point, I say, poetry cuts through the undergrowth. It makes space. It opens up connections.

I like number three, he says. Innovation and creativity. Let's go with that. It's time to test some of the ideas with a wider business public.

So how would you make an argument for poetry and creativity? the CEO asks me. How would you differentiate it from any of the other fads out there? Telling fairy stories? Playing with building blocks?

"Creativity" is big business, a fashionable watchword. There are books and articles galore, all hyping creativity as the concept of the moment. There are features on it in *Business Week*, where I pick up the following quotations.[1]

"The Knowledge Economy as we know it is being eclipsed by something new—call it the Creativity Economy."

"What was once central to corporations—price, quality, and much of the left-brain, digitized analytical work associated with knowledge—is fast being shipped off. . . . Increasingly, the new core competence is creativity."

A great deal has been written about creativity theory. Much of it is dense and earnest, often aimed at students in MBA courses, and written by their professors. At the other end of the scale, creativity as it relates to business practitioners is often envisaged as a kind of cure-all, the latest must-have that will magically transform the proportions of any ailing bottom line. It's the perceived *product* of creativity—innovation—that so many of the business articles are hyping, as well as the perceived *processes*. How you can get it bolted onto your organization? Who delivers it? Who are the gurus? What will it cost? What are they saying?

The *what* of creativity—what it is, what it feels like, where it comes from, how you handle it, how you nurture it as a vital and systemic ingredient in your organization—these and other important aspects often take a backseat.

The Fox and the Lair

One of *the* poems of the twentieth century that captures the creative instant in all its complexity is "The Thought Fox" by Ted Hughes.

The Thought Fox
by TED HUGHES

I imagine this midnight moment's forest:
Something else is alive
Besides the clock's loneliness
And this blank page where my fingers move.

Through the window I see no star:
Something more near
Though deeper within darkness
Is entering the loneliness:

Cold, delicately as the dark snow,
A fox's nose touches twig, leaf;
Two eyes serve a movement, that now
And again now, and now, and now

Sets neat prints into the snow
Between trees, and warily a lame
Shadow lags by stump and in hollow
Of a body that is bold to come

Across clearings, an eye,
A widening deepening greenness,
Brilliantly, concentratedly,
Coming about its own business

Till, with sudden sharp hot stink of fox
It enters the dark hole of the head.
The window is starless still; the clock ticks,
The page is printed.

This is the light the poem casts for me on creativity:

The When of Creativity

Thinking is something we do all the time. Focused thinking is something we do at will: "I must give some thought to the problem of. . . . I must make a decision about . . ." Creative or inventive thinking, on the other hand, is not something we can do at will.

"The Thought Fox" shows how the moment of creative insight creeps up on you. The fox is out there in the night, as a fox, and the power of creative vision transforms fox into poem.

When is the moment of transformation?

When the "two eyes" become "an eye, / A widening, deepening greenness." This is the moment when reality is reenvisioned and the living creature is, through a kind of magic—the imaginative fusions of inside (poet) and outside (fox)—metamorphosed into the stuff of the poem.

The Where of Creativity

Creative thought happens in silence and isolation; it comes out of a kind of enclosure and blankness. Often it happens when you feel as though nothing is there ("I see no star"). You have to be mentally somewhere far out on your own. It doesn't happen all at once but in installments (Now, and now, and now).

The Delicacy of Creativity

Those paw prints on the white snow: they point up the respect you need for the creative process. You can't go in there in big boots and stamp around. The pattern of the fox's paws in the white snow: this is the first carving out of a track in new territory. It needs to be carefully handled, judiciously approached, if you're not to spoil it, maybe even inadvertently trample it. Patience is required while the fox creeps up on you.

The Mystery of Creativity

Developing a creative thought is opening yourself up to a kind of invasion. It's mysterious. The thought is outside then suddenly inside your head. It's almost as if you were on autopilot. You're not in control of it. "It" is in control of you, crossing your boundaries, becoming part of yourself.

Creative Thinking Is a Violent Process

The breaking of barriers and boundaries is a violent change process. What's "outside" and what's "inside" fuse by means of a strong osmotic force. Impermeable layers have to become permeable. Discomfort or downright pain can be/are part of the process. Where has that "hole in the head" come from? It's like a birth in reverse, a painful opening up to allow entry, which gives rise to the life force, the new idea or created entity.

Creativity Is Not Just an Intellectual Activity

Creative thinking involves more than just the exercise of that abstract-sounding thing, "the intellect." Creativity is a gutsy business. It's sensuous. Everything about you has to be keyed up and keen, tuned in and ready. That "hot sharp stink of fox" is part process—the fruition of the idea—and part recognition—knowing what's happened and where in the process you are.

The four senses at work here are touch, smell (the nose at the twig, the coldness), sight (the green eye widening), and hearing (the ticking clock). But there's more than that. The whole body is involved, a tired, "lame" body, a "wary" body, the fox's, yes, but ultimately yours, too, because you are the "lair" of this seeking creature. Your mind has to shape itself to the lineaments and the mood of what is approaching you. And in this the feelings must be hard at work, too, the emotions, those antennae that pick up tiny signals outside our conscious reach. Wary, bold: these are attitudes of the fox, but also necessary characteristics of the creator. A wariness characterizes the patient observation of the fox approaching (Will he turn away? Will the very situation of being observed spook him?), and a boldness informs the intensity of engagement that allows for the dramatic entry of the fox into the head—the ultimate fusion of creativity.

The Strategy of Creativity

Having a creative thought is making a movement from one state to another. The poem suggests there's a strategy involved. The strategy involves a predisposition of attitude: (1) boldness, keeping on even though you're "wary"; (2) tolerance of delay, keeping going through the lean patches when nothing is coming, maintaining that intensity while knowing what approaches may come to nothing; (3) opportunism, not only *seeing* the fox but *tuning in to perceiving* its relevance, *recognizing* its significance, *opening up* for its entry, *translating/utilizing/capitalizing on* what it offers, *cherishing* its otherness; and (4) holding perception in an acute state of readiness: having your antennae on the alert to pick up signals.

Where Is Creativity?

Is the moment Hughes describes in his poem *really* all there is to creativity? my reader asks.

We're sitting in a restaurant on the corner of Greenwich and Franklin, the menus are open, and we're sitting down to a convivial dinner and a discussion of how things are going so far. I've shared with him the news of an exciting development, that The BCG Strategy Institute and a major UK microchip company—ARM Holdings, PLC—will be jointly hosting a forum on "Thinking Strategies" and poetry will be one of the three areas explored. I've told him about the relationships I'm wrestling with among poetry, business, and creativity.

The challenge, I say, is in making the linkages explicit yet exploratory enough to get the attention of the audience at the forum.

The ethos of the event, he says, what is it?

Fresh, fun, and informative, I tell him. If it's a little bit controversial, so much the better. We can't afford to go too far into complex ideas and theories.

But it must have weight and substance? he says. That will be essential.

It will have plenty of weight and substance, I tell him, but dispensed, as the champagne will be, with a light hand.

The fifty people coming to the seminar will want value for an afternoon spent listening in Cambridge is his view.

I tell him there will be three strands at the forum. I've elected to present poetry first. Culture and then dialectics are to follow me. Forty minutes of presentation and twenty minutes of questions. A break for tea, and then, after the last presentation and questions, a reception with champagne and canapés. The hope is that it will be at once a showcase for the unusual approaches of The Strategy Institute, a new look at approaches to creativity, a test bed for the ideas on offer, a branding operation for the two principal companies, a valuable networking opportunity, and a celebration of the potential for diversity in the profit-driven day-to-day business of the participants.

What about ARM? he says. What are they hoping to get out of it?

I tell him that ARM has a reputation as a company at the forefront of opening up new avenues. They'll want the standard of the presentations to do justice to that reputation.

I show him the invitation to the forum, which I've spent an afternoon designing with a Strategy Institute colleague.

The central theme of the event, I tell him, is "Thinking Strategies," the motor "innovation and creativity." The invitation focuses on new approaches to thinking. Away with tools and matrices and benchmarks. In with some more unconventional approaches. Dialectics. Culture. And—in my part of the program—language, thought, creativity—under the banner of poetry.

It's a bold step, he says, for two successful companies to embrace in public these less than readily quantifiable approaches. And poetry especially, he says, even more than the other headings, is a long way from anything you could call mainstream.

He's sympathetic, though, overall, to the aims of the forum. A lot of the

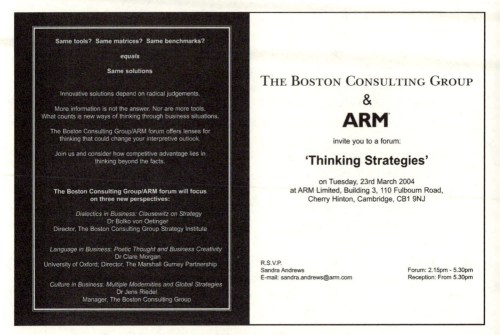

Fig. 2. "Thinking Strategies" invitation

younger people coming into his organization are looking for evidence that the creative skills and tendencies they have will be made use of. Some of the more rigid, balance-sheet orientations that have characterized how companies operate in the past are subject to revision.

The new recruits are looking for a culture that looks forward not back, he says to me, one that can demonstrate a keen awareness of the bottom line but has more than that to it. It could be useful to have something like poetry as an aspect of their training program.

Perhaps we could catch some of that brightness, he says, that willingness to take risks and try new approaches, before it gets diluted. He's aware, though, that the traditionalists in his company would need to be brought around.

They'd probably say to me, he says, that creativity isn't the same for a businessperson as it is for a poet.

I tell him what I'm planning to tell my audience: that creativity is a revolution in seeing, whoever you are and whatever your need to be creative.

And what is a revolution in seeing made up of? he asks me. Is it just the Eureka moment people usually say it is? Is it just that moment of inspiration that "The Thought Fox" is talking about? (He likes the poem; it reminds him of how he used to feel about things, the intensity, when he was still a very young man.)

The moment of inspiration is essential, I say to him. But it's a small part of it. That high-point moment seldom comes without patient preparation of the new-envisioning ground.

My reader makes a gesture with his head, somewhere between nodding it and shaking it. He's made some notes on creativity that he'd like to share with me.

Take a look at this, he says. It might be of interest.

The three comments on creativity that he's noted from his recent reading of the business pages are as follows.

- The pace of global change means "we must become as good at changing our perceptions as we have become at changing reality."
- Inspiring creativity is one of the most pressing needs for corporations.
- True creativity can only be had if you are willing to break the rules that have locked you in a set way of thinking.

If all or any of this is true, he says, you'll still need to answer two questions for your ARM/BCG Strategy Institute Forum audience.

1. How does poetry help prepare the ground for creativity?
2. How does poetry encourage you to break the rules?

❧ *The Islanders*

by PHILIP BOOTH

Winters when we set our traps offshore,
we saw an island further out than ours,
miraged in midday haze, but lifting clear
at dawn, or late flat light, in cliffs that might
have been sheer ice. It seemed, then, so near,

that each man, turning home with his slim catch,
made promises beyond the limits of his gear
and boat. But mornings we cast off to watch
the memory blur as we attempted it,
and set and hauled on ledges we could fetch

and still come home. Summers, when we washed
inshore again, not one of us would say
the island's name, though none at anchor sloshed
the gurry from his deck without one eye
on that magnetic course the ospreys fished.

Winters, then, we knew which way to steer
beyond marked charts, and saw the island, as
first islanders first saw it: who watched it blur
at noon, yet harbored knowing it was real;
and fished, like us, offshore, as if it were.

❦ 3 ❧

A Revolution in Seeing

we woke up in a gale
that was reasoning with our tent,
and all the persuaded snow
streaked along, guessing the ground.

Creative Transformation

Is the moment Hughes describes in his poem all there is to creativity? Not really. "The Thought Fox" reveals the extreme moment of creative accomplishment. This is the insight moment, the Eureka moment (although the poet represents it as a subdued event, characterized more by tension and exhaustion than by triumph). Is creativity to be found in the Eureka moment, the moment of revelation that leads to a step change?

I turn to a well-used model of how thinking works and how creativity fits within it. Graham Wallas's 1926 "thought act" model of how an idea works sets out four stages.

Preparation
Incubation
Inspiration
Verification

This four-stage model has been much modified by subsequent thinkers but still holds good as a basic scheme of how ideas happen. Inspiration—the Eureka moment—is the visible island, with the palm tree, the peak of one or more suboceanic ranges. But that peak depends very much on a context. The creative transformation seldom happens without surrounding changes. The preparation and incubation stages are essential precursors to the big step up. Creativity in this sense can be seen as a form of competence rather than a discontinuous (miraculous) and brief leap from one state of perceiving to another. Like other competencies, it needs to be fueled and nurtured. It thrives on learning methods that offer questions, surprises, and incomplete answers.

I meet Luc de Brabandere, a BCG partner, whose book *The Forgotten Half of Change* approaches creativity from a philosopher's viewpoint but also from the standpoint of the consultant/businessman. We talk over tea in a hotel in central Brussels. Creativity, he argues, is central to change in an organization. And central to creativity is the ability to shift perceptions. Changes in perception make way for imaginative leaps that generate the new ideas that fuel organizational changes. He is using poetry to exemplify some of the challenges of creativity.

How did you use it, I ask Luc. The poetry?

I took some alexandrines of Victor Hugo, he tells me, and I talked about how rigor is essential to the creative process. How rigor and creativity are two sides of the same coin.

And how did it go? I ask him. Was your audience receptive?

It went well, he tells me. They saw it immediately. How you create through discipline. How it isn't wishy-washy. How creativity is a very tough and muscular thing.

It's when I ask him why he decided to use poetry that a surprising fact comes up. The major hotel chain he's working with put out its request for proposals from consultants *in the form of a poem.* They chose the poetic form for their initial approach because they wanted to unearth consultants who could bring unusual breadth and freshness to the project, and poetry, it seemed to them, was an appropriate test, an apposite benchmark by which to separate the traditionalists from those who would be up to enacting and implementing a groundbreaking approach.

I ask Luc whether he used poetry in any wider way in the project, perhaps as a mechanism for helping bring about the desired changes in perception that could facilitate creativity.

He didn't do that, he says, he's a philosopher not a poet, but he thinks there would have been plenty of room for a wider application of poetry in the project. The essential thing is facilitating a change in perception. Change doesn't just happen. It exists at the level of ideas, and ideas come out of the groundswell of flexibility. Poetry could well be a very useful addition to that.

Breaking the Rules: Poetry and Meaning

How could poetry help facilitate a change in perception? By, in a sense, breaking some of the rules that business generally operates within—or at least alerting the practitioners in the organization to the taken-for-granted forms they're habitually working within. One of the rules poetry breaks is that it isn't looking for the same kinds of meaning as the business executive usually does. According to Sir Philip Sidney, "The poet never lieth, since he asserteth nothing." The aim of the discourse of poetry is not the statement of logical "fact."

Is the statement of logical fact an aim of business discourse? Generally, yes. And quite rightly. But there has to be a place for fancy, not just fact, out there in the thinking realm of the so-called creativity economy, a place where the rules of the dominant discourse are broken, at the right time and in the right place, by the rules of a discourse with a different endgame. Different, in particular, because for poetry there is no endgame beyond the production of the poem. The poem (in the words of Archibald MacLeish) "should not mean but be."

Case Study: A Revolution in Seeing:
Colorless Green Ideas Sleep Furiously

Take the famous phrase, coined by the language theorist Noam Chomsky, "colorless green ideas sleep furiously." Does the phrase have any meaning?

If my reader answers no straightaway, this book hasn't been doing what it should.

The answer I'm hoping for is: *That depends on the question "whose meaning"?* Or, if I'm very lucky, *That depends on the question "whose discourse"?* Either will do. The point at issue is just whose rules of meaning, aims of utterance, do we want to apply?

"Colorless green ideas sleep furiously" is probably never going to mean anything to

- People who operate primarily in a language game whose aim is "proof"
- The baker's daughter
- The baker himself

Why not?

The kind of rationale that would inform the judgment that "colorless green ideas sleep furiously" makes no sense, would posit that because the words *colorless* and *green* are incompatible, canceling each other out in a clash of irreconcilables, the phrase can amount to no set of notions that might be of any value.

Could the phrase make sense in a language game with a radically different aim?

Yes. It *could* make sense within the language game of poetry.

Why?

In poetry, the logical incompatibility of *colorless* and *green* does not matter. This is because poetry is a mode that has more to do with the associative than the deductive capacity and whose expectations therefore circumvent the predictability of everyday logic.

How could you go about making sense of the phrase?

The best way to make sense of "Colorless green ideas sleep furiously" is to ask a series of interlinked questions.

Can an idea sleep furiously?

Can an idea be green?

Can anything be colorless and green at the same time?

Have you ever slept furiously, tossing and turning, throwing off the covers because something (possibly a gritty strategic problem) is troubling you?

Have you ever been green with envy or become perilously green (seasick) on a sailing trip?

Paradox is where two things that concurrently exist seem mutually exclusive. It's a part of life. We must expand, but the market is saturated, so we can't expand. So maybe the paradoxically "colorless" and "green" state of the idea is what's keeping us tossing and turning: something we can't solve is haunting us.

Colorless and *green*, though, isn't there something else about them? Something fantastical? Could those ideas be not quite in our usual realm—be fantasies? So maybe fantasies, ideas beyond our grasp, unrealizable in our ordinary world, are what's keeping us awake. Or are we (in Freudian terms) repressing something that's just below the surface, just about to boil up and overflow?

These are the kinds of "meanings" that begin to accrue when we look at Chomsky's phrase in the terms of poetry rather than any dominant model of logic or proof. (Whether the phrase would, in fact, ever turn into a poem depends on the form and direction in which it was developed.)

What's called for is not so much the pursuit of proof as a conjuring of *associations* that *evoke* images and *generate ideas* related to those images. This is a fundamental way poetry works.

෨ʘ────────────────────────────────

Creativity and the Business Environment

This is all fine, my reader says, as far as it goes. I'm with you (although I guess you've still got quite a lot to tell me about how poetry inspires creativity). But lots of things are happening in business generally that are aimed at encouraging a creative environment. Take office layout, for example. All those state-of-the-art thinking areas with palm trees in pots. Some places even have a water feature. Running water gets the creative juices flowing, I've heard people say. And trainers and facilitators come in and work with paintings and building blocks.

But these, I say, are what I would call situational responses to the need for creativity. Reading poetry offers something different. Reading a poem won't in general immediately provoke a Eureka moment (though it might). What it will do is foster the development of a strong competence in discovering and perceiving new paths and connections. It can help develop a mind-set that explores and questions rather than accepts.

What are some of the ways in which you're suggesting the business environment works against creativity? he asks me. I think you'd be hard-pressed to prove that the exploration of ideas isn't encouraged these days.

I agree that's true, I say. But don't you think there are ways in which the business mind-set in general fosters a cut-to-the-chase, a-to-b, approach? Speed and outcome—much prized in organizations for legitimate reasons—aren't really conducive to creativity. The road to a new way of seeing is full of false starts and blind alleys. Rather than offering a straight passage, it's characterized by twists and turns.

On my laptop is something I wrote a while ago about executive summaries. There has been considerable discussion with my BCG colleagues about their place and value in an organization that is seeking to foster creativity. It turned out to be a kind of polemic, a diatribe. I wrote:

> *Executive summaries are paraphrases designed for people in a hurry. They were designed, perhaps, to address the conundrum: "I don't know whether I want to read this until I know what it says." Executive summaries save time in avoiding useless ploughing through irrelevant material. But they also pander to the culture*

which prizes "fact" (what's in this) above exploration (what might be in this).
They cater for people whose minds have become lazy. Lazy, that is, in being content
to take the (apparently) shortest line between two points.

As a statement on its own, of course, it's utterly unacceptable. Like many
polemics it addresses only half the truth. So why are executive summaries,
which often make simplified nonsense of complex and intricate material,
so prevalent? Nothing to do with laziness. More, maybe, to do with what's
valued in business—speed, concision, accessibility, immediate applicabil-
ity? More to do with the values that inform the way things have to be
expressed?

The argument goes like this. I need an executive summary because it's
quite possible I won't get anything out of this or that article or argu-
ment. Maybe what I find there won't be relevant to me and my situation.
Then I will have wasted precious time, which could have been spent more
productively.

That's quite a persuasive argument. Time is limited. Life is finite.
There are many pressing deadlines that have to be met. However, there
are two difficulties implicit in the argument.

Difficulty 1. What does *productively* mean? Does it mean producing a
product? Or producing results? Or producing ideas? Or could it mean, just
possibly (and essential in terms of creativity), a patient feeding of the
ground out of which ideas may or may not be forthcoming now or in the
future?

Difficulty 2. Whose summary is it? Whose perception has been brought
to bear that decides *this* is what an article or chapter or news item is about?
Many times in the course of writing this book I've been told "this or that
article or book just isn't relevant." Many times I have been told it addresses
"a," but when I go myself and read it I find that "z" is (for my purposes
right now, for this stage in the thinking) what it addresses.

Case Study: "Stop All the Clocks" versus the Executive Summary

"Stop All the Clocks," the 1953 poem by W. H. Auden, occupies a central
moment in the moneymaking 1990s movie *Four Weddings and a Funeral.* At
the height of the funeral, which is also the height of the film, the bereaved
lover of the deceased stands up and recites the poem.

Stop All the Clocks
by W. H. AUDEN

Stop all the clocks, cut off the telephone,
Prevent the dog from barking with a juicy bone,
Silence the pianos and with muffled drum
Bring out the coffin, let the mourners come.

Let aeroplanes circle moaning overhead
Scribbling on the sky the message He Is Dead,
Put the crepe bows around the white necks of the public doves,
Let the traffic policemen wear black cotton gloves.

He was my North, my South, my East and West,
My working week and my Sunday rest,
My noon, my midnight, my talk, my song;
I thought that love would last forever: I was wrong.

The stars are not wanted now: put out every one;
Pack up the moon and dismantle the sun;
Pour away the ocean and sweep up the wood.
For nothing now can ever come to any good.

What is this poem "about"?

If you had to summarize it in not more than a few words, what would you say?

Discussion:
What the poem is about: a summary

• When someone you love dies, it feels like the end of the world.

Objection:
Is that all the poem is about? Couldn't you also summarize it as:

• Personal grief feels like it ought to be public at the time.
• When somebody dies, depression inevitably kicks in.
• Isolation is the natural and desired state of the bereaved.
• People have a tendency to aggrandize their grief.
• Grief makes you pessimistic.

- It's dangerous to build your life around one person.
- Death makes you feel powerless, so you overcompensate.

And so on.

What the poem is about: an exploration

Here's what a student of mine wrote about the piece. He is forty-five years old, a computer scientist running his own company:

> The poem has expressed—in an understandable language whose beauty and resonance surpasses "everyday" language—what we might call "the inexpressible." The poem has gathered the audience into the experience of bereavement and shared it with them, involved them in "how it feels," expanded their apprehension of what "it" is.
>
> How has this happened? This expansion happens differently for different people. But many listeners are struck by that "juicy bone" that's offered to the dog. For many, the image generates a certain discomfort, even a sense of latent horror: "Prevent the dog from barking with a juicy bone." What's that "juicy bone" doing there? What do we see? Well, perhaps we see, or nearly see at the edge of our vision, the former fleshliness of the dead and loved person, but now dehumanized, discarded, reduced to something that's gnawed on a mat by a family pet. That "juicy bone" causes us to confront, at some level, the cadaver. The horror of the absence of that loved person from his fleshly self is held up before us in a single image. We're not told it. We don't deduce it "rationally." We infer it from the choice of words situated in the vacancy between STOP and SILENCE. The shock—the nightmare quality of loss, hits us—head-on.

> Is what the student/computer scientist wrote more illuminating, more thought-provoking than the summaries?
> Were any of the attempts at summary adequate?
> Maybe you can do better. Why not try it, but keep within the terms that executive summaries usually conform to: brief and *either* instructive *or* descriptive.
> Here is a different take on the poem, a magazine news article written with the business reader in mind.

> Want to hike up your bottom line and enjoy a good movie? The big name in big-time box office growth is W. H. Auden. Wystan Hugh, as he's known to

his friends, has come up with the cool way to turn Movie (ME) into Moving (MG). He's one of the new breed of late-comer box office gurus. And he's come up with the latest thing to make audiences swoon. The low budget English film has hit the headlines. Forget wide screen extra-max feelies. Wystan has got it all beat. It's the simplest thing, he says, I just wrote a poem. This little beauty has out-grossed MGM. And the secret of its success? According to Wystan Hugh, it's easy: "I reconceptualized the movie-goer from someone wanting entertainment and a night out, to someone hungry to surf the way life's feeling. Sure, the film does that, but it takes one hour fifty seven minutes. The poem had it all in a sound-byte. Eighty-two seconds and the whole of Real Life. That's what they paid for, that's what they took away with them. Every film should have one. It's the new black. It's the must-have of the moment. It's the best decision I ever made."

One thing's for certain: it grossed big, box-office. Wystan Hugh is a rich man these days. He just bought his own island off Barbados and a ten seater jet. Great add-ons too: CDs made seven figures, and the recording studio's gross profits were up 70%. Anthony P. Waterstone of Waterstone's bookstores is jumping for joy. Auden was always a steady seller, he says, but there were queues out in the street for this one.

He attributes the success of the poem to the breadth of its consumer appeal. Who could resist those cutesy little doves with the bows on? Poets and moviemakers everywhere—better get your skates on. By this time next year, you won't be seen without one. Take a word from the wise and get going: you'll be glad you're ahead of the curve.

✍ *Executive*

by JOHN BETJEMAN

I am a young executive. No cuffs than mine are cleaner;
I have a Slimline brief-case and I use the firm's Cortina.
In every roadside hostelry from here to Burgess Hill
The *maitres d'hotel* all know me well and let me sign the bill.

You ask me what it is I do. Well, actually, you know,
I'm partly a liaison man and partly P.R.O.   *[public relations officer]*
Essentially I integrate the current export drive
And basically I'm viable from ten o'clock till five.

For vital off-the-record work—that's talking transport-wise—
I've a scarlet Aston-Martin—and does she go? She flies!
Pedestrians and dogs and cats—we mark them down for slaughter.
I also own a speed-boat which has never touched the water.

She's built of fibre-glass, of course. I call her "Mandy Jane"
After a bird I used to know—No soda, please, just plain—
And how did I acquire her? Well to tell you about that
And to put you in the picture I must wear my other hat.

I did some mild developing. The sort of place I need
Is a quiet country market town that's rather run to seed.
A luncheon and a drink or two, a little *savoir faire*—
I fix the Planning Officer, the Town Clerk and the Mayor.

And if some preservationist attempts to interfere
A "dangerous structure" notice from the Borough Engineer
Will settle any buildings that are standing in our way—
The modern style, sir, with respect, has really come to stay.

Poetry versus the Thought Police

Was he free? Was he happy? The question is absurd:
Had anything been wrong, we should certainly have heard.

The Grammar of Possibility

The grammar of poetry—how its words and images, its sounds and silences, its rhythms and pauses and ambiguities operate, what they amount to—is one that opens up new possibilities. The presence of new possibilities inevitably alters the ground on which we see things, changes the relationship between the things on the ground, and shifts the relationship between the ground and other grounds, present, past, future, possible, impossible.

The ability to envisage new possibilities—what is not *yet*—is a fundamental aspect of creativity.

Strategic thinking is, or should be, a deeply creative activity. A strategy is surely based on writing a new story, one that hasn't been told yet, with an imagined outcome. You may use facts and characters from real life, but so does the fiction writer. These are the raw materials that are turned to an end.

I am determined to answer my reader's question: is creativity the same for a poet as for a business executive? It amounts to considering whether the strategist is in some way also a poet. The strategist could or should be a poet in some respects because the common areas of composition for the poet and the strategist include:

- Balance
- Timing

- Constraints of form
- Precision of components
- Rhythm
- A notional "user"
- An image (however indistinct initially) of the completed "it"
- An overwhelming sense of purpose
- Skill in handling a form as yet unrealized
- A provisional order plucked out of flux and chaos
- A specific unity painstakingly achieved

But what if something is holding the strategist back, causing her thinking to happen "inside the box"? What if something is stopping her envisioning the new possibilities, preventing her from tapping into what is not—*yet?* Like a pair of spectacles blurring the fine distinctions between things, making *a* look very much like *b*, casting differences into shadow, and ironing out differentials in color and tone?

Dominant systems of knowledge based in dominant discourses that control and direct the way we think act like these spectacles and constrain our ability to be creative.

These dominant systems constrain our creativity because they inhibit not only how we express ourselves but also *what we see.* We tend to structure the world we inhabit though the models of the dominant system. This isn't just a matter of individual perception. Groups tend to transform their own models in terms of the received (dominant) ones. The ability of individuals and groups to "see," in other words, is heavily influenced by the dominant knowledge systems within which they operate. The philosopher Michel Foucault's encapsulation of this dilemma is summed up by Michael Ryan as follows.

> The way knowledge is organized in the discourses of western society is allied with the organization of power in society. Power seeps into the pores of society . . . over time, power becomes part of the habitual everyday procedures and operations of such *social institutions as . . . the workplace* (italics added).[1]

This is what I write, how I intend to sum it up for my BCG-ARM forum audience.

If strategic thinking has at its center the expression of scenarios (possible ways things might be) that are not only alternative to those that currently exist but alternative to each other, then dominant ways of seeing that impede or hamper the conceptualization of new models in their own terms must be detrimental to the pursuit of that breadth of possibility out of which successful strategies grow.

Words and Power

George Orwell drew a frightening picture of the relationship between words and power in his famous novel *Nineteen Eighty-four.* Big Brother and his security forces, the Thought Police, created a state in which there was no opposition. Their tools of oppression were not truncheons or electrodes but words. If you controlled words, you controlled history. More than that, you controlled what could happen in the future; you also took charge of the present—family relations, friendships, living patterns—even sex and death were ultimately in your power. How? Because words, the theory went, control our thinking; we cannot formulate an idea unless the words are there for the idea to arise from. Our whole world exists, so to speak, *within* our language.

The argument I'm forming is that poetry has a role in resisting the word-thought tyranny. Poetry shakes you up, questions your assumptions, offers a subversive little voice that keeps asking: Why? What? How? For whom? In particular, reading poetry opens up a different mind-set, a mind-set that can tuck itself away from, dodge, and oppose those Thought Police, balaclava clad, wielding their guns and truncheons.

How can it do this? By providing a fresh observational space in which to pause and consider the nuance and subtlety of language and what it does to us, how we can use it, and how that use may corrall us into accustomed ways of thinking, ways that are counterproductive and seemingly inevitable. Ways related, perhaps, to those that Aristotle referred to when he said that poetry could challenge the stability of the well-run state.

The idea of relative perception is fundamental to this idea of a fresh observational space (or, in the terms of the discussion with my reader, a revolution in seeing).

I find a poem by Wallace Stevens that sets out quite compellingly some issues around the idea of relative perception. Stevens was a businessman as well as a poet, and I wonder whether his experiences in the world of business informed his exploration of the effects of what happens when a single idea becomes unduly dominant.

Anecdote of the Jar
by WALLACE STEVENS

I placed a jar in Tennessee,
And round it was, upon a hill.
It made the slovenly wilderness
Surround that hill.

The wilderness rose up to it,
And sprawled around, no longer wild.
The jar was round upon the ground
And tall, and of a port in air.

It took dominion everywhere.
The jar was gray and bare.
It did not give of bird or bush,
Like nothing else in Tennessee.

I imagine the three of us sitting in a room, me, the poem, and my reader.

"The jar and the hill," I say. "What's the relation between them?"

"It changes," my reader says. "First it's a good thing, then it's a bad thing."

"How is it a bad thing?"

"It takes over."

"Where's the problem?"

"In the bareness. It spoils things."

"So which is the true perception?" I ask.

My reader shakes his head.

"Both perceptions are true," he says. "And neither. Same jar, different view of it. It all depends where you're standing, what you're looking for."

At its simplest (I write), *the relation between jar and hill alters according to the viewer's perception of their relative dominance. The setting of the jar in nature at first seems to tame nature, making it "no longer wild." But as the viewer looks longer, the very unnaturalness of the jar makes it seem a poor thing compared to the lush possibilities of the natural world. The jar is "gray and bare," not giving "of bird and bush," the stuff of nature and of life.*

The negative impact of the overdominant idea has to do with how the jar starts out and how it ends up. The jar, in the first stanza, acts as a lens that usefully tames the apparent chaos beyond it. The view through it has, in some manner or other, ordered the "slovenly wilderness." So for a while this positive effect renders the jar important and valuable: "tall, and of a port in air." This positive effect edges over in the word *port* because *port* has attached to it notions of "haven" or "safe place" or "resting place." It also has connotations of a portal or gateway. So the jar is both a welcome point of repose and an invitation to future discovery.

However, after a while, the jar "took dominion everywhere." In becoming all powerful, it loses its magic. It becomes "gray and bare," and, even worse, it *doesn't faithfully reveal the detail of life anymore*. It's the only thing that doesn't "give of bird or bush." The jar doesn't conjure up, whisk into being, the vital ingredient of the scene—Life. So what starts off as a positive filter between the viewer and the world has turned into a negative means of obfuscation. Beware! the poem is saying. If you look too often through the lens of the upturned jar, you're going to get an entirely false and misleading impression of the world.

I save a note to my memory stick: *Communication inevitably takes place within sets of power relations; these power relations are enacted through the designated acceptability (or not) of ways of expressing ourselves.*

On the screen in front of me I have a quote I found in the London

Fig. 3. T. S. Eliot

Observer. It's the words of Anthony Hopwood, founding head of the Said Business School in Oxford: *"Language preempts and deforms "managing,"* he says. *It can be used to deny the possibility of an alternative."*

I call up next to the Hopwood quote the black and white image of T. S. Eliot in his three-piece suit circa 1954. Banker, publisher, poet extraordinaire. *"Poetry keeps clean the tools of thought,"* Eliot says to me, blinking and nodding behind his steel-rimmed glasses. Some kind of answer is beginning to form itself, to the question of what rules poetry breaks.

Clothing the Emperor

Here is a tale that shows just what kind of effect dominant knowledge systems can have when there's no one to oppose them, when they're allowed to get out of control.

The story of the emperor's new clothes is a familiar one. The emperor needs some new vestments for a tremendously important public event that's just around the corner. He finds two new tailors who promise him the most gorgeous vestments anyone could imagine. These two tailors have an eye to their profits and aren't above a little creative thinking of their own. They can't or don't want to or can't afford to get in any marvelous new fabric. They certainly have nothing that could meet the emperor's vanity and satisfy his need to be the most gorgeously arrayed nobleman in the country.

So they pretend they have a fabric so wonderful that only the cleverest people in the land can see it. If you can't see it (the word goes around) you're just plain stupid. No two ways about it.

The emperor, not wanting to appear stupid, "sees" the beautiful new garments that are being prepared for him. He has a moment's misgiving when at the last minute before the procession the tailors help him into his gorgeous (and nonexistent) new outfit. I guess it must be there, he thinks to himself. If it weren't, surely someone would have told me?

His courtiers and all the noblemen congratulate him on the beauty of his outfit. Sublime! they say. Immeasurably lovely! And the peasants who line the processional route, equally steeped in a system where what you "see" depends on the authority of someone else's superior knowledge, echo how awesome is the fabric, how elegant the attire. No one, they say, is more worthy of veneration than our leader.

But one little girl at the back cranes her neck, stands on tiptoe and says, "Oh, how funny! That man is naked."

"Hush!" says her father. To his neighbors he says, "You must excuse my daughter. It is but the blindness and stupidity of a child!"

But the word has got out. Nothing on. Nothing on! It's the truth, look! (one nudges the other in the ribs). All that fine talking. The emperor has been taken for a ride, if you ask me.

And the laughter swells up, and the fingers start pointing. Nothing on! Nothing on!

The courtiers look at each other, uneasily. If this is sedition, it should be dealt with.

But it's true, the whisper goes round.

We had best brave it out.

But behind their fans and their hands and their upturned collars of fine lawn they are laughing.

We have our clothes on. The emperor is naked.

The emperor hears all of it. He hears the whispers and the laughter; he sees the nudging and the squint-eyed stares after his nakedness.

I will keep on, he says, until I get back to the castle.

But it is not recorded whether he did that because he believed in the clothes still. Nor is it recorded what he did when he got back to the castle at the end of the procession and ordered the closing of the doors.

⚬ The Unknown Citizen

by W. H. AUDEN

To JS/07/378
This Marble Monument Is Erected by the State

He was found by the Bureau of Statistics to be
One against whom there was no official complaint,
And all the reports on his conduct agree
That, in the modern sense of the old-fashioned word, he was a saint,
For in everything he did he served the Greater Community.
Except for the War till the day he retired
He worked in a factory and never got fired,
But satisfied his employers, Fudge Motors Inc.
Yet he wasn't a scab or odd in his views,
For his Union reports that he paid his dues,
(Our report on his Union shows it was sound)
And his social Psychology workers found
That he was popular with his mates and liked a drink.
The Press are convinced that he bought a paper every day
And that his reactions to advertisements were normal in every way.
Policies taken out in his name prove that he was fully insured,
And his Health-card shows he was once in hospital but left it cured.
Both Producers Research and High Grade Living declare
He was fully sensible to the advantages of the Installment Plan
And had everything necessary to the Modern Man,
A phonograph, a radio, a car and a frigidaire.
Our researchers into Public Opinion are content
That he held the proper opinions for the time of year;
When there was peace, he was for peace; when there was war, he went.
He was married and added five children to the population,
Which our Eugenicist says was the right number for a parent of his
        generation,
And our teachers report that he never interfered with their Education.
Was he free? Was he happy? The question is absurd:
Had anything been wrong, we should certainly have heard.

⤺ 5 ⤾

Hot Cognition

We'll . . . say some contract has been signed
With what lies under, and that that occurred
Which has no human gesture and no word.

Stripping Off the Rubber Coat

A poem causes you to strip off received ways of looking at things. It says take a long, hard look at that emperor. Is he, or is he not, wearing any clothes? Forget what you've been told, forget what you've been instructed to believe, forget (if you can) all the subtle bindings and trappings of the differential expectations our complex living and operating systems bring with them. Look at him and his situation newly, freshly. Look at him with the immediacy and freedom of a child's eye.

The child in the emperor's tale perceived something that ran contrary to what all her elders and betters "knew." She was the one who broke through the barriers created by the dominant group model, a model based on the primacy of received wisdom, respect for authority, and fear of dissent.

Language theorists and in particular theorists about poetry came to the conclusion a long time ago that poetry can change our way of looking at things. "We live as if coated with rubber," Viktor Schklovsky said. "We must recover the world. Perhaps all the horror (which is little felt) of our days . . . can be explained by our lack of feeling for the world, by the absence of an extensive art."[1]

This is the central point I want to get across to my forum audience. Poetry is an extensive art because:

- A poem stretches itself, reaches out beyond its own boundaries, enlarging and expanding the terms of its own label, "poem," constantly, in the words of Ezra Pound, making itself new.
- A poem prolongs itself in terms of its meaning. It's an entity whose meaning boundaries are difficult to define, whose precise precincts are difficult to categorize.
- A poem taxes its own medium, that is, language, to the utmost. As Schklovsky put it, "We must first of all 'shake up' things. . . . We must rip things from their ordinary sequence of associations. Things must be turned over like logs in a fire." How does poetry bring about this hoped-for revolution? "The poet removes the labels from things. . . . Things rebel, casting off their old names and taking on a new aspect together with their new names."
- A poem extends its readers, requiring of them patience, persistence, flexibility, adaptability, humility, a taste for paradox, a thirst for precision, and comfort in chaos.

Figure 4 is the slide I put together for the ARM-BCG Strategy Institute forum, with a quote from Roman Jacobson, which, I hope, will point up the strength of impact poetry can really have.

A revolution in seeing depends on sharpening the way we *feel* about things. Intellectual and emotional responses need to work hand in hand to

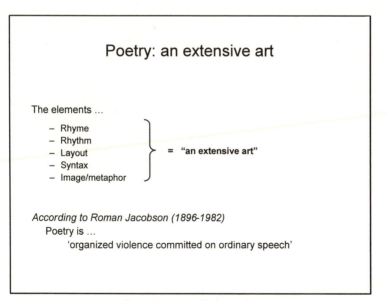

Fig. 4. Poetry: An Extensive Art

enable us to move from knowledge to perception. You can "know" a lot of things through rational deduction. But very often the enlarged capacity implicit in "perceiving" things won't be achieved by rational deduction alone.

Perceiving something requires more of you, or at least something different. than knowing does. Because perception includes the idea of "awareness." And awareness takes you straightaway into the realm of the senses and the emotions. *Aware* is the all-around response field, the full-on antennae, that Ted Hughes brought to bear in "The Thought Fox."

Would you rather be called knowledgeable or perceptive?

I'd like to be both, but if I had to choose one or the other I'd rather be called perceptive.

Why?

Knowledge is a state. Knowledge is time and situation relative. It can be overtaken; it can become outmoded.

Perception is a form of competence. Perception is an enduring quality. It is an adaptive mechanism that is never going to be passé.

Both knowledge and perception are enablers. Perception enables you to use knowledge creatively. Knowledge gives you something concrete to which you can apply your perceptive capability. Perception has to do with the removal of the rubber coat.

Poetical Emotion

I encounter in rapid succession two arguments, both cited by John Fudjack and Patricia Dinkelaker, that help me refine my own.

1. *Emotion is the ground of creation; it makes creation possible. Just how emotion works in the creative process is a mysterious and stupendous issue involving such questions as the nature of inspiration, prophecy, and the creative act.*
2. *Emotion is itself change . . . TRANSFORMATION. . . . Emotion is not just a change in conscious representations but a transformation of them in terms of symbolic reality.*

And then I unearth one more quotation, by Jacques Hadamard, that makes explicit the link between poetry and creativity for which I have been searching.

3. *[A]n affective element is an essential part in every discovery or invention. . . . no truth is born of the genius of an Archimedes or a Newton without a poetical emotion.*[2]

Emotions conceived of in what psychologists call "hot cognition" are adaptive devices that help us negotiate our environment. They operate in perception by grabbing and directing attention. They scan the landscape of our knowledge and thought to prioritize the material we encounter. They act as antennae, if you like, in terms of how we order and apprehend the world. Emotion helps us place things in the world without any knowledge of how we place them. A whole world of pathways and signposts and dwelling places and intersections is set up out of our sight, outside our (rational) ability to "know."

We're using this out-of-sight, emotion-perception resource all the time. We can often intuit the way things work more readily than we can account for or explain how they work.

I can make my laptop do all the things I need it to do. I could not say how I know what to do or describe to others what I do or what they can do to achieve the same ends. I just know that a certain set of actions feels right, another does not.

Psychologists have conducted an experiment that sheds light on how what we feel relates to what we don't know we know.

Case Study: Knowing and Feeling

Psychologists created an artificial language by specifying in advance a finite set of allowable transitions between letters. On the basis of this "grammar," fifteen acceptable letter strings were generated to be employed as training stimuli, and twenty-eight additional letter strings were generated to be employed for an anagram task.

Subjects memorized the stimulus materials and were later able to identify NEW strings of syllables as "well formed" (conforming to the "grammar") without knowing HOW they were performing this task.

Often subjects who demonstrated high levels of accuracy would verbalize incorrect rules or indicate that they had chosen an answer because it "felt" right. This experiment indicates that the "rules" governing the new grammar were internalized by the participants without having been logically followed or overtly understood.[3]

You could say perception is like a craft we travel in and hot cognition is a GPS facility we're quite unaware of, sending back information all the time about where we are in relation to everything around us. We trim our course by it in a cumulative way, with each change of tack minutely modifying how we see our position and therefore the precise impact of the next piece of GPS information we are fed.

Knowledge, Power, and Perception: Two Responses in Health Care

Example 1

Throughout much of the twentieth century, scientific discourse, intent on evidence, proof, and a demonstrable relationship between cause and effect, vilified "alternate" (or "quack") medicine. Only since the discourse of science has been called more into question and an associated realignment of power taken place, has alternative medicine gained a certain respectability. In drugstores and pharmacies there are shelves full of products that would formerly have been unsanctioned. Doctors' surgeries have adjunct areas for homeopathy and healing. "Alternative" has been reconceptualized as "complementary." And a new and powerful market has been opened.

Example 2

In Irvine, California, Professor Johanna Shapiro takes us for a delicious lunch. She has twenty years' experience teaching medicine. She is director of the Program in Medical Humanities and Arts at the University of California, Irvine. She has, for more than seven years, used poetry as an important means of widening doctors' understanding of patient care.

Professor Shapiro has a great understanding of the care of two weary travelers who have been delayed by a blank in the radar systems of the West Coast and spent an uncomfortable night in a motel adjacent to Chicago's O'Hare Airport. There was no soap or hair wash in the bathroom, breakfast consisted of an overfried doughnut, and the bed linen—and the cleaning services generally—had seen better days.

Johanna's lunch of salad and a glass of wine was the epitome, after the motel experience, of civilization. Her considered and humane approach has characterized the development of her medical humanities program. She is a poet herself and has successfully utilized poetry in helping doctors and patients to reenvision the nature of illness and aspects of patient care.

She is convinced that poetry creates an emotional engagement that can be lacking in scientific discourse. The clinical language of psychology, for example, teaches you—in an intellectual sense—what depression is. That is useful and valuable, Johanna believes, but it's not the same as actually putting you in touch with the experience of depression. This "putting in touch with experience" is what poetry does, she believes. Poetry enables you to *perceive* what you may already *know*.

There are no long-term studies of the effects of working with poetry, but Johanna and her colleagues at Irvine are convinced that poetry's opening up of the imaginative and creative potential of medical students, the refining of perception of those whose scientific knowledge is already second to none, is of fundamental significance in the future of patient care.

A Christmas Scenario

It's a few months later, a crisp Munich morning before I head out to the airport. We've had a two-day team meeting on the progress of the poetry project. Everyone is agreed that it's a long haul, but feelings are positive. Right by the Rathaus-Glockenspiel clock in the square, with its family of miniature people stiffly emerging from their boxes and taking their bows, we take a look at the Christmas market.

After two days of intensive discussion, it's good to be out in the air. We breathe deeply. The project seems to me just then like one of the carefully blown glass balls so festively displayed in the sales stalls. Their colors resist definition; their shape and delicacy invite but give warning against unconsidered touch.

"We throw away quite a few of these," the glassblower says to me.

I ask why, and he says, "They don't quite work out. They get lumpy or the thickness is wrong."

My BCG colleague expresses the hope, as we walk away from the market, that our project won't be subject to quite as much wastage as the glassblower seems to think is acceptable. He wants to press on with the book just as fast as we can. A nice, clean first draft in six months or so. Hopefully, not to be followed by too many revisions.

I share his enthusiasm but differ on what will ultimately be the shape of the process. I don't say what is in my head, that getting to the meaning of this project will be like peeling off layers, like gingerly unwrapping something with care and due respect for the discarded material. I don't tell him what I think about gradually getting the heart of the matter revealed to us or a version of that heart that will serve our purpose but not be the only possible version. That would be talking too much like a poet, not enough like a businessperson with her eye firmly on the ball.

༄ The Diver
by E. L. MAYO

Dressed in his clumsy, stiff, aquatic clothes,
His helmet screwed fast on so that he can
Do, say, see nothing in the world of man,
The diver shambles to the boatside, goes
Down the ladder, and the waters close
Over the steel that seals his sacred brain.
Over the boatside lean, his shadow scan
As it descends, shapeless and wavering.
It is no devilfish, is still a man—
But now it's gone.
                  Creatures beyond our ken
He will describe in words on his return—
Pale words for objects seen—
The inhuman life that swirled before his sight,
Or fled, or fought. The treasure he seeks out
May yet be lifted up by creaking crane,
Splashing, out of the green, but in his brain
The jungles of the sea must flower still,
Whose hook has drawn the pale blood of the shark,
And when his streaming bulk climbs back aboard,
We'll mutter, say some contract has been signed
With what lies under, and that that occurred
Which has no human gesture and no word.

6

Thinking Strategies: Poetry in Public

I land to stay here;
And the windows flock open
And the curtains fly out like doves
And a past dries in a wind.

The ARM-BCG Strategy Institute Forum

Can reading poems make a deeply uncreative person creative?

It's a voice from the back left of the auditorium.

No, I say. But it can maximize potential for seeing things freshly and so for contributing to creative potential and participating in creative debate.

Is creativity a group activity, then, as well as an individual one?

It's another voice, farther forward this time, in the middle of the third row.

That depends on the situation, I say. The creative leap more often than not is made in the individual mind: Archimedes jumping out of his bathtub, Friedrich Kekulé envisioning the shape of the benzene rings. But there's little doubt that creativity benefits from stimulation, from an environment where ideas rub off each other and create a spark.

The ARM-BCG Strategy Institute Forum is going well. It has the scent and taste of a successful event. There are about fifty people in the room; they've come from the opening offering of tea and coffee in a long reception area with enough windows to let in plenty of light. They've settled themselves on the dark blue chairs; they've greeted people they know and introduced themselves to people they don't know. Among the attendees are representatives of the Automobile Association and British Aerospace and the chair of the biggest engineering and IT professional organization in the UK, the IEE.

How can you find a common ground between you and the audience when you're dealing with a topic as apparently far removed from their everyday interests as poetry? I've decided to break the barrier by involving them in the process. I've persuaded four members of the audience to read out loud the four poems I'll talk about in the presentation. I give them the nod at the appropriate moment. They stand up. They begin.

They've read well and with feeling. It's stirred up interest, created an atmosphere of involvement, and bridged the divide between deliverer and receiver.

For the poetry project this forum is a first broad-scale public airing. I am expecting searching questions, but what I'm getting, generally, is:

- Enthusiasm for a possible new means of encouraging creative capacity
- Suggestions for situations in which poetry might be used in training and creativity development
- Expressions of enjoyment of the experience of poetry in an unexpected setting
- Endorsement for the BCG Strategy Institute's boldness in addressing such an unusual means

But there are lots of "aids to creativity" out there, says Robin Saxby, chair of ARM Holdings, PLC, and founder of the company. For me, painting is the one. That's what creates the space for creativity. Isn't it just horses for courses? Can you say what's special about poetry, what marks it out as a different and desirable means?

Poetry, I say, is the means that focuses most closely on the mechanisms by which we construct ideas, the mechanisms of language. There is a variety of "creativity tools" out there, most of which can be stimulating and beneficial. But poetry, being made up of language and yet going beyond language, addresses the borderland in our thinking where a vague apprehension can be turned into an idea. Of course, poetry isn't an "instead of"; it's a valuable addition. By its unusual juxtapositions, it constantly surprises, it encourages questions and connections, it develops, over time, a lasting thinking skill.

The chair of the IEE, who was one of the poetry readers, says, I would say one of the unique features is the way poetry grabs you. It sounds corny to say it, but I felt a tear in my eye when I was listening to "Stop All the Clocks."

A voice over in the corner says, Yeah, that makes sense to me. I did one of those things with building blocks, a group of us, and it was fun, and I think we got a lot out of it. But it certainly didn't engage me emotionally. It was like a game or a puzzle. There wasn't any sense of a competence having been developed, or an awareness, that would enable you to do a similar thing again. Once you've solved it, that's it.

One of the things, I say, that really makes poetry unique is how handle-able it is in material scope (a single sheet of paper, say, thirty lines or so of text in the general run) yet how very large it is as a ground for exploration. You can't exhaust a poem in one discussion or even ten discussions. And because it engages you you'll very often want to go back.

Are you suggesting, says someone who I later discover is a venture capitalist, that we use poems to throw light on specific issues? I mean, like, "The Road Not Taken" to tell us things about making decisions? Isn't it ultimately a content rather than a process thing?

It's very important, I say, to work with poems that have a ground for common interest with the group or audience. A poem like "The Road Not Taken" is a great stimulant for discussion of the decision-making issue. It's likely to tease out all sorts of complexities and nuances that might be missed in a discussion that didn't have the intricacies and contradictions of the poem as a starting mechanism.

But the thing of major importance is what the investigation of the poem does for your thinking processes. In terms of creativity predisposition, the kind of connections you have to make, the often unusual questions you ask, are there embedded in the structures and intricacies of the poem's form and language. You could see the poem as a kind of language and meaning maze that seems to change its disposition every time you step into it. It's said that a precondition for creativity is to go through the world in a constant state of surprise. Most peoples' lives contain, for good or ill, what look like some very unsurprising elements. Poetry encourages surprise not only about issues but also about itself; about yourself, about other people's reactions and readings, and, with any luck and if the poetry is good enough, about the world in general.

There's a buzz in the room; poetry has passed the interest and relevance test, with this audience at least. It's achieved acceptance as an idea and is potentially seen as a usable mechanism in the intellect, knowledge, and creativity realms of business operation. The *difference* of poetry, rather than creating indifference or antagonism, has created a sense of excitement. The head of the IEE is wondering, aloud, whether something like this ought to be included in the general training of his engineering and IT executives.

What I feel, chiefly, is pleasure at the tenor and level of people's responses and relief that the first large-scale public airing of the topic has gone well. I can sit back and enjoy the next two presentations. They both attract good questions, good interest. The supper is elegant, the champagne plentiful. Several people give me their e-mail addresses so that I can recommend some poetry to them; they want to read more, to think about things a bit differently.

Relative Perception

The beautiful young lady or the crone, the duck or the rabbit, the page of blotches or the cowboy riding. Which do you see? Which should you see?

This is the standard way to open a discussion about perception, about how the world isn't a static thing "out there" that we interact with; about how we create our own worlds through the way we see.

In the ARM-BCG forum the question of relative perception has been moved from considering standard pictures to inhabiting nonstandard words. What has been taken on by the audience is the way we create our world through language. They've accepted the message that language is where you formulate and make ready your ideas. They've taken onboard the notion

Fig. 5. Cowboy-riding inkblot

that the poem, being made up of language, is a different kind of entity from the duck and the rabbit. And very different from the mazes or pendulums or building blocks. We seem to be, the audience and I, in agreement that the poem is not:

a. A test in ingenuity
b. A new kind of problem with an answer you can reach
c. A trick you can figure out

That's fair enough, my reader says. You've made considerable headway. The idea that the poem is full of surprises, that it's a revolution in seeing, is a good one. It has traction. It appeals to the active desire for engagement that, in general, business practitioners demonstrate. A poem, in using language newly, makes you see newly. And think newly. But what about applicability? What are you going to say about that?

I suggest to her that through reading poetry the MBA graduate and her father in "Da Vinci and Daughter" would have been able, perhaps, to think beyond the duck, the rabbit, the blotches, the cowboy, the crone, and the young lady. They'd have been able to explore some mental ground that could amalgamate all these things or dispense with them or use the light from the window poetry created to look into the white space beyond the inked-in areas and *imagine*.

Imagine what? she asks me.

One thing or many things. Something that no one, so far, has imagined in that situation.

That's all very well, she says. But what does it mean in practice? How could that new way of looking at things be put to work to change things in my company? It's fine to say "emotion is transformation." I don't disagree with that. You've convinced me about poetry helping to strip off the rubber coat. But there's still the issue to be resolved of how it can be made to work in action. If you want to win people over, I think you'll need to be convincing about the real stuff of the value proposition.

Case Study: How Poetry Could Have Helped in Accor

The shift in emphasis from what the product will do to how the user feels about it is a crucial driver in the creativity economy.[1] Meeting what is fast becoming the Holy Grail of innovation—the "unmet, unarticulated" needs of consumers—is paramount. It underlies the successful shifts in perception that have changed corner coffee shops into Starbucks; old radio into new satellite radio; old crowded electronics stores into new Apple computer stores; old traditional, rather seedy circuses into the new Cirque du Soleil; old big, expensive airlines into new cheap, low-cost carriers; old Macy's into new Target; old earth-toned Birkenstock sandals into new colorful beach "Birkis."[2]

The hotel chain Accor had treated its hotel clients as just that—people staying the night and using hotel facilities. In a change process involving eight thousand employees across several continents, it reconceptualized its constituency. No longer clients but travelers. No longer one-night-standers but voyagers shuttling the roads and airways of a busy world.

There were three levels of change that Accor aimed to implement.

- From functional to human emphasis
- From logic of structure (hotel) to logic of flow (journey)
- From practical tie to emotional tie

Along with these aims Accor wanted to encourage a management style that:

- Favored creativity
- Could accommodate ideas about change and flux

In the context of Accor's diffuse management structure, the process it chose to achieve these ends was a "collective dynamic of interrogation" that involved inviting around eight thousand propositions around the theme *the pleasures of travel*. The reinvigorated notions of the client that came out of this exercise would act as the federating theme in the change process.

What could poetry offer in this process?

There are three places in particular where poetry might be an ideal mechanism for facilitating the achievement of aims such as Accor's.

1. *As the creative instrument in the collective dynamic of interrogation.* Imagine a selection of poems, all taking their own unique view of travel, traveler, destination, aim, means, context. Imagine them used as a basis for discussion over a period of time and across countries. The poems, in all their diversity around the common theme, would provide a live and lively forum for ideas generation, opening new ground, revisiting tried and tested conceptions, and coming up with unique but not static envisionings of who the client is.

2. *As a mechanism for a perceptual shift or expansion in the role of the "hotel."* Just as the ground for perceiving the hotel client would have shifted, so,

too, would space have been created to reconsider the role of "the hotel." An additional series of poems around the theme of hospitality, leisure, work, foreign places, or temporary spaces would open new spaces for conceiving the nature of the hotel as a dynamic entity caught for Accor's purposes in a specific contemporary moment that, like all moments, is subject to change.

3. *As a mechanism for generating an emotional sensibility in relation to the issues.* Exploring poetry's depiction of traveling and the traveler, and of the temporary place of repose that the hotel is in its different guises, could cause the participants to feel and experience the issues rather than merely contemplating them from a safe distance. What is the inner world of the traveller composed of? What might his emotional needs be? What range of expectations and hope might she bring with her? What fears and insecurities?

A summary of what poetry could have added: A series of interlinking common grounds for contemplation, discussion, and the sharing of views that are readily disseminable, of manageable size, not susceptible to refutation, transferable across culture zones, able to provide perspectives beyond the contemporary, able to strip off accustomed labels and provide fresh sight, require emotional engagement, and leave conceptions openended for future revision.

The fourth aim of Accor could also have been addressed: participants would be habituated to the instabilities of fluctuating view. Because reading and discussing the poems would encourage a layered and malleable notion of the traveller, his needs, her concerns, their expectations, a notion that moves when you work with it and requires you constantly to bring to the process of envisioning a willingness to be surprised, flexibility, and a questioning attitude that *does not allow for stasis in the conception of the traveler.*

⁓

A Very Particular Kind of Traveler

The Listeners
by WALTER DE LA MARE

"Is there anybody there?" said the Traveller,
　　Knocking on the moonlit door;
And his horse in the silence champ'd the grasses
　　Of the forest's ferny floor:
And a bird flew up out of the turret,
　　Above the Traveller's head:

And he smote upon the door again a second time;
    "Is there anybody there?" he said.
But no one descended to the Traveller;
    No head from the leaf-fringed sill
Lean'd over and look'd into his grey eyes,
    Where he stood perplex'd and still.
But only a host of phantom listeners
    That dwelt in the lone house then
Stood listening in the quiet of the moonlight
    To that voice from the world of men:
Stood thronging the faint moonbeams on the dark stair,
    That goes down to the empty hall,
Hearkening in an air stirr'd and shaken
    By the lonely Traveller's call.
And he felt in his heart their strangeness,
    Their stillness answering his cry,
While his horse moved, cropping the dark turf,
    'Neath the starr'd and leafy sky;
For he suddenly smote on the door, even
    Louder, and lifted his head:—
"Tell them I came, and no one answer'd,
    That I kept my word," he said.
Never the least stir made the listeners,
    Though every word he spake
Fell echoing through the shadowiness of the still house
    From the one man left awake:
Ay, they heard his foot upon the stirrup,
    And the sound of iron on stone,
And how the silence surged softly backward,
    When the plunging hoofs were gone.

I love the poem, my reader says, it's great. It creates an amazing atmosphere, and it's really evocative. But I'm worried about relevance. The twenty-first-century hotel client isn't going to turn up on horseback. Furthermore, it's a house in this poem—or even a kind of castle maybe?—not a hotel.

But, I say, don't those "faint moonbeams on the dark stair" have resonance with just about everybody? Isn't this a poem about a state of mind as much as a place or event?

I suppose it could be, she says. He's certainly lonely, the traveler, and we can all identify with that.

And he's trying to make amends for something?

Yes, that looks persuasive. He wants to make amends for something he didn't do in the past.

It seems to me, I say, that the comparison between movement and stillness is an important one. There's something very disconcerting about bringing a world of movement and action into stillness and silence and nonresponse.

Yeah, she says. I recognize that. That's how I feel sometimes when I check into a second-grade hotel. You turn up at reception and it's a ghost town. One assistant on the phone in the corner, a guy who looks like a loser in a brown mackintosh scanning the taxicab ads in the corner, the bell captain's desk with a layer of dust on it. I can tell you, it's times like that, 11:30 p.m. and the flight's been held over in Tucson, you begin to wonder, you feel like doing something.

It's a question of worlds with no linkage between them, I say. Both worlds are there, the traveler's and the listeners', but there's no way to bridge them.

It's the traveler, isn't it, who wants to bridge? she says. The listeners are holding themselves away from him.

That's certainly how I read it.

So there are very different aims and emphases on the two sides of the divide?

That's it.

The traveler seems like he's working to some old contract. There's a new contract in place that doesn't include him.

So the traveler and the listeners used to be in sync but they aren't any longer?

Kind of, she says. That would be one way of looking at it. Timing is all.

What interests me, I say, is where those "plunging hooves" are going to take him next.

I know where I'd like them to take him, she says, to somewhere warm, welcoming, and interactive. Somewhere with a big log fire, comfortable chairs, and people who step forward and say, Welcome!

Yes, I say, a space with warmth, light, and the timbre of people going about their ordinary business in a positive way.

Those stars, she says. That sky. The place he goes to next would need to be a kind of haven. He's going to need to recoup, get back on an even keel, reestablish himself in a world going forward not backward.

It's not just that traveler, though, is it? It's almost in the nature of travel itself to become disoriented, to see yourself as the existential outsider. Sometimes you wonder, in a funny kind of way, if you're ever going to get home.

So the place he goes to next—that should be somewhere that makes him believe coming home is possible?

And allows him space to choose how he handles the experience he's been through.

And looks after his horse, too. That horse! The ultimate time traveler.

So d'you think this poem might be worth using after all? I ask her.

She tells me she thinks I should use it. It has such a poignant atmosphere, it's very arresting. And you know what? she says. I'm on the lookout for other poems about traveling. I don't think I'm going to be thinking the same way about travel again.

Criteria for Success: Satisfying the Executive

Q: So what if I buy that poetry can help make a ground for creativity? How do I measure whether or not I've been successful?

A: You don't. Initiatives like this aren't verifiable though measurement. They are, though, verifiable through the application of criteria.

Some general criteria for the success of a poetry-creativity initiative:

- You think about an issue in more and different ways than you used to.
- You find absence of closure a stimulant rather than an irritant.
- You define the success of a discussion in terms that do not necessarily include closure.
- You multiply and revel in ambiguities rather than resolve them.
- You use paradox as a means of exploration.
- You take issue with the precise meaning of words and sentences.
- You deconstruct executive summaries and find them inadequate to certain purposes.
- You perceive the unusual in the usual.
- You question rather than accept norms and normalities; you don't take things for granted.
- You treat fact and reality and data as valuable provisional assessments of a world in motion.
- You feel the world as well as analyze it.

- You seek out poetry and read poems independently.
- You consider how certain poems can illuminate themes at hand.

And the organization that includes poetic competence in its creativity armory will, under appropriate and specifically chosen circumstances:

- Postpone the requirements for "results" and closure
- Include downtime for thinking in its definition of *productive*
- Modify its expectation of the logical progression of a project

✑ The Makers

by HOWARD NEMEROV

Who can remember back to the first poets,
The greatest ones, greater even than Orpheus?
No one has remembered that far back
Or now considers, among the artifacts
And bones and cantilevered inference
The past is made of, those first and greatest poets,
So lofty and disdainful of renown
They left us not a name to know them by.

They were the ones that in whatever tongue
Worded the world, that were the first to say
Star, water, stone, that said the visible
And made it bring invisibles to view
In wind and time and change, and in the mind
Itself that minded the hitherto idiot world
And spoke the speechless world and sang the towers
Of the city into the astonished sky.

They were the first great listeners, attuned
To interval, relationship and scale,
The first to say above, beneath, beyond,
Conjurers with love, death, sleep, with bread and wine,
Who having uttered vanished from the world
Leaving no memory but the marvelous
Magical elements, the breathing shapes
And stops of breath we build our Babels of.

7

A Poem Too Far

And, as in uffish thought he stood,
   The Jabberwock, with eyes of flame,
Came whiffling through the tulgey wood,
   And burbled as it came!

Where Order Meets Chaos: Two Kinds of Creativity

There's a theory that says there are two kinds of creativity: P-creative: this is where you conceptualize or do or engender something that's absolutely new to you. And H-creative: where what you conceptualize or do or engender is totally new. New not just to you but to everybody.[1]

Two things have to be in place for either of these to be operative. First, your emotions have to be involved, those compelling agents in generating creativity and change. Second, a new *generative grammar* has to be in place.

A generative grammar is, broadly speaking, a set of possible pathways (as yet untrodden) down which you can go to discover new intersections, byways, and vistas you didn't know could exist.

I discover an important link between this kind of grammar and what a poem has to offer in the work of Jerome Bruner. Bruner is one of the most eminent educational psychologists of the twentieth century. "The conventional apparatus of the psychologist," he says, "leaves one approach unexplored. . . . It is a way that grows happy hunches and 'lucky' guesses, that is stirred into connective activity by the poet and the necromancer looking sidewise rather than directly. *Their hunches and intuitions generate a grammar of their own—searching out connections.*"[2]

That "poet's" grammar, "searching out connections," is there some-where we can place it, some way to conceptualize it that could help eluci-date just what it is?

The linguist Ferdinand de Saussure places poetry on the outer bound-ary of "meaning" and how we construct it. He puts it where the order of organized language starts to break down. Different poets at different times have displayed more, or less, of the tendency to break down language. But one thing is certain: a characteristic of poetry is that it takes language into places it doesn't usually go.

One of several oppositions Saussure uses to elucidate his theories of language are syntagmatic (pertaining to the sentence) and paradigmatic (pertaining to the choices of unit used to make up the sentence). Thus, in the syntagm (or sentence) "I am afraid," the word *afraid* has a syntagmatic relationship with "I am," but a paradigmatic relationship with the words *frightened, scared,* and *fearful.* The logic of grammar is held in balance, in Saussure's opposition, with the chaotic world of possibility that encom-passes all the unchosen units that could have been used to make up the ut-terance. So, for example, table 3.

	TOM					
(syntagmatic →)	**THE** **CAT**	**SAT**	**ON**	**THE**	**MAT**	
	KITTEN					
	LYNX					
	JAGUAR					

(paradigmatic ↑)

The direct utterance of the sentence focusing on *cat* has occurred at the expense of alternatives, *tom, kitten, lynx,* and *jaguar,* among many others. The paradigmatic, therefore, suggests all kinds of possibilities that could have taken place, might perhaps take place at some time in the future, or are taking place in other situations all the time, which are outside our view and apparently outside our remit.

Saussure believes that these two axes, the syntagmatic and paradig-matic, are brought much closer together in poetry than in any other lan-guage mode. For everything that's said in a poem, there is a whole host of other possible utterances jostling just under the surface. The difference between the poem and "ordinary speech" is that the poem draws attention to the possibilities that the logic of language (the syntagm) has necessarily held in check (see the diagram on "the possibilities of language").

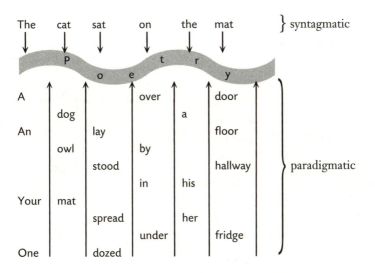

So poetry, more than other language constructions, encourages us to see "what is" in terms of "what might be" or even "what might have been." What *isn't*, in poetry's use of language, is always whispering its messages, always tapping on the door of what is.[3]

Case Study: Remodeling Meaning

Jabberwocky
by LEWIS CARROLL

'Twas brillig and the slithy toves
   Did gyre and gimble in the wabe:
All mimsy were the borogroves,
   And the mome rath outgrabe.

"Beware the Jabberwock, my son!
   The jaws that bite, the claws that catch!
Beware the Jubjub bird, and shun
   The frumious Bandersnatch!"

He took his vorpal sword in hand;
   Long time the manxome foe he sought—
So rested he by the Tumtum tree,
   And stood a while in thought.

And, as in uffish thought he stood,
   The Jabberwock, with eyes of flame,
Came whiffling through the tulgey wood,
   And burbled as it came!

One, two! One, two! And through and through
   The vorpal blade went snicker-snack!
He left it dead, and with its head
   He went galumphing back.

"And hast thou slain the Jabberwock?
   Come to my arms, my beamish boy!
O frabjous day! Callooh, Callay!"
   He chortled in his joy.

'Twas brillig, and the slithy toves
   Did gyre and gimble in the wabe:
All mimsy were the borogroves,
   And the mome raths outgrabe.

A Digression

I wonder why you're taking such a risk, my reader says to me.

We are walking down Fifth Avenue, it's a blustery day in March. She's holding her coat together and balancing a Louis Vuitton computer bag on her right arm.

You mean by including "Jabberwocky"?

I mean, she says, by including something that isn't going to make any sense at all to a lot of your readers.

But it's there for a reason, I say. It's making a serious point about perception, about what Saussure is saying a poem does.

I don't doubt the seriousness, she says. But don't you think you're taxing your readership with this unduly? I mean, I can see how some of my colleagues might take a look at "Jabberwocky" and say, *What is this? I thought this was a book about business thinking. Why am I being asked to read nonsense verse?* I appreciate there's more to it than that, but don't you think they'd have a point?

I'd hope by this time, I say, that most people would have taken onboard the element of playfulness that's a necessary ingredient of relating to language. In one way or another, playfulness is a characteristic that you need to cultivate if you're going to enter the joys and pains, the intense intricacies, that language can offer you. And entering those intricacies—reveling in them, really—is a necessary ingredient of acquiring the mind-set that can begin to resist the persuasions of the thought police.

A long-suffering look comes over her face. Her eyes water. Is it the wind coming up over the ocean from lot of cold places? She slows down a little.

Do you really think an acquaintance with "Jabberwocky" can be of applicable use to the business practitioner?

I believe it can help foster an agility with language and an awareness of impossible combinations that can lead to a beneficially freer mind-set.

OK, she says, let's try it. I've been involved with this thing almost from the beginning. I do think a freer mind-set could benefit many of us. The environment in which we do business is changing. I'm fairly convinced that we need to harness some of the more unusual ways of developing capability so that we can move with the times.

We walk on, more slowly now, till we get to the Convention Center. We climb the steps, and all those flags are flapping above us. We go around the corner and sit down in the shelter on a bench.

A Discussion

As a matter of literary history, Lewis Carroll was satirizing a certain kind of Victorian poetry, in particular the genre put forward by his peer Algernon Swinburne, who was famous for creating "emotional atmosphere" out of very little "substance." "Jabberwocky" is part of Carroll's *Alice in Wonderland* and *Alice through the Looking Glass* sequence. Those sequences were, in one way or another, about perception. Someone very big becomes someone very small, and the world alters.

This is what I would say the poem is doing.

- Asking me to look behind the words on the page to a whole host of other words that might have been written there
- Demanding imagination, requesting that I suspend assumptions about what (doesn't) make sense
- Placing meaning fairly and squarely in my own hands

Take that "brillig" situation. What's "brillig"? Maybe "brilliant" or "illegal" or "illegitimate"? Or maybe all three, all at the same time. Or maybe some other quite different combination. The possibilities are endless. And they depend on what's there, to be worked on, in each of our minds. As Saussure suggested, the poem is saying here's what's on the page; it's deliberately just off center. What can you see that's behind or beyond or below the things that are presented? Labeling it "nonsense verse" says no to all the possible connections. And says no to putting your mind to work in a different way.

Killing the Jabberwock: An Imaginary Discussion with My Reader

Those "slithy toves," she says to me. They make me uneasy.

Me, too, I say. I'm wondering if the speaker is one of them? Or the "he" with the sword?

It's the way they "gimble" along the seashore that bothers me, she says. And how "slithy" makes me think "slithery."

The "mome raths" add to it, I say.

They do? I thought they were OK. I didn't have a problem.

But don't they hang there between "moth" and "rat"? And that activity they're involved in, "outgrabe." Is it "grab," "grave," or "rabies"?

I see what you mean, she says. They seem like a pretty grasping lot. And there's also the question of the Jabberwock. They're all against him, but do we believe them? Are their motives pure?

Well, I say, the Jabberwock has "eyes of flame," so he looks quite threatening or frightening—

But then that's undercut, isn't it, by the "whiffling" and "burbled"? That seems inoffensive enough?

By the time we get to the "snicker-snack" sound of blade on neck bone, the killing stroke delivered with such "through and through" relish, the "galumphing" and chortling of the hero really bother me.

I agree, she says. Not very endearing. And what about the kind of "winding up" of the final stanza? Where things are repeated?

Isn't it a restoration, after a heroic interlude, of that opening, peaceful scene?

That's how I took it first of all, she says. But then, when I looked again, it took on a more sinister ring. After all that violence, those less than attractive "slithey toves" and "raths" go on uninterruptedly gyring and gimbling. They don't exactly have a moral conscience. Isn't there some danger they could be (I hate to say it) playing beach ball with the severed head of the Jabberwock?

An Alternative Reading: "Jabberwocky" as a Market Share Metaphor

Just who controls this island anyway? (We "know" it's a tropical island because of the Jubjub bird, the Tumtum tree, and those "borogroves"—redolent of "mangrove"—bringing to mind the steamy swamplands in which Ian Fleming's secret agent 007 enacts his battles against evil in *Dr. No.*) Our "hero" (the VP for marketing?), encouraged by hearsay and received opinion, goes forth to vanquish the force that's threatening his company's market supremacy. He's successful, too; the "opposition" is wiped out, and he returns to a rapturous welcome. But has his effort really been spent in the right way? *Was* the Jabberwock really a "threat"? Are the opinions on which his strategy of extermination was based reliable opinions? Are there stagnatory implications in the resulting retention of the status quo?

Taking It Further: Trying It Out

But sometime we will turn
back to the curtain and go
by plan through an unplanned storm,
disappearing into the cold,
meanings in search of a world.

Leda and the Swan
by W. B. YEATS

A sudden blow: the great wings beating still
Above the staggering girl, her thighs caressed
By the dark webs, her nape caught in his bill,
He holds her helpless breast upon his breast.

How can those terrified vague fingers push
The feathered glory from her loosening thighs?
And how can body, laid in that white rush,
But feel the strange heart beating where it lies?

A shudder in the loins engenders there
The broken wall, the burning roof and tower
And Agamemnon dead.

          Being so caught up,
So mastered by the brute blood of the air,
Did she put on his knowledge with his power
Before the indifferent beak could let her drop?

About "Leda and the Swan" and W. B. Yeats

"Leda and the Swan" was written in the same year W. B. Yeats was awarded the Nobel Prize for Literature, 1923. Its apocalyptic theme and tone reflect his concern both with the ongoing civil war in his native Ireland and the instability of political events on the world stage. In the mythical rape of Leda by the god Zeus disguised as a swan, which resulted in the birth of Helen of Troy and the subsequent destruction of early Greek civilization, Yeats places the question of power in a dimension that goes beyond the confines of space and time. But is the poem concerned with the rise and fall of states and nations and the role of a single event in tectonic change or with something more personal and individual? "It was the predicament of the lady that captured my imagination," Yeats admitted. "In thinking about her I rather forgot about the politics."

W. B. Yeats was one of the most prolific and influential poets of the twentieth century, publishing numerous collections ranging from *The Wind among the Reeds* (1899), which reflected his keen interest in Irish mythology and folklore, to the more robust and overtly modern *Last Poems* (1939). Essays and plays formed a significant part of his literary output, and his work overall reflects his interest not only in Irish politics and history but in the occult and myth. He was made a senator of the Irish Free State in 1922 and died in France in 1939. He wrote, toward the beginning of his career, "Everything exists, everything is true, and the earth is only a little dust under our feet."

Life Cycle of Common Man
by HOWARD NEMEROV

Roughly figured, this man of moderate habits,
This average consumer of the middle class,
Consumed in the course of his average life span
Just under half a million cigarettes,
Four thousand fifths of gin and about
A quarter as much vermouth; he drank
Maybe a hundred thousand cups of coffee,
And counting his parents' share it cost
Something like half a million dollars
To put him through life. How many beasts died
To provide him with meat, belt and shoes
Cannot be certainly said.
                              But anyhow,
It is in this way that a man travels through time,
Leaving behind him a lengthening trail
Of empty bottles and bones, of broken shoes,
Frayed collars and worn out or outgrown
Diapers and dinnerjackets, silk ties and slickers.

Given the energy and security thus achieved,
He did . . . ? What? The usual things, of course,
The eating, dreaming, drinking and begetting,
And he worked for the money which was to pay
For the eating, etcetera, which were necessary
If he were to go on working for the money, etcetera,
But chiefly he talked. As the bottles and bones
Accumulated behind him, the words proceeded
Steadily from the front of his face as he
Advanced into the silence and made it verbal.
Who can tally the tale of his words? A lifetime
Would barely suffice for their repetition;
If you merely printed all his commas the result
Would be a very large volume, and the number of times
He said "thank you" or "very little sugar please,"
Would stagger the imagination. There were also
Witticisms, platitudes, and statements beginning
"It seems to me" or "As I always say."

Consider the courage in all that, and behold the man
Walking into deep silence, with the ectoplastic
Cartoon's balloon of speech proceeding
Steadily out in front of his face, the words
Borne along on the breath which is his spirit
Telling the numberless tale of his untold Word
Which makes the world his apple, and forces him to eat.

About "Life Cycle of Common Man" and Howard Nemerov

The quasi-scientific feel of factual reporting gives to this satirical considera-
tion of a contemporary life much of its pathos and power. Nemerov's unease
with technology and the machine age, his concerns about the dehumanizing
effects of scientific materialism, are reflected in his parodic use of the pared-
back language of statistical analysis. And yet, is the poem chiefly an attack on
materialism or is its focus the extraordinary courage required to live be-
tween the two existential givens of birth and death? Critics have commented
on how the laconic mode of the narration, the lack of pyrotechnics in tone
and method, lend to the poem and its subject a moving dignity.

Howard Nemerov was awarded the Pulitzer Prize for his *Collected Poems*
in 1978. He was a pilot with the Royal Canadian unit of the U.S. Army Air
Force in World War II, after which he devoted himself to writing and teach-
ing. Among the many honors he received were a Guggenheim Foundation
fellowship and the National Medal for the Arts, and he was poet laureate of
the United States from 1988 to 1990. He died in Missouri in 1991.

∾ *Found in a Storm*
by W I L L I A M   S T A F F O R D

A storm that needed a mountain
met it where we were:
we woke up in a gale
that was reasoning with our tent,
and all the persuaded snow
streaked along, guessing the ground.

We turned from that curtain, down.
But sometime we will turn
back to the curtain and go
by plan through an unplanned storm,
disappearing into the cold,
meanings in search of a world.

About "Found in a Storm" and William Stafford

This short poem relies on an extreme situation for its dramatic effect.
Stafford has frequently written about man in nature, reflecting his long-
time residence in the large landscapes of the western United States. There
are parallels here with "Traveling through the Dark" in the exploration of
the responses of the human when deprived of the usual comforts of the
"civilized" world. Just how the orderings of cause and effect give meaning
to human existence is also, perhaps, being questioned in a gently enigmatic
manner that leaves interpretation wide open. The speaker of the poem
promises a return to the mountain at some later date, but are there reso-
nances of a greater journey of a more mystical kind, one that must ulti-
mately be undertaken?

William Stafford's first major collection of poetry, *Traveling through the
Dark*, was published when he was forty-eight years old. After working in
forest camps during World War II, when he was a conscientious objector,
he lived and taught for many years in Oregon, where he died in 1991. "A
writer," Stafford believed, "is not so much someone who has something to
say as he is someone who has found a process that will bring about new
things he would not have thought of if he had not started to say them."

❧ *Night-Time: Starting to Write*
by BERNARD SPENCER

Over the mountains a plane bumbles in;
down in the city a watchman's iron-topped stick
bounces and rings on the pavement. Late returners
must be waiting now, by me unseen

To enter shadowed doorways. A dog's pitched
barking flakes and flakes away at the sky.
Sounds and night-sounds, no more; but then I catch
my lamp burn fiercer like a thing bewitched,

Table and chairs expectant like a play:
and—if that Unknown, Demon, what you will
stalks on the scene—must live with sounds and echoes,
be damned the call to sleep, the needs of day,

Love a dark city; then for some bare bones
of motive, strange perhaps to beast or traveller,
with all I am and all that I have been
sweat the night into words, as who cracks stones.

About "Night-Time: Starting to Write" and Bernard Spencer

The British poet Bernard Spencer composed "Night-Time: Starting to Write" in the shadow of World War II. The sense of expectancy that resonates through these four stanzas is palpable. Perhaps also there is a slight feeling of menace with the watchman, the barking dog, and the bewitched light. Is this the menace of a country at war, a city in blackout during the blitz? Or is the process of artistic creation itself a battlefield? The poem is readily comparable with Ted Hughes's "The Thought Fox," but the emphasis on the sheer hard work of writing is particular to this poem.

Bernard Spencer published three volumes of poetry between 1946 and his death, under mysterious circumstances in Vienna, in 1963. He was educated at Corpus Christi College, Oxford, and edited the prestigious magazine *Oxford Poets* in the early 1930s. His poetic output was rather overshadowed by that of his more illustrious contemporaries, W. H. Auden and Stephen Spender.

The Fish

by ELIZABETH BISHOP

I caught a tremendous fish
and held him beside the boat
half out of water, with my hook
fast in the corner of his mouth.
He didn't fight.
He hadn't fought at all.
He hung a grunting weight,
battered and venerable
and homely. Here and there
his brown skin hung in strips
like ancient wall-paper,
and its pattern of darker brown
was like wall-paper:
shapes like full-blown roses
stained and lost through age.
He was speckled with barnacles,
fine rosettes of lime,
and infested
with tiny white sea-lice,
and underneath two or three
rags of green weed hung down.
While his gills were breathing in
the terrible oxygen
—the frightening gills
fresh and crisp with blood,
that can cut so badly—
I thought of the coarse white flesh
packed like little feathers,
the big bones and the little bones,
the dramatic reds and blacks
of his shiny entrails,
and the pink swim-bladder
like a big peony.
I looked into his eyes
which were far larger than mine
but shallower, and yellowed,

the irises backed and packed
with tarnished tinfoil
seen through the lenses
of old scratched isinglass.
They shifted a little, but not
to return my stare.
—It was more like the tipping
of an object toward the light.
I admired his sullen face,
the mechanism of his jaw,
and then I saw
that from his lower lip
—if you could call it a lip—
grim, wet and weapon-like,
hung five old pieces of fish-line,
or four and a wire leader
with the swivel still attached,
with all their five big hooks
grown firmly in his mouth.
A green line, frayed at the end
where he broke it, two heavier lines,
and a fine black thread
still crimped from the strain and snap
when it broke and he got away.
Like medals with their ribbons
frayed and wavering,
a five-haired beard of wisdom
trailing from his aching jaw.
I stared and stared
and victory filled up
the little rented boat,
from the pool of bilge
where the oil had spread a rainbow
around the rusted engine
to the bailer rusted orange,
the sun-cracked thwarts,
the oarlocks on their strings,
the gunnels—until everything
was rainbow, rainbow, rainbow!
And I let the fish go.

About "The Fish" and Elizabeth Bishop

The American poet Elizabeth Bishop became a popular subject for academic consideration during the later years of twentieth century. "The Fish" is one of her best-known poems, its brilliant accumulation of visual detail combining with a headlong mêlée of short lines and long sentences to produce a breathlessly hypnotic effect. The single incident of catching—and releasing—a fish seems to have a wealth of significance attached to it. Some commentators see the theme of perception as being central to the poem, while others focus on what they see as a moral journey. Is the realization of the importance of the fish as another sentient being a growth in the speaker's humanity or a regression into an overly squeamish attitude toward the necessities of life?

After graduating from Vassar in 1934, Elizabeth Bishop pursued a nomadic existence, traveling in North and South America as well as Europe and Canada. She eschewed the "confessional" style made popular by some of her contemporaries and focused on precise impressions of the physical world for her poetic explorations. Although she wrote sparingly and published only four volumes of poetry, her reputation as a strongly influential force on contemporary poetry has continued to grow. She died in Cambridge, Massachusetts, in 1979.

ல *Arrival*
by PHILIP LARKIN

Morning, a glass door, flashes
Gold names off the new city,
Whose white shelves and domes travel
The slow sky all day.
I land to stay here;
And the windows flock open
And the curtains fly out like doves
And a past dries in a wind.

Now let me lie down, under
A wide-branched indifference,
Shovel-faces like pennies
Down the back of the mind,
Find voices coined to
An argot of motor-horns,
And let the cluttered-up houses
Keep their thick lives to themselves.

For this ignorance of me
Seems a kind of innocence.
Fast enough I shall wound it:
Let me breathe till then
Its milk-aired Eden,
Till my own life impound it—
Slow-falling; grey-veil-hung; a theft,
A style of dying only.

About "Arrival" and Philip Larkin

Philip Larkin's brand of English understatement is a hallmark of his poetry, which first came to public attention in the 1950s. He is renowned for writing about individual loneliness and the inability of the human being to connect. While his imagination is generally rooted in England and Englishness, this poem explores, and perhaps undercuts, the possibilities of a new start in what may be a foreign destination. Larkin has sometimes been criticized for his pessimism, and the somewhat downbeat tone of this and other poems has given rise to accusations of an unduly negative view of human relations. Jean-Paul Sartre's comment that "hell is other people" certainly seems to find echoes in this poem. But is "Arrival" in the end a theater for the demonstration of a huge egocentricity or a moving exposition of isolation and despair?

"Arrival" was written soon after Larkin went to Queen's University, Belfast, where he spent the first half of the 1950s as sublibrarian. While in Ireland he developed and refined his laconic yet moving style and produced some of his best-known poems. He admitted that he had spent too much time in his youth "trying to write like Yeats" and later realized that Yeats wrote in a "particularly potent music, as pervasive as garlic." He was one of the foremost figures in twentieth-century poetry and was offered the opportunity to become poet laureate of the United Kingdom, which he declined. He spent much of his life as librarian at the University of Hull, and died in 1985.

Part 3

Thinking Values

*Posing and describing a question
can be much more valuable in the
long run than finding a solution.
Its focus away from closure toward
exploration is very much in tune with
the mind-set poetry can facilitate.*

The Trust Gap

I used to be Just Looking Round,
I used to be How Much, and
Have You Got it in Beige.

Now I devour whole stores—

The "New Black": Corporate Social Responsibility

Corporate Social Responsibility is big business. It is 5.30 p.m., a gray day in February. It has been dark for some time; the yellow stone walls and the narrow alleys of Oxford look rather insubstantial. The lights of Kellogg College spill down the steps and over the pavement in St. John Street. I am a few minutes late for the seminar. As I push open the glass doors of Mawby Pavilion and sit down at the back of the room, I hear those words or something like them.

José Arratia, senior corporate responsibility manager for Vodafone, has come to talk to us. Vodafone's image as a responsible corporation is central to the company's philosophy and positioning. Vodafone, a global cell-phone service provider, is wholly aware of the sensitivities surrounding such issues as the disclosure of call information to repressive regimes. Access to the Internet via cell phones has opened up a new ethical dimension, which the corporation is addressing. There are complex safeguards to help protect minors against the dangers of Internet pornography.

Mr. Arratia has an hour to speak. The planned format is a forty-five-minute PowerPoint presentation (he has a very full and informative slide deck, which will take his audience through the essential elements of Vodafone's corporate responsibility agenda) plus fifteen minutes for questions.

We will then adjourn to the bar for half an hour's informal discussion before dinner. Mr. Arratia was in the U.S. yesterday. He will be in Brussels tomorrow.

Forty minutes into his allotted time Mr. Arratia has not yet begun his presentation. He is still fielding questions about the ethical and social dimensions of corporate policy. To whom or what does a corporation owe allegiance? To shareholders? To stakeholders? To the ordinary men and women of the country it's operating in? To the policy standards of its home government? To the wider ethical agenda of "the West"? To the ideal of a globalization that will (ultimately) bring peace and plenty to the world?

His audience is not exactly hostile. But it is not exactly friendly either. It is poised on the cusp of what could be called a skeptical welcome. This is Oxford. The forms of politesse are in place with a vengeance. Mr. Arratia is our guest and will be given his due hearing, his due courtesy. Such courtesy does not preclude tough questions. The questions range from probing the way certain figures have been presented in the latest balance sheets (from an MBA student at the Said Business School) to issues of the ethical appropriateness of the company's policies in Africa (from an international human rights lawyer).

One thing comes across clearly. The MBA students around the table, who form the majority of the audience, are unanimous in their agreement that it is "uncool" to work for a company that does not have a significant and workable corporate social responsibility policy. Corporate social responsibility (or at least a policy calling itself that) is the "new black." To what extent the new black is merely a fashion is open to question. What it amounts to, its processes, and how it can be embedded in an organization, these are the issues that float in the air, never quite caught, over claret, over gigot of lamb, over coffee. Can Mr. Arratia send me two of the slides about TRUST that featured in his presentation? He can; he will be delighted. Two days later the e-mail address on his card delivers my message right back to me. Several permutations of the same address yield nothing better. I check the address and discover it is the correct one. I decide to try again later. Mr. Arratia (who has been courteous, open, and as helpful as possible in answering all the questions that have been addressed to him) has a lot to handle. Maybe his mailbox is full.

Poetry in the Global Framework

In the bar between seminar and dinner I have told Mr. Arratia that I am working on an argument that poetry can facilitate shifts in opinion. "You mean change people's minds?" he asks. I tell him it can provide something called a ground for surrender that acts as a basis for reframing and revisioning apparently intractable issues. Reframing and revisioning are essential first steps in opening up the possibility of a change of mind. And that possibility, in turn, can act as a catalyst in the trust process.

He laughs, then thinks about it for a minute. "Maybe you can encourage our customers to read poetry," he says.

The chamberlain announces that dinner is served. As we make our way through to the long table with its damask cloths and silver candles, I tell him it is highly likely that quite a few of them already do.

The slide he put up about TRUST is the one that sticks in my mind. Longer than the images of happily smiling Ugandan fishermen texting details of their catch to the market two hundred miles away. More even than the images of the selections parents can make to prevent their seven year olds being exposed to the ubiquitous influence of porn star culture. The simple bar graph showing that 33 percent of U.S. citizens trust President George Bush while only 3 percent trust large corporations is at once startling and yet not unexpected. This is what we are up against, Mr. Arratia has said. These are the facts of the matter.

It occurs to me that these facts and this matter underlie the nature of the reception Mr. Arratia is experiencing. Most people in the room are skeptical of Mr. Arratia's message because they are skeptical about the motives of large corporations.

The split between how corporations see themselves and how the world sees them is increasingly evident. It's also increasingly relevant to how a corporation sets about organizing itself, its positioning and its strategies for differentiating itself in the marketplace.

I consult a BCG Strategy Institute project that addresses precisely this issue. The Strategy Institute's Business and Society initiative focuses around consumer belief that large corporations are untrustworthy and are working contrary to the good of society at large. The consumer of pharmaceutical products, for example, worries about the price gap and provision of medication to developing countries. Excessive profits are a concern, and there is unease about the focus on products that enhance lifestyle rather than addressing disease. In the food industry, consumers are increasingly concerned about the escalation of obesity and how that may relate to the wider question of marketing to children. A general problem about food safety is perceived, and globally there are issues about fair trade. Increased preoccupation with climate change resulting from industrialization is already provoking significant economic consequences. According to BCG's Bolko von Oetinger and Martin Reeves:

The serious preoccupation with climate damage due to industrialization is also triggering a reappraisal of what economists term externalities. . . . The more we realize how sick the planet is, the greater will be the pressure to counteract it. . . . Insurance companies like Münchener Rück, Allianz and Swiss Re have for a long time been passing on to their customers the additional costs caused by climate changes.

The Business and Society project predicts that the potential effects of the trust gap are increased regulation, price controls, consumer pressure, and ultimately litigation.

High-profile comment is increasingly laying bare the problem. The implications of a company failing to pay sufficient attention to corporate social responsibility are already being felt. Jack Welch, the longtime CEO at General Electric (GE), recently said that talented executives prefer employers who "have understood that what's good for society is good for business."

It's clear that these are some of the reasons why companies are taking the idea of corporate social responsibility seriously.

Lack of trust (I write) *isn't just a state of play. It's a virulent dynamic in a changing field of operation.* I sit back, quite pleased with the phrase: *virulent dynamic.*

A Word of Caution from My Reader

Hang on, my reader says. Surely this book isn't setting out to question the economic structures of contemporary society? A corporation is, after all, an economic rather than a social unit. Without profit, the engine of the corporation will not run.

He is sitting across the aisle of the 767, two months later, on the way to Tokyo. It's taken a long time to get the workshop in Tokyo set up. Why do I need it? is the general feeling. Can't I just get on with it and write the final section of the book? There have been one or two voicings of unease about the project. This poetry thing—isn't it a little soft-edged, a little too noncommercial in emphasis? Is poetry *really* an appropriate subject for a major business consultancy?

My reader has hung in there with me. We're becoming friends, almost, a wary camaraderie has grown up between us aligned with a burgeoning degree of mutual respect. He's told me that as long as we're together he never gets bored.

I assure him that the book is not setting out to question the economic structures of contemporary society. I reiterate that it aims to tease out links between reading poetry and thinking strategically. The link it's currently focusing on is how a corporation might adapt to the multiple competing exigencies of the modern world in terms of the ever more evident lack-of-trust issue.

I understand the problem, he says. This is a challenge that global corporations are facing. It's true that "trust" and "corporate social responsibility" are increasingly recognized as important issues. But I'm not quite sure, in this instance, about the connection you were making between reframing and trust.

One of the things that makes trust difficult, I say, is when you believe the other person is incapable of entering your way of approaching things. If you find a ground for surrendering your hold on a preconceived view, there's room for maneuver. If you look at a poem on risk, or making a tough decision, or the value of work, or any other of a myriad of difficult issues, it won't let you rest on what you're comfortable with. So if you're discussing it with other people, everyone's view is explored and held up to question. Since the poem doesn't give a single answer, the balance of where the weight falls (Is this right? Is this wrong? What do I think about this?) is constantly changing. You're revisioning your view, together, in discussion. The poem is a ground for nonconfrontational exploration of values and attitudes.

That may be so, he says, but I guess in this instance you're thinking of context?

He frowns a little, holds out his glass for a refill as the cabin crew passes by.

Context, I say. Yes. A broader applicability.

And that's what we're doing here—poetry in the global framework?

I nod. When he says it like that, it seems more than a little preposterous.

My argument, I say, is that reading poetry feeds into the expansion of ethical sensibility.

You mean individually? he asks.

Yes, I say, but there's another layer. I want to do something more and see how reading poetry can work between cultures. Are compatible ways of looking at things going to come up? Will a poem translated into Japanese generate the same questions as that very poem does on the page in English? The "ground for surrender" idea—will it hold water? Can discussing a poem in the transcultural corporate arena overcome some of the barriers, exchange statement for question, argument for exploration?

Not that I want to counsel undue caution, he says. But that sounds like a pretty tall order. You'll need to bear in mind that people don't like to be preached to. Values. Ethics. Morals. Phew! You could just be opening a real can of worms.

That's one of the reasons, I say, that I'm glad you're with me. I want to make sure I don't overdo things. I need you there as a sounding board.

He grins and waves his *Wall Street Journal* at me.

You can borrow this when I've finished with it, he says to me. There's a neat piece in here on the power of poetry.

Changing Minds

Poetry by its nature, I write, *invites you to enter mind-sets opposed to your own. This is akin to why Socrates thought the poets were of doubtful value. The mind-set you're invited to enter is the fanciful, what-if mind-set. When philosophers talk about how the arts work in framing values, they talk about imaginative and emotional engagement. In art you have to enter how it feels to think or be or experience other than you are.*

Psychologists say these imaginative formations orient us in holding and acting on the values we believe we have. The well-known World War 1 poet Wilfred Owen put it this way: "My subject is war, and the pity of war. The poetry is in the pity."

But the way art can work as a change mechanism is a subject of discussion for contemporary commentators, too. Howard Gardner, building on his influential notion of multiple intelligences, has been considering how artists change people's minds *indirectly*. In his book *Changing Minds*, he argues that artists change minds differently from scientists and leaders of nations. Artists, rather than employing "theories, ideas and concepts," tend to "introduce new ideas, skills and practices."

Professor Gardner believes that through these means art effects a *change in sensibility*. He suggests that new movements in art, such as the great early-twentieth-century upheaval known as modernism (peopled by artists like Paul Cézanne and writers like Virginia Woolf) create paradigm shifts in the way we can see the world and human relations and the nature of humanity itself. (*Not for nothing*, I think as I read this, *did Virginia Woolf pronounce, having seen Cézanne's and the other postimpressionists' paintings, "In or around December 1910 human character changed."*)

Movements in art create, foster—or at least accompany—shifts in the way we see ourselves and the world. But while the tectonic shifts make highly visible differences, a fundamental justification for art itself is that the artwork enables multiple ways of looking at the world that are often new to the individual and, in the exhaustibility of "good" art, continue to be new, to offer fresh revelations, however long the individual may go on interacting with the work. As Ezra Pound put it, Literature is News that STAYS News.

I do not know it yet, but two opposing views will be expressed in Tokyo that become a kind of fulcrum in the hypothesis that poetry is relevant to changing business minds.

Tokyo, March 2006, view 1. At the end of the poetry evening, a senior vice president of BCG tells me his view: poetry is great, and valuable in its own right, but is opposed to business. What he actually says is, "Poetry is one thing. Business is another. What they are aiming at is fundamentally different."

Tokyo, March 2006, view 2. "I read poetry every day," another senior partner says. "Poetry is extremely valuable to me. It helps me connect to reality, to place things, to know what's important." He stops and thinks for a moment. "But then," he says, "my wife says I read it to take me away from reality. I don't know. I don't think she is right."

Shopping Blown Open

Over Outer Mongolia (the flight tracker tells me) I decide on an experiment.

A poem about shopping, I say to my long-suffering reader. He has his eyeshade out. He looks at it, looks at me, and reluctantly puts it away.

It was up on the Coudal Partners Web site. You know? That initiative they have where you phone in your poem and they have it up on the Web site to share?

Coudal? He says. They have a reputation for being an interesting company.

They are. I spoke to Jim Coudal. I'll tell you about that later.

The cabin attendant says her name is Jane and she's happy to join us. We go up to the quiet part by the door, next to the galley. Nothing is happening. It's one of those nontimes in a flight.

A poem? Jane says. It's been quite a long time since I've looked at any poetry.

Shopper
by CONNIE BENSLEY

I am spending my way out
of a recession. The road chokes
on delivery vans

I used to be Just Looking Round,
I used to be How Much, and
Have You Got it in Beige.

Now I devour whole stores—
high speed spin; giant size; chunky gold;
de luxe springing. Things.

I drag them round me into a stockade.
It is dark inside; but my credit cards
are incandescent.

Rationale for discussing Connie Bensley's "Shopper." Shopping is a big part of many people's lives. We enjoy it. It is recreational. Our ability to spend defines who we are in society. "High Street" confidence is an indicator of the state of the economy. The relative states of the major economies are indicators of the health and stability of the world. The desire to consume is what companies thrive on. Without consumers there are no companies. A free society is (to one extent or another) a consumer society. A happy consumer is an essential element in the growth of democracy, the spread of peace and opportunity. Truly, it might be said, if the customer is king, the shopper is sovereign.

Connie Bensley's Shopper: A Discussion

JANE: It looks to me like this woman has had a bad hair day. She loves being out there, doing it. But now her feet are tired. She's gone home alone. She doesn't care as much as she thought she might for the things she's purchased. So she questions everything. But in the end she finds her spending power comforting.

READER: Isn't it a bit wider than that? I mean, she starts off spending her way "out" but ends up well and truly "in." Behind a kind of barrier.

C. M.: A "stockade"—that's the word that's used there.

J.: Yeah, "stockade" sounds like she's defending herself from something.

R.: And what she's purchased. All that stuff—she drags it in there with her.

C. M.: I wonder what she's defending it from?

R.: Well, she's the only thing that's alive in the poem. The rest of it is "things."

J.: Except the road—that sounds kind of human when it "chokes."

C. M.: Something about where she ends that line seems important.

J.: On "chokes"? Leaving it hanging at the end of the line?

R.: It seems like "chokes" is an action all on its own, and then we have to change the meaning of the word from really choking, like gasping for air, into the way we use *choke* every day, for traffic, like gridlock, the ordinary use.

J.: The same thing happens with *spending*. She's "spending her way out"—like out of something really big, out of something she's trapped in. Then, because the "out" hangs at the end of the line, we have to adjust to "the recession." It's like a big, general thing made into an ordinary thing again. A recession. Just something that comes. Something that goes.

C. M.: What's the atmosphere of the piece? How is she feeling?

R.: Weary.

J.: Kind of skeptical and fed up with the whole thing.

C. M.: What makes you say that?

R.: It's the repetition of "used to be." The normal, ordinary things that happened before compared to the frightening things now. That's how she's feeling in the end, I think. Frightened.

J.: Yeah, that word *incandescent*. It sounds like a firework going off. But just a single thing burning, you know? Not like in a celebration. Not with other people. She's just alone, inside something, shut away with her things.

R.: And I'm wondering how the ordinary things—just looking round, and so on—fit with the "devour." She's suddenly changed into a monster? There's a feeling of *King Kong* in here or *Jurassic Park*. But I'm not sure how we got to there from "shopping."

C. M.: Could it have something to do with the way the ordinary activities are presented? Just Looking Round. How Much. Have You Got it in Beige?

J.: You mean the capitals?

R.: It's true, the capitals make it quite menacing. She's mixing up how people speak now—how young people speak now—with something really important. She's joining up the activity you're doing with the thing you are—

J.: Sort of "I'm, like, Don't give me grief here"—

R.: Yes, that, that's what I mean—she's mixing up how people speak now, and the capitals, to make it seem like she's *become* her shopping. She *is* Just

Looking Round. How Much. Have You Got it in Beige. So the ordinary things you say when you're shopping have taken you over, rubbed you out.

C. M.: But something's happened, hasn't it? "Used to" has become "Now"?

J.: Everything's bigger. She's turned into this monster that "devours whole stores"—

R.: It's become fantastical. It isn't real anymore. It's like a nightmare.

J.: Everything's bigger-better, "high-speed," "chunky," "giant size," "de luxe springing"—

R.: Except it's not better. That "springing," it's starting to make me think of a giant cat, a prehistoric tiger. The world's changed here. We've gone back to something. We're not going forward.

C. M.: Maybe the "stockade" fits in here?

J.: You mean, back to the Stone Age?

R.: So all that "spending your way out"—that going forward, progress, brightly lit malls—the idea is that it's taking us backward?

J.: It certainly isn't making this person happy. But the credit cards, aren't they like a beacon in the darkness?

C. M.: "Incandescent"?

R.: Well, one meaning I get from *incandescent* is "angry." If I say "I'm incandescent." I mean "with fury."

J.: So the credit cards are partly the destroyers; they're what makes the roads "choke." But they're also, aren't they, the only light in the darkness?

C. M.: Doesn't *incandescent* also mean "up in a big and blinding flurry of light and then gone again"?

R.: So beyond the credit cards is even more darkness?

J.: I don't think I'm ever going to feel the same way about the Bicester Village shopping mall again.

ൟ *Traders' Call to Arms*
by EUGENE SCHLANGER

(for Constantine Economos)

Our apparent greed mocked by the media;
Our insatiable need condemned by professors,
Who condemn materiality, lest their
Discussions of Foucault affect nothing.
Until you are part of a trading floor
You will not understand the excitement of
Real-time screens, of offers to buy that
Bid up dealers' prices around the globe
Instantaneously, uniting buyers and
Sellers in an enterprise that promotes
Enterprise. 3,000 dead by terrorists.
I'm short on Afghanistan, long on bonds.
Liberty is specious without a sound
And active economy. Position yourselves.

Eugene Schlanger dedicated "Traders' Call to Arms" to Constantine
Economos, a forty-one-year-old partner at Sandler O'Neill & Partners who
worked on the 104th floor of the World Trade Center's south tower and
perished on September 11, 2001.

Reconnecting Poetry

Does the poet
Evade us, as in a senseless element?

Evade, this hot, dependent orator,
The spokesman at our bluntest barriers

Destabilizing Meaning: Poetry and Knowledge

The unease Socrates felt about the poets hasn't abated in the two thousand years since he put his views forward. Aristotle's sense that the poetic temperament could upset the balance and order of a civilized state finds echoes in the notion, expressed by the BCG partner in Tokyo, that poetry and business have nothing to offer each other.

But why should this be? Given that poetry addresses complex issues of the human condition, that it questions givens and destabilizes meaning, that it challenges assumptions by making unexpected associations that can't be pinned down, that it focuses on precision in communication while at the same time encouraging refinement and expansion of available frames or fields of perception, and that in placing itself on the cusp of language usage it requires of its readers a continually cutting-edge replenishment of modes of thought and expression, what is the unbridgeable chasm that separates poetry from business activity?

Somewhere in the two millennia since Aristotle suggested that poetry posed a danger to the well-run state, science outstripped poetry and the other literary forms in investigating and presenting the facts of the contemporary world.

The debate about the relative values of poetry and science has centered around the relation of each to *facts.* Here is I. A. Richards, one of the most influential literary critics of the twentieth century.

> It will be admitted—by those who distinguish between scientific statement, where truth is ultimately a matter of verification as this is understood in the laboratory, and emotive utterance, where "truth" is primarily acceptability *by* some attitude, and more remotely is the acceptability *of* this attitude itself—that it is *not* the poet's business to make scientific statements. . . . *A pseudo statement is a form of words which is justified entirely by its effect in releasing or organizing our impulses and attitudes.* . . ; a statement on the other hand, is justified by its truth, *i.e.,* its correspondence, in a highly technical sense, with the fact to which it points. . . . A pseudo-statement, as I use the term, is not necessarily false in any sense. It is merely a form of words whose scientific truth or falsity is irrelevant to the purpose in hand.[1]

A poem is, in these terms, a pseudo statement. Richards didn't mean anything remotely pejorative by this. He meant that poetry is trying to do something different from what science is trying to do.

Richards has been accused of suggesting that poetry is dealing in a different *kind* of knowledge from the knowledge science deals with. I think he is saying that the *forms* in which poetry *approaches* knowledge are different from the forms in which science approaches knowledge. And that the expectations attached to that approach, and to its value and importance and fruitfulness, should be similarly different.

One thing that's highlighted in what Richards says: the importance of poetry in *releasing or organizing our impulses and attitudes.* For impulses and attitudes we could substitute "feelings and values." Contemporary philosophers such as Martha Nussbaum have written extensively on the role literature, including poetry, plays in our value systems. The process of catharsis (variously interpreted as clarification, illumination, or purification) implies that in undergoing imaginatively the emotional situation of a poem, story, or play we emerge from the experience as though we had "really" undergone it; and so we've undergone the commensurate expansion of our understanding of the issues involved in the situation and our attitudes and values in relation to the situation have been developed accordingly.

Plato feared that poetry's access to feelings opened up a concentration on the baser, nonrational aspects of the human psyche. We now know that feeling and reason work together; our emotions are vital in orienting us in the world and fundamental to our value systems and the decisions we make.

One of the central powers of literature in helping us reach a deep understanding through this as-if mechanism lies in what we *are not told* in the literary work. The philosopher David Hume wrote, "The sentiments of others can never affect us but by becoming, in some measure, our own."[2]

In what ways can a poem make the sentiments of others become, in some measure, our own?"

Reframing Values

Emotions are evolutionary devices for identifying significance and adapting to the environment. They are vital in orienting us toward the holding of values. They trigger reevaluation of goals, plans, and concerns. Such reevaluation is the basis for a changing of mind or, in Howard Gardner's terms, developing a new sensibility. A poem, by taking us into a heightened and contained emotional arena, can intervene significantly in this process.

In part 1 of this book I made the case for "poetic competence" being a mode of cognitive response that is based in a ready movement between the logical-deductive (rational) and nonlogical or intuitive (emotional) realms. I made the argument in part 2 for how the "hot cognition" generated by reading poetry can encourage creativity. In this section of the book my argument centers on the role poetry has in generating the particular perceptions (perhaps these could be called the "deep realization") that may help inform ethical and social sensibilities.

The development of ethical sensibility is a mind-changing process. The changing of mind is partly dependent on a reframing of viewpoint in which the transformative potential of art can be a major motor. Martha Nussbaum encapsulates this potential in her belief that artworks

> both show us and engender in us a process of reflection and (self-) discovery that works through a persistent attention to and a (re-) interpretation of concrete words, images and incidents. . . . Every horizontal link contributes to the depth of our view of the particular, and every new depth creates new horizontal links.

How does this work? Nussbaum draws attention to Aristotle's view that ethical knowledge comes via perceptions of the particular rather than from generalizations. These perceptions of the particular are arrived at by means of a cognition that includes emotional response.

These are not new ideas, although in Nussbaum's hands they are given contemporary urgency and relevance. The case for the moral force of poetry has long been argued. As long ago as the 1580s, Sir Philip Sidney, in his *Apology for Poetry*, made an explicit case that moral philosophers and historians cannot compete with the "speaking picture" the poet offers. Their wordy approaches to the realms of abstraction (philosophy) or exemplification (history) must inevitably be outshone by the mediating force of poetry, which "setteth virtue so out in her best colours . . . that one must needs be enamoured of her." It is the power poetry has to move its reader, in other words its requirement to access feeling and emotion as well as logic and reason, that makes it the more likely vehicle for exercising moral change.

There's more to it than this, though. The absence of a simple, singular message in the artwork is part of its value in developing an ethical sensibility. The alternatives art offers—which often seem incompatible—should be part of what commentators have called "mature ethical deliberation." This deliberation helps foster individual judgments against the grain of the sometimes crude generalizations that surround us in everyday cultural exchange.

How does a poem help foster such individual judgments? By engaging the imagination as a working vehicle. Samuel Taylor Coleridge, in his famous *Biographia Literaria* (1817), puts forward the idea that the imagination "reveals itself in the balance and reconciliation of opposite or discordant qualities." If empathy or imaginative engagement is necessary for the development of ethical knowledge, then the never-ending attempt at reconciliation that is involved in making sense of a poem, however partial and incomplete this must inevitably be, must give considerable exercise to the faculty of imaginative engagement.

"Poetry leads us to the unstructured sources of our beings, to the unknown, and returns us to our structured, rational selves refreshed."

Do you believe that? My reader's voice speaks that, just a whisper, quite close to my ear.

I put down the article by A. R. Ammons, whose work, up to now, I haven't been familiar with.

"Poetry is a verbal means to a non-verbal source," I whisper back. *"That's what Ammons says. It is a motion to no-motion, to the still point of contemplation and deep realization."*

There's a short silence, I can hear nothing but hiss and crackle, like the ether maybe, like listening to the airwaves. Eventually my reader comes back to me. His voice is small and distant.

Given the context, he says, *I think that makes sense.*

How Poems Change Minds

Rhyme, rhythm, image, layout, and syntax are vital ingredients of a poem and are what take it "beyond language." They are also vital ingredients in making a world you can enter, one where you can flex your imaginative muscles and breathe the heady freedoms of undictated air. They are, perhaps most vitally for this part of my argument, the mechanisms through which the ready movement between language logic and feelings and intuition (poetic competence) can be brought about.

The poet Wallace Stevens, himself a businessman, put this question about what a poem is and does.

Is the poem both peculiar and general?
There's a meditation there, in which there seems

To be an evasion, a thing not apprehended or
Not apprehended well. Does the poet
Evade us, as in a senseless element?

Evade, this hot, dependent orator,
The spokesman at our bluntest barriers,
Exponent by a form of speech, the speaker

Of a speech only a little of the tongue?

from "Notes toward a Supreme Fiction: It Must Change, IX"

Is the poet evading us by constantly moving between the peculiar (particular) and the general? Or is this movement (if we can tune in to it) precisely where the value of the poet lies—as the spokesman for something most of us can only grope after?

One of the poems we are going to look at in Tokyo is Robert Frost's "Stopping by Woods on a Snowy Evening." I first read and thought about this poem when I was eight years old. I was attracted in particular by the harness bells, the snow, and the mystery, not necessarily in that order. Since then I have lived and relived Frost's midwinter moment of stillness again and again. But how will the Tokyo BCG group respond to such an enigmatic poem, with no strongly apparent direct link to a business theme?

Stopping by Woods on a Snowy Evening
by ROBERT FROST

Whose woods these are I think I know.
His house is in the village though;
He will not see me stopping here
To watch his woods fill up with snow.

My little horse must think it queer
To stop without a farmhouse near
Between the woods and frozen lake
The darkest evening of the year.

He gives his harness bells a shake
To ask if there is some mistake.
The only other sound's the sweep
Of easy wind and downy flake.

The woods are lovely, dark and deep.
But I have promises to keep,
And miles to go before I sleep,
And miles to go before I sleep.

"Stopping by Woods on a Snowy Evening" seems pretty straightforward. When you first read it, you wouldn't think it's speaking about very much, certainly not anything about which there are "barriers," nothing we really need a "spokesman" for. The words on the page give the impression that what's being told of here is a simple incident. A man in a horse drawn cart is on his way from somewhere to somewhere. It's the middle of winter, the end of a short day. He stops and savors the silence of nature. His horse wonders why they are stopping. The man knows he must continue on his journey.

But for most people there is also an immediate feeling that something else is going on. There's a sense of mystery and doubt, of teetering on the brink of something deeply important but unexplainable. Whether the mystery and doubt—and, in Sidney's terms, the delight and beauty—of the poem will be strong enough inducements to interest the Tokyo BCGers is uncertain. It's a risk. I decide to take it.

Why take the risk?

Frost's poem is a wonderfully compact vehicle for opening up the mechanisms that effect a change in sensibility. All its aspects add up to a representational redescription that can never be exhausted, a meaning in motion that can never really be pinned down.

How does this meaning in motion work? What are the elements?

a) Syntactical ambiguity. Right from the first line the poem hovers between statement and question, between knowing and doubting. "I think I know" is a sequence that usually leads to certainty rather than away from it. But here the thinking seems to be leading away from the knowing, the implied "but" bringing unease and a feeling of disorientation. Has the speaker been away and is now returning? Or is he leaving a familiar world and already reaching the end of his knowledge?

b) Rhythmic countertow. If the language seeks to unsettle, the steady beats—four stresses per line in the first four lines—indicate an opposing stability and firmness: da-**dah**, da-**dah**, da-**dah**, da-**dah**—rather like the reassuring beat of the horse's hooves walking steadily along that winter-evening road. You get pulled—at a "feelings" level—between the two without really being aware of it.

Allied to this is the way the sentences slow down the movement. Line 1 is a complete sentence, then lines 2 to 4 are as well. Lines 4 to 8 are also a complete sentence. Lines 9 and 10 are a complete, shorter sentence. Lines 11 and 12 ditto. Line 13 is a very short sentence all its own. The speaker is on a journey (he has "miles to go"), but the poem is about *stopping*. And that's just what the sentences do: bring the reader to a halt right on "The woods are lovely, dark and deep."

c) Paradox. But there's something here that doesn't quite work out, emotionally. Do "lovely" and "dark and deep" really go together? Unless you're a deep-sea diver or a caver, the words *dark* and *deep* are generally more threatening than inviting. But that won't do either because the loveliness of those dark, deep woods *does* make sense. How many of us have not, at one time or another, thought about striking out into the unknown challenges of the uncharted world? Could this poem be addressing just that—sticking to the known way, the tried and tested, the mapped out—or striking out into the dangers and excitements of the unexplored?

d) Image. It's as though from the moment the "frozen lake" emerges out of the dusk and into our view things begin to slow down and falter. Forward motion has ceased. The speaker's journey is on hold. Beautiful certainly, treacherous maybe. But above all, the image of a frozen lake suggests *stasis*. A temporary state of enforced immobility and sub-zero dormancy appertains here. And Frost has placed this image right at the heart of his poem—line seven out of sixteen. What the image leads straight to is "the darkest evening of the year" (in the northern hemisphere, the shortest day, the point of least light and growth, the nadir of the year compared to midsummer's zenith of expansion and abundance). What the frozen lake image leads to in terms of the shape of the poem is precisely those increasingly shortened lines, which lead to the pivotal, singular, enigmatic statement "The woods are lovely, dark and deep."

e) Sound patterns. The countertow principle takes us forward into how the rhyme works. The full and open end rhymes of *know, though,* and *snow* wrap themselves into a firm container for the thinner and more discordant *here.* But then, in the second set of four lines, that uneasy vowel sound is taken up and put into the foreground via a word that emphasizes the unease of it: *queer. Queer, near,* and *year* work as the off-key rhyme container of the centrally important *lake.* That lake, corralled by the *ee* sounds of *queer, near,* and *year,* is a "frozen lake"—the *o* of *frozen* chiming in with those full rhymes of *know, though,* and *snow,* taking them sideways, agreeing yet disagreeing, notching up the emotional temperature of the poem, adding at the inexplicit, feeling-state level of the auditory imagination a complex layering that allows the reader no certain conclusion or rest.

The Cusp of Mind Change: Poetry in Motion

The shake of the harness bells is the cusp on which the poem turns. The only other living entity in the poem is the "little horse." It is his harness bells that "ask if there is some mistake." Whether there is a mistake and what the nature of that mistake might be is never addressed or answered directly in the poem. The shake of the harness bells acts as a wake-up call from a kind of reverie, an input from the living, breathing world into the breathless world of white, still dormancy. That world—and the speaker—seem both to hold their breath as the shake of the bells echoes in the imagination. "The only other sound's the sweep / Of easy wind and downy flake." *Easy* and *downy* are both malleable words with meanings behind the immediately straightforward ones. *Ease* means rest and *down* is what pillows and quilts are made of, suggesting, along with those elongated, steady rhythms, the call of sleep, the rest beyond effort.

The breathless moment of listening is rewarded by a kind of answer, although the nature of the question is never made explicit. A corner has been turned. A psychological corner? An emotional corner? Those woods are "lovely, dark and deep," wonderfully enticing and a strong draw to the speaker (and to the reader, who is caused to inhabit the speaker's emotional and imaginative shoes for the space of the scene the poem evokes and encapsulates)—BUT.

The spell of silence and stasis, of inhuman communication, is broken by an abstract notion, the intrusion of a moral universe: "I have promises to keep." It is those promises that set the speaker and the poem in motion again via another shift of meaning, a regearing of the plates of significance: the desired state of ease or rest or sleep has now been transferred to the future to be enjoyed some time at the end of the journey after all the "miles" have been traversed. More than that, though, the idea of the miles has itself turned into something soothing, a lullaby of sorts. "And miles to go before I sleep, / And miles to go before I sleep" has become a promise that the repeated vowel sound *ee* of *keep, sleep,* and *sleep* have picked up from the earlier *easy wind.* Don't do it now, the poem says; the reward of peace and rest will be waiting later. It's the journey that's calling now, the way forward that needs your energy and attention.

Something momentous has happened. A point of realization has been reached and passed through. The horse, the speaker, and the journey are in train again. Neither the speaker nor the situation is given any detailed substance or description. The poem addresses a state of being that is interpretable in many ways. It is precisely its unpinned-down quality, the gaps it leaves for the reader to respond to, ponder, and maneuver, that makes it something you can enter and become part of.

The poet T. S. Eliot expressed this complex mode, which is fundamental to how poetry works, in the following manner.

> The only way of expressing emotion in the form of art is by finding an "objective correlative"; in other words, a set of objects, a situation, a chain of events which shall be the formula of that *particular* emotion; such that when the external facts, which must terminate in sensory experience, are given, the emotion is immediately evoked.[3]

This notion of the *objective correlative* helps to explain how the poem is particular and general at the same time and how this mixture of particularity and generality can make the poet a "spokesman at our bluntest barriers." Image, rhythm, sound pattern, and syntax add up to the complex of *emotions* that gives rise to *feelings,* which inform how we *value* the complexities the poem proposes to us. I have returned to this poem again and again in the not inconsiderable number of years that have passed since I first read it. This is what I've taken away from it.

It's made me think deeply and from numerous different angles about how it feels to be cut adrift, momentarily, in a detached observational space on one's life.

It's made me consider the relation of the immediate to the long term.

It's made me hunger after a clarity that perhaps only comes with isolation.

It's made me think about time, truth, and duty.

It's made me think about the intuitive relationship between human and animal.

It's made me think about the importance of stopping to consider the particular when I am in pursuit of a general goal.

These thoughts and considerations have come directly out of the intensity with which I continue to "feel" myself stopping by those woods. That intensity comes back to me sometimes when I am passing real woods, when I am driving through the Royal Forest of Dean in England, or through the extensive woodlands of western Massachusetts, or through the pine forests on the Swedish-Norwegian border.

I think about it as I am flying farther and farther north on my way to Tokyo. A sunny afternoon, chasing the day forward through time zones. No reader is in sight. Robert Frost's snowy woods are below me as well as in front of me. I wonder what relevance they will have for the group in Tokyo. How transportable is emotion? How common is the feeling generated by image, rhythm, and the intricate patterning of sound? How much will be lost, or found, in translation? The horse shakes his harness bells again, and the iced lake glitters.

✑ *On First Looking into Chapman's Homer*
by JOHN KEATS

Much have I traveled in the realms of gold
    And many goodly states and kingdoms seen;
    Round many western islands have I been
Which bards in fealty to Apollo hold.
Oft of one wide expanse had I been told
    That deep-browed Homer ruled as his demesne;
    Yet never did I breathe its pure serene
Till I heard Chapman speak out loud and bold:
Then I felt like some watcher of the skies
    When a new planet swims into his ken;
Or like stout Cortez when with eagle eyes
    He stared at the Pacific—and all his men
Looked at each other with a wild surmise—
    Silent, upon a peak in Darien.

Intelligent Movement

For poetry makes nothing happen: it survives
In the valley of its making where executives
Would never want to tamper

West Point Leadership

One fundamental difference between poetry thinking and business think-
ing is that business thinking is supposed to have *action* as an outcome. If, as
W. H. Auden said, "Poetry makes nothing happen," then poetry is, has to
be, cannot avoid being, irrelevant to the exigencies of the business world.

Except, of course, it is not as simple as that.

The most action-oriented realm in which you could be involved is,
arguably, the military. Nothing could be further from the speaking picture
of a poem than the carefully orchestrated mayhem of the battlefield. And
nothing, surely, ought to be more removed from the precision of military
strategy than the emotional or aesthetic or ethical considerations the lyric
poem addresses?

Lt. Gen. James Lennox disagrees. General Lennox, who has had cen-
tral responsibility for the development of the West Point curriculum since
1990, believes the study of poetry is vital to the development of the high-
est possible caliber of military leaders. "Poetry gives our cadets," he says,
"a new and vital way of seeing the world . . . . Since *The Iliad*, poetry has
allowed its writers to capture war's chaos and horror with a power that
other artists lacked."[1]

The value of this, according to Lennox, is that it enables future military leaders to engage with new ideas that challenge their worldviews by offering "differing perspectives, competing values and conflicting emotions."

Cadets at West Point spend sixteen weeks studying poetry from the ancients to the present day. This study, as well as sharpening their communication abilities ("good communication is essential to every leader," General Lennox believes), also helps military graduates face the practical challenges of on the ground combat, "whether to fire at a sniper hiding in a mosque, or how to negotiate agreements between competing tribal leaders." Standard answers to these questions are never enough. In the absence of standard solutions to these complex dilemmas, poetry has a vital role to play. The nature of that role is, according to General Lennox, that "in teaching cadets poetry we teach them not what to think, but how to think." The "how to think" that he points to bears a distinct resemblance to the "higher powers of mind" referred to by another general, Carl von Clausewitz, in his magnum opus *On War* (1832). The powers of mind Clausewitz believes are vital to the strategist include "a wondrous pitch of vision that readily touches on and sets aside a thousand half-obscure notions that a more common intellect would bring to light only with enormous effort, and that would become exhausted in the process."

But it goes deeper, even, than that. General Lennox makes the case for poetry as a mediating force in the following, persuasive way. The "romance" of war is one thing, the reality another. Poetry strips away the trappings of "romance" (could he mean, here, something close to stereotype?) and makes you see, clearly, the reality. This is very like what Victor Schklovsky said about poetry stripping off the rubber coat. And it's just what Wallace Stevens means when he talks about the poet as "spokesman at our bluntest barriers."

Our bluntest barriers tend, perhaps, to be the things we believe in most fully, the things we *feel* to be right, often without really considering them. So for the West Point cadets notions of patriotism, duty, and glory, may be uppermost in their belief systems at the start of their military careers. Poetry shows them the other side, too. Wilfred Owen's bitterly antiheroic "Dulce et Decorum Est" is on their curriculum. Tennyson's "Charge of the Light Brigade" opens up the futility and waste of life inherent in all war. These issues are presented to America's military elite in the form of *poetry* because the "competing values and conflicting emotions" discoverable in the compressed language entity of the poem can positively inform the same conflicting values and emotions that will face the leader in battle situations. What General Lennox seems to be implying is that military leaders should be humane, informed, and well-rounded individuals with an ethical system based in well-considered oppositions rather than simple dogmas. If these are the lessons deemed suitable for America's future combat leaders, heading their nation's military imperatives in ever more complex global conflict situations, might there not also be something of value to business leaders, setting out to handle the dense complexities of the cross-cultural commercial world?

The Kind of News Poetry Brings

If America's future combat leaders are caused to spend considerable amounts of time studying poetry, ought the prospect to be as alien to business leaders as is often supposed?

Dana Gioia, former businessman and chair of the National Endowment for the Arts, makes this unequivocal statement about the value he has found in poetry.

> In terms of shaping the individual imagination, [Auden's] poetry certainly changed my life, enlarging my sense of the world, language, and the human heart.

The role of the poet as bringer of important tidings that are likely to be ignored by the executive is summed up by W. H. Auden in his poem "In Memory of W. B. Yeats," in this way:

> For poetry makes nothing happen: it survives
> In the valley of its making where executives
> Would never want to tamper, flows on south
> From ranches of isolation and the busy griefs,
> Raw towns that we believe and die in; it survives,
> A way of happening, a mouth.

The contention of this book is that executives should tamper in the valley of poetry and that their executive selves will benefit from this engagement. In particular, part 3 of the book argues that the estrangement of the executive world from the general world could be lessened by an engagement with poetry. That the trust gap that has undoubtedly opened up alarmingly between global corporations and the object of their existence—the man or woman in the street—could begin to be addressed. In this, the role of values, or "ethical sensibility," is seen to be central.

William Carlos Williams, poet and medical practitioner, made the link between ethics and living in the world and poetry's role in creating a conduit in the following persuasive way in "Asphodel, That Greeny Flower."

> My heart rouses
> > thinking to bring you news
> > > of something
>
> that concerns you
> > and concerns many men. Look at
> > > what passes for the new.
>
> You will not find it there but in
> > despised poems.
> > > It is difficult
>
> to get the news from poems
> > yet men die miserably every day
> > > for lack
>
> of what is found there.

What "concerns you / and concerns many men" are *values*, the "how to think" that General Lennox was referring to, the set of intangibles that subsist in the rational-logic/intuitive-emotional dynamic the poem creates. No one is suggesting that reading a poem or two will turn you into a deep-thinking, contemplative individual with a live and constantly developing ethical sense. But the "way of happening" Auden refers to has something important to say about what poetry offers. The poet and critic George Szirtes puts it this way:

> The sweetest sound in all the world, said Finn MacCool of Irish legend, was the music of what happens. The music of what happens is the sensation of being alive to any event, from insects running about in a square of grass and the sun moving down a brick wall, to the power of a volcano, the fall of a temple or the death of a child. Or the deaths of thousands. The human mind encounters and accommodates all this.

The "music of what happens" is nothing, though, until it's cast into language. And this is just what the poet does, makes the happening in the world transmute into the happening in language, and so this vital "happening" is a shareable entity. You as reader can experience it, too, as the complex and unsayable takes on the mantle of happening in action. This is the kind of "legislation" (to use Shelley's term) that General Lennox wants his West Point cadets to participate in and benefit from. As George Szirtes says:

> It is poetry's unique task to say exactly what it means by singing it and dancing it, by carving some crystalline pattern on the thin, cold surface of language, thereby keeping language audible and usable. That is its straightness. That is its legislation.

Poetry News *versus* Business News?

Case 1: The Need for Ethical Leadership

The need for business leaders to be more ethically aware is being made consistently. Sometimes the case is made overtly, sometimes covertly.

Joseph L Badaracco Jr. is John Shad Professor of Business Ethics at the Harvard Business School. He believes the balance between pragmatism and ethics in business situations needs to be readdressed. The issues that face modern leaders are complex and contradictory, often requiring a fresh take on the appropriate balance between pragmatic and moral elements of decisions. The moral structures a leader brings have to be developed, flexible, and adaptive. What you learned in your childhood and grew up with is unlikely to be enough anymore. Increased focus on the inner lives of leaders needs to be on the curriculum.

The teaching of formalized management tools on MBA programs should be balanced with "a little more in the way of good judgement and self-knowledge, as well as a deeper understanding of human nature." The scientific model has gone too far, and the fact that "business students are nowadays not, for the most part, poets" needs to be counterbalanced with an increased attention to literature.

Badaracco proposes literature as a means of exploring the inner lives of leaders. He uses Joseph Conrad's novel *Lord Jim* as a way of addressing the complex ethical dimensions and contexts in which leaders and their strategies operate: "It may well be that becoming a leader involves learning to grapple with very hard trade-offs and almost reckless testing of your limits. . . . Taking responsibility means coming to grips with your reflective side. . . . There are a lot of unexplored selves that you have to integrate before you become a leader."

For Badaracco a very important thing about serious literature is that it rarely endorses black and white morality. The need to embrace a complex code of ethical behavior is paramount for the contemporary leader: "Leaders should learn more about themselves if they want to succeed. . . . Productive deliberation is a chaotic process of going back and forth, zigzagging between feelings, thoughts, facts and analysis. It resists the temptation to grasp hold of a single grand principle and allow it to tyrannize all other considerations."

Case 2: Poetry Helps Protect Intelligent Comprehension

The way management expresses itself—what you could call its "rhetoric"—is focused around the quantitative, the analytical, the decisive. This is good for motivating and getting actions implemented. But the paradoxes, ambiguities, contradictions, and ambivalences of life are less well approached via the managerial rhetoric of decisiveness. Jim March, Emeritus Professor of Business Strategy at Stanford University, believes that "intelligent comprehension" needs to be protected from "the simplifying necessities of managerial life." Although managers experience duality and complexity in their own lives, in the workplace they are expected to "represent confusions as clarified, contradictions as resolved, estimates as certain, and doubts as driven out." Simplicity of expression and action have to be held back from oversimplifying the structures of managerial thought. Poetry is the antidote Jim March proposes. In other words, poetry news—"the music of what happens"—needs to be brought in alongside business news. You might say that the "romance" of business—the bottom line, market share, competition—needs to be balanced with the "reality" of the world in which business activity has necessarily to take place. A world of people, motives, needs, hopes, desires, despairs, affections. A world of power, of problems, of aspirations, of inequalities. A world of violently differing views and voices, of beliefs, standards and ethical dimensions. A complex, shifting world where boundaries are constantly crossed and frontiers dissolve almost as soon as we look at them. A world in which the "incandescent" credit cards of the consumer may not be enough to illuminate which way, in the myriad possibilities, is a right way to go.

✍ *Dulce et Decorum Est*
by WILFRED OWEN

Bent double, like old beggars under sacks,
Knock-kneed, coughing like hags, we cursed through sludge,
Till on the haunting flares we turned our backs,
And towards our distant rest began to trudge.
Men marched asleep. Many had lost their boots,
But limped on, blood-shod. All went lame, all blind;
Drunk with fatigue; deaf even to the hoots
Of gas-shells dropping softly behind.

Gas! *Gas!* Quick, boys!—An ecstasy of fumbling
Fitting the clumsy helmets just in time,
But someone still was yelling out and stumbling
And flound'ring like a man in fire or lime.—
Dim through the misty panes and thick green light,
As under a green sea, I saw him drowning.

In all my dreams before my helpless sight
He plunges at me, guttering, choking, drowning.

If in some smothering dreams, you too could pace
Behind the wagon that we flung him in,
And watch the white eyes writhing in his face,
His hanging face, like a devil's sick of sin,
If you could hear, at every jolt, the blood
Come gargling from the froth-corrupted lungs
Bitter as the cud
Of vile, incurable sores on innocent tongues,—
My friend, you would not tell with such high zest
To children ardent for some desperate glory,
The old Lie: Dulce et decorum est
Pro patria mori.

The Soldier

by RUPERT BROOKE

If I should die, think only this of me:
That there's some corner of a foreign field
That is for ever England. There shall be
In that rich earth a richer dust concealed;
A dust whom England bore, shaped, made aware,
Gave, once, her flowers to love, her ways to roam,
A body of England's, breathing English air,
Washed by the rivers, blest by suns of home.

And think, this heart, all evil shed away,
A pulse in the eternal mind, no less
Gives somewhere back the thoughts by England given;
Her sights and sounds; dreams happy as her day;
And laughter, learnt of friends; and gentleness,
In hearts at peace, under an English heaven.

4

The Music of What Happens

But who
will study alphabets for hands? Who gives

a damn what goes into
a good wheelchair?

On the Way to Tokyo

Hideaki Imamura is a pleasure to work with. He has used poetry to explore issues of communication in his team with a successful outcome. The aim there was to use poetry as a ground for opening up issues that didn't usually receive full and open discussion in the business environment. How people felt about things. How certain things were almost never spoken of, taboo subjects. How important it was to generate open exchange.

This will be different. An exploration. An experiment. What can poetry offer to strategy? How might it impact on strategic thinking? And—a particularly important question for what I am currently writing—is there some way poetry reaches across cultures and promotes understanding at a much deeper level than do facts about local customs, habits, and manners?

It is to be held in an evening, at Trader Vic's, at the New Otani hotel complex, just around the corner from the BCG offices. Hideaki and I exchange e-mails and speak on the phone. My Oxford office seems, suddenly, a long way from BCG Tokyo.

The Japanese are a poetic nation, Hideaki Imamura says. But it is a different thing, getting poetry into a corporation.

I ask him why he thinks that is.

They are a poetic nation, he says, they like to juxtapose things, they like balance and beauty. But the method of commerce is science, more or less. The quantitative, analytical method. It is linked, too, to the idea of decisiveness, to the black and white culture.

Maybe it is changing? I ask him.

He shrugs.

Maybe.

The workshop is to be open to all levels of employees in the company. Interest is trawled; about twenty people would like to participate. In the end, because of dates clashing, we have ten participants. They range from receptionist to senior partner. This is to be a discussion without reference to hierarchy. The poems will make this possible. There are no right or wrong answers in discussing a poem. The danger of losing face is disposed of. The poem is an adventure. The aim of the evening is to explore.

We choose four poems and put together a further twelve for an anthology participants will take away. Robert Frost is much translated into Japanese. Billy Collins, too; his "Introduction to Poetry" is where we'll start. We'll look at Stafford's "Traveling through the Dark." ("Yes, the moral dimension here will be interesting," Hideaki says.) And we'll choose from Robert Frost's "Stopping by Woods on a Snowy Evening" and Ted Hughes's "The Thought Fox." "Frost is dealing with the idea of 'mission' in an interesting way," Hideaki says. "And 'Thought Fox' captures so beautifully and perfectly the moment when inspiration happens."

Two and a half hours will be allocated to the event. We'll see how it goes. We'll see what the reactions are and play it by ear about how far we go, how long we keep going. "And the language capability?" I ask him. "Well," he says, "quite mixed. The understanding of English will generally be quite good. But the ability to contribute in English will be lower. I'll get in a translator. You will need a translator, I think. I will be very much in the background. You will be facilitating this. It will be interesting. It will be very interesting."

Three Straws in the Wind and a Conversation

The argument looks quite persuasive so far, my reader says. The need for a developed ethical sensibility in leadership. Ways of protecting intelligent comprehension. But isn't there a sense in which these are just pronouncements? It all seems a long way from business on the ground, from how I operate, every day, when I walk through the door of my office building, and the e-mails confront me and the meetings, the decisions, the issues, the shareholder expectations, the bottom line.

Are you sure? I say, that it's really such a long way from where you operate?

Well, he says. An awful lot of complex things come over my desk, and sometimes I think I'm expected to sit somewhere between being a judge, a politician, and a manufacturer of dollar bills. But in general, with the global economy functioning the way it is, people are pretty happy with how things stand. That can change, of course. The challenge you're facing with this material is whether there's enough of a perceived need to warrant it.

The feedback I'm getting, I say, is that there is a perceived need out there. It's not huge, but it's growing. I ran a poetry workshop recently in Prague for a global auto manufacturer.

My reader raises his eyebrows. Global auto? One of those mixed groups coming in? I'll bet that was a tough one.

The feedback, I say, indicated that among the younger practitioners particularly there was a strong wish for more initiatives that stretched their thinking, that opened up, like poetry, unusual views of things.

I guess there's always going to be a spread of response, he says. I think what's going to be vital in gaining acceptance for this is how you position it. The sense of just how to do that will develop as you go on.

I tell him I've also run a series of workshops for a major British government department as part of its fast-track development program for senior executives.

How did it go down there? he asks me.

The group, I say, was pretty receptive. Five out of eight participants said in debriefing that they felt working with poetry was a valuable experience in broadening their thinking skills.

Well, he says, that's good. That's really promising. But I think you'll find that the organizations that are out ahead of the game may be the ones that are most likely to readily take to it. Maybe those that need it most—the ones behind the lead a little—will be so intent on catching up with the competition that there won't be room.

Tokyo, March 2006: the beginning of the poetry workshop evening. Twelve people around a restaurant table. Interested faces. Potentially skeptical responses.

"Why have you come?" I ask. "What are you hoping to find here?"

"I am looking for difference. This is not the way we usually approach things in business."

That is one answer. Another is:

"I am looking for a new way to discuss things. When I step into the BCG office in the morning I have to leave a whole lot of myself behind. They demand a lot of you. A certain kind of focus. I want to know where this different kind of focus could fit in."

New York, February 2005. The "Poetry Workout." Come and discuss how poetry can change things, that was the invitation. A kind of test, a let's-see-what-this-poetry-thing-can-offer. There's a mixed group of fifteen BCGers around the table. A consultant says, "One of the things I've noticed is what happens when recruits come in and we say put away your slide deck. Just tell us what you want to say in your own words. They are dumbfounded. They can't think away from the slide deck. We have to do something to alter that."

Oxford, April 2006. I arrange to have lunch with a communications officer from Munich Re. She was in the audience at the original presentation of the poetry project ideas, three years ago, an informal gathering in Munich. "Poetry," she said then. "This is exciting. Yes. An indirect way to come to an understanding."

Now it's Branca in Oxford, a London-style café, bar, and restaurant, busy, cosmopolitan. We discuss the necessity for different perspectives in business. New observation points that can develop the fresh perceptions successful strategies require. "That is what we need," she says. "Indirection. For this, reflection is necessary. But where are the mechanisms for 'reflection' in the contemporary business world? Where practical action, pragmatism, quick response are at a premium, how does the manager find the space in which to reflect? And how does she develop the skills of reflection when she is in a habitually results-oriented world?

What CEOs say they want is a creative organization. Flexible thinking, new approaches, the kind of mind-set that reaches across obstacles. But it's risky. And they get rather alarmed when you do things to facilitate this. What is this soft-edged stuff? They say. How can we justify it to our shareholders? What is its relevance to the bottom line?"

"So What" for Business?

I rehearse my argument.

1. Empathy and imaginative engagement are necessary for the development of an ethical sensibility.

2. Ethical sensibility is an important component in the development of business leaders who can address the burgeoning complexities of contemporary commercial and economic activity.

The question. Is the thinking capacity needed for imaginative engagement and ethical sensibility necessarily and inevitably opposed to the thinking that informs successful operations in relation to the bottom line?

A provisional answer. The way businesspeople think about themselves is not static. "Business" has re-created itself over and over again to accommodate the practical exigencies of changing social and ethical, as well as economic, emphases. From the Bubble Act through New Deal legislation to the late-twentieth-century boom in regulation, the environment companies operate in has been shaped by the ethical climate of the age they encounter. The twenty-first-century context for this shaping is one of burgeoning global awareness of the power of the corporation (as powerful in some cases as an elected government) and a growing perception that the corporation should be using its power as a vehicle for good in the global society. In light of this, another level of corporate self-awareness has begun to reveal itself, one that calls for a new breadth and flexibility that links values and strategic advantage.

Jim March and Joseph Badaracco are among those who have pointed out the need for, and potential advantages accruing from, a rebalancing of the hierarchy of thinking modes in the corporation. Along with them, a chorus of practitioner voices is beginning to argue that just as imaginative engagement is a motor of ethical sensibility, so, too, is it a powerful element in how an organization can set about differentiating itself. The kind of thinking that foregrounds imaginative engagement is increasingly seen as a core skill.

This is because a tendency in leadership thinking to reduce the unknown to the known, and thus act in ways that are tried and tested, has been identified as characteristic of approaches by many contemporary strategists. However, incremental improvement, which so often results from the application of the tried and tested, is no longer enough.

Roger Martin, dean of Toronto's Rotman School of Management, calls the thinking that foregrounds imaginative engagement "abductive thinking" or "design thinking," and he's amalgamating it with MBA studies. His view is that the MBA curriculum—with its emphasis on administration—tends to focus on a more-of-the-same approach. The abductive thinking that people such as designers bring to the challenges that confront them could act as a valuable refocusing mechanism in business studies because designers (like poets) think in a way that looks at "mysteries" and capitalizes on them. That's what he believes business thinking needs more of.

Roger Martin is not a lone voice in his unease about trends in business education and his desire to address or redress the shortcomings he sees. The capacity to value imaginative engagement as a fundamental skill that organizations need to develop alongside their action-oriented pragmatism is increasingly recognized as vital, not only to questions of values and ethics but also to the processes that underpin strategic differentiation and along with it corporate success.

The question arises, however: might not a noticeable shift in emphasis from the rational-deductive to the imaginative engagement mode upset the bottom line orientation of business endeavors to an appreciable degree?

There is, perhaps unsurprisingly, no agreement on the answer. BCG's work on corporate social responsibility shows some companies sticking hard to the economics and others willing to explore new roads not yet taken. Some big oil companies, for example, deny the need to develop other sources of energy while others trumpet their intention to diversify beyond oil and be both more successful and better corporate citizens as a result.

Where does this leave the issue of ethical action through imaginative engagement? What's the "right" thing to do about closing factories in communities that depend on them? About providing health care to those who can't get it? About the increasingly high-profile but still (some would say) unsubstantiated threats of global warming?

The right thing, of course, is to find a viable economic answer to these issues. But perhaps the road to that answer requires a broader and more empathetic embrace of all the aspects and a willingness to entertain the intractable and go beyond the words of the common debate.

There are, increasingly, examples of this willingness. Several major international financial institutions, according to one of BCG's advisers, have adopted "Equator principles" on sustainability, which they apply to project finance proposals. If the project fails to meet certain standards of environmental friendliness, it is not financed regardless of its economic attractiveness. This may simply be a matter of calculated public relations, but it may well be that these institutions have espoused new environmental values because they have begun to recognize their social responsibilities as global corporations.

Perhaps an increasing realization of this shift toward the need for a wholeness of response in business decisions was instrumental in the choice of Coudal Partners to run a poetry feature as a central hook on their Web site.

Verse by Voice

Coudal Partners' Verse by Voice initiative (2005–6) is a roaring success. Coudal is a design company based in Chicago. The Coudal Partners' Web site was one of *Time* magazine's "fifty coolest Web sites" in 2005 and regularly attracts ten thousand hits a day. Why bring poetry into the equation? By Jim Coudal's own admission, it started as a stab in the dark. The company invited people "itching to recite" a favorite poem to call in and record it for possible inclusion in the Verse by Voice feature. The result was "many, many entries" and an inclusion in Yahoo's "picks" for April 2006. Visitors to the site can click on the featured poems for text or audio, and participants range from the man or woman on the street to the novelist Zadie Smith reading Frank O'Hara's "Animals."

Animals
by FRANK O'HARA

Have you forgotten what we were like then
when we were still first rate
and the day came fat with an apple in its mouth

it's no use worrying about Time
but we did have a few tricks up our sleeves
and turned some sharp corners

the whole pasture looked like our meal
we didn't need speedometers
we could manage cocktails out of ice and water

I wouldn't want to be faster
or greener than now if you were with me O you
were the best of all my days

Listening to a reading like this on a nonpoetry Web site is strangely arresting, particularly unexpected. But why Frank O'Hara's "Animals"? Why poetry? What has the initiative achieved for Coudal? Jim Coudal says the company is always looking for new ways to connect with its audience. To keep on top you have to "stay sharp and learn," and that includes, for Coudal, being tuned in to the pulse of the way the world is. He wants people to explore and enjoy his Web site: "We want to be the seller AND the audience. We want to target ourselves so to speak. Building a large and loyal audience to our site was the first part, creating products that they AND we need." So mutuality and inclusiveness are part of the brand image, as well as being central to Coudal's own belief system. The poetry acted as a mode of communication between audience and company. Coudal could tune in to and learn from the preoccupations of its audience as expressed in the poem choices. And at the same time Coudal could show itself as an organization concerned with expression, emotion, the reflective moment and the poem's ability to *connect*.

Could the poem be a kind of ground for the company and audience to occupy and mutually explore what each other values? Jim Coudal believes that "assignments [from clients] are given based on the dynamic between the people involved first and the actual work you've done for other people second." Poetry is one of the means he and his team chose to move that dynamic forward.

One could say that poetry is at work here as part of an ethical framework that seeks to promote trust and respect through a partnership between company and customer. Poetry is a way of demonstrating mutuality—of empowering and engaging the customer on a common ground.

The Oven Loves the TV Set
by HEATHER MCHUGH

Stuck on the fridge, our favourite pin-up girl
is anorexic. On the radio we have a riff

of Muzak sax, and on the mind
a self-help book. We sprawl all evening, all

alone, in an unraised ranch;
all day the company we kept

kept on incorporating. As for worlds
of poverty, we do our best, thanks

to a fund of Christian feeling
and mementos from

Ameila, the foster child, who has
the rags and seven photogenic sisters we require

in someone to be saved. She's proof
Americans have got a heart

to go with all that happy
acumen you read about. We love

a million little prettinesses,
decency, and ribbon on

the cockapoo. But who
will study alphabets for hands? Who gives

a damn what goes into
a good wheelchair? Who lugs the rice

from its umpteen stores
to the ends of the earth, to even one

dead-end? Not we.
Our constitutional pursuit

is happiness, i.e.
somebody nice, and not

too fat, we can have
for our personal friend.

5

The Hall of Mirrors

Who can face the winds, till the panes crack in their frames?
And if a man faced them, what in the end would he do
But look for shelter like all the rest?

Connection through Metaphor

In his introduction to *Hansel and Gretel and the Cuban Missile Crisis*, Bolko von Oetinger proposes metaphor as a means of meeting the need for managers to increase their reflective capacity. "If slightly more metaphoric thinking could be introduced into the daily lives of managers," von Oetinger believes, "and if this way of thinking were to become an inspiring companion to analytic and economic thinking and to a pragmatic approach, a lot would have been gained."

Poetry, perhaps more than any other written form, has a strong and intense engagement with the vehicle of metaphor. This makes it particularly well suited to exploring complex issues of value.

What is a metaphor? A metaphor is a mechanism of language that compares things that are generally seen as incomparable or unlike. It juxtaposes things we don't usually juxtapose. It says—look, see how one thing is approachable in terms of another? You didn't think it was like that. Maybe it isn't. But maybe it is—or could be. And even if it isn't, that possibility of comparison has opened a number of important doors.

Metaphor defies the attempt to make any simple or thoroughgoing division between logical and intuitive in the thinking process. A metaphor connects things in a way that "makes sense" but doesn't follow the cause and effect route of logic. Metaphors propel your attention outward to the "what might be." They tend to resist what the philosopher Martin Heidegger referred to as the "concealment" that accompanies each "disclosure." What he meant was when you come to an idea of what is "true," that inevitably blocks off other possible ways in which the matter under consideration might be "true." As Friedrich Nietzsche said, "On every metaphor you ride to every truth."[1] The metaphor works against that block—concealment—because it won't let the truth you arrive at sit still.

Much has been written about how metaphor works and what value it might have in the workplace. But the way metaphor is often used in business contexts is as a kind of illustration of a problem, a mapping of metaphor onto an organizational dilemma. Tiha von Ghyczy has pointed out in the *Harvard Business Review* that the importance of metaphor for business thinkers is precisely where it doesn't fit rather than in the mappable coincidences between metaphor and the facts of a situation.

This is another way of saying that business has tended to use metaphor in a way that strains against the very substance of what metaphor is; that pulls in a contrary direction to what metaphor has to offer.

Mapping the Edge

Stanford University's Jim March thinks that poetry can be valuable in adding new dimensions to business thinking, and he has done much groundbreaking work through a concentration on interpreting the relevance for business of certain poetic metaphors and themes.

Professor March has stated, however, that the poetry dimension should be kept separate from the everyday, up-front business of *business*. The rhetoric of poetry has a place in the private ruminations of the leader, and in this private place it will be complementary to, and nonthreatening of, the more thrusting, public, results-oriented rhetoric of management.

This book is proposing something rather different. It is saying that the rhetoric of poetry *should* be brought into the rhetoric of management, not in an attempt to usurp it but to act as a frame or mirror—a rebalancer and refresher—in other words to show that the rhetoric of management is, like management itself, like the notion of corporation or capitalism, a mutable entity, a resilient structure that has to adapt to survive.

Perhaps Jim March's desire for separation is aligned to how he approaches the business of analyzing poetry, and in particular to how he utilizes its metaphoric content. In the article I'm looking at, "Poetry and the Rhetoric of Management," he focuses on the nature of revolutionary leaders. What is their motivation? What is their morality? He concentrates on mapping the ambiguities of W. B. Yeats's poem "Easter 1916." The poem is about the Easter Rising in Ireland, the Irish against their English masters, nearly a hundred years ago.

This is how the poem opens.

> I have met them at close of day
> Coming with vivid faces
> From counter or desk among grey
> Eighteenth-century houses.
> I have passed with a nod of the head
> Or polite meaningless words,
> Or have lingered awhile and said
> Polite meaningless words,
> And thought before I had done
> Of a mocking tale or a gibe
> To please a companion
> Around the fire at the club,
> Being certain that they and I
> But lived where motley is worn:
> All changed, changed utterly:
> A terrible beauty is born.

For Jim March, the poem is "a tribute to fanatical visionaries for their contribution to Irish independence" but one that points up the cost of this fanaticism as a moral and emotional stasis. The business value of the poem, for March, lies in the way its themes cause the reader to revisit issues of complexity and ambiguity in the way life's important currents run: "The poem invites an awareness that the leaders involved in radical change are saints only by subsequent reconstruction. . . . The implicit claim of the poem is that . . . every virtue has its vice, and every vice its virtue."

These are no doubt valuable "lessons" or reminders as far as they go. But there is a great danger that the "mapping" approach to poetry and business may leave reservoirs of relevance untapped. Such mapping techniques—looking at the relevance of metaphoric *content* to the substance of business issues—carries with it the danger of saying "Look at this, it's important" while leaving the "*how* to think" that General Lennox believes is so important relatively unaddressed.

In this case, the surface relevance of the metaphor is in the "message" or theme that visionary leadership is a complicated issue and may have negative as well as positive impacts. But why use a poem to explore this? There are many ways in which this apprehension could be brought to the attention of the leader. A study of history that included a consideration of Hitler's rise and fall could be one striking example.

Where Terror Meets Beauty

The poem addresses the questions it raises about ambiguity in a striking and memorable way. But even more striking and arguably more memorable are the poem's own ambiguities and paradoxes, those elements of the "poem as a poem" that the reader has to engage with if she is to come away with more than a surface message. The central motor of ambiguity and paradox in "Easter 1916" is the metaphor of the stone.

The third section of the poem utilizes this metaphor to focus on the complex topic of the nature of a leader-martyr.

> Hearts with one purpose alone
> Through summer and winter seem
> Enchanted to a stone
> To trouble the living stream.
> The horse that comes from the road.
> The rider, the birds that range
> From cloud to tumbling cloud,
> Minute by minute they change;
> A shadow of cloud on the stream
> Changes minute by minute;
> A horse-hoof slides on the brim,
> And a horse plashes within it;
> The long-legged moor-hens dive,
> And hens to moor-cocks call;
> Minute by minute they live:
> The stone's in the midst of all.
>
> Too long a sacrifice
> Can make a stone of the heart.
> O when may it suffice?
> That is Heaven's part, our part
> To murmur name upon name,
> As a mother names her child
> When sleep at last has come
> On limbs that had run wild.

This section of the poem is based around the metaphor of the heart as a stone. The "warning" of the poem—"too long a sacrifice can make a stone of the heart"—is counterbalanced by the notion of "enchantment." What is enchantment? A wonderful thing and a terrible thing. The stuff of fairyland and alluring glitter, the output of wicked witches and the dark powers of the underworld. There's another factor, too. A loving attentiveness to language and image joins with the emotional crescendo of the music. The rider, the birds, the tumbling clouds—precisely George Szirtes's "music of what happens"—is conjured up in a snapshot of peace, beauty, harmony, and the details of ordinary life. In the end, terror and beauty can be seen to coexist in the stone-hearted martyr.

How can this be? The stone as metaphor is constantly shifting its shape in the imagination. What is the usual meaning of a heart turning to stone? Loss of feeling, a negative thing, a dehumanization that most of us would fear rather than relish. But as Yeats presents it to us, this sense is counterpointed by the way the stone is positioned in the central stanza. That central stanza ("Hearts with one purpose alone") is one of transcendent beauty, through its images of the natural world, and the stone in the stream is part of that beauty, an emblem of power and lastingness in the unstoppable "stream" of life. The stone is also primordial; it has been thrust up to the surface of the earth's crust to last through aeons and become part of a natural idyll around which and through which everyday life, the passing of the horse and rider, the procreating of the moorhen, burgeon and bloom. In these terms the stone has attributes of grandness, monumentality, and enduringness. The twisting aspect of its metaphoric usage means that the stone is contradictory, is many things, is negative and positive at the same time.

The paradox that the stone is all the things suggested but none of them entirely, is central to the complexity the reader has to grapple with. The martyred political leader is ugly and beautiful; separate but conjoined; unfeeling yet necessary; part of time yet outside time; essential perhaps, inevitable certainly, to the "terrible beauty" that we humans create in the mêlée of our conflicting ideals.

"Easter 1916" operates on the mapping level of relevance. But the uniqueness of the poem as a vehicle for exploring the notion of the radical leader lies in its densely woven ambiguities, its metaphorical intricacies. And the metaphor has a knock-on effect through the whole poem. The stone, the heart, is a conduit between the martyrs and the people who make them. How complicit is "the public" in constructing the visionary leader? Is it the "love" the visionary leader feels for the *cause* that "bewilders" him (confuses him, makes him "wild")? Or is it the love the *people* have for the leader that bewilders him? Or both? And if both, in what order of magnitude? What is the nature of the responsibility the people bear for creating their leaders and martyrs?

Telling Rhythm

Metaphor doesn't operate on its own. I suggested earlier that an emotional crescendo in the poem works along with metaphor to generate effects that engage the reader in a nonstatic, imaginative interchange with the poem— precisely that interchange that can help bring about a reframing of view. That emotional crescendo depends in part on the rhythm of the poem, how "the music of what happens" works *as music.*

Just as there was a countertow in "Stopping by Woods on a Snowy Evening" between the forward momentum of the horse-hoof rhythm and the braking effect of the rise and fall of the lines, so here there is a similar interplay between surge and fallback. There's a rhythm that brings you all the time to the brink of something but doesn't let you go over.

Hearts with one **pur**-pose—a-**lone**	1
Through **sum**-mer and **win**-ter **seem**	2
En-**chan**-ted to a **stone**	3
To **trou**-ble the **liv**-ing **stream**.	4
The **horse** that **comes** from the **road**.	5
The **rid**-er, the **birds** that **range**	6
From **cloud** to **tumb**-ling **cloud**,	7
Min-ute by **min**-ute they **change**;	8
A **shad**ow of **cloud** on the **stream**	9
Changes min-ute by **min**-ute;	10
A **horse-hoof slides** on the **brim**,	11
And a **horse plashes** with-**in it;**	12
The **long-legged moor-hens dive**,	13
And **hens** to **moor-cocks call;**	14
Min-ute by **min**-ute they **live:**	15
The **stone's** in the **midst** of **all**.	16

In lines 11, 12 ,13, and 14 particularly, there's a rhythmic weight, a re-configuring of rhythmic importance. You can see the pattern of it in the increased solidity of the bold print. Suddenly the boldface words are following on from each other; there are fewer "light" or unstressed beats breaking up the weight of the language. Instead of a predominant three beats per line, there are four; instead of the beats being interspersed with light, unstressed elements, line 13 culminates in the increased weight of five stresses in a row. From the stressed word *changes* at the beginning of line 10, matched with the opening stressed word *hearts* in line 1 (the only other two opening stresses are the half words *min* in lines 8 and 15), we are taken—via sliding, plashing, and diving—where? Into a world where "the stone's in the midst of all."

This observation on its own is in danger of generating a massive "so what" question. The student of English literature, the writer, the theorist, or the philosopher may be keenly, excitedly, expectantly, wholeheartedly interested in such minutiae, but why should anyone else care for a second?

Because the rhythmic structures of poetry are an important part of its ability to reframe, are keenly relevant to an assertion, such as Gardner's, that art can change minds. William Blake believed that poetry cleansed the doors of perception. The tension between the opposing forces in a poem— between the transparent and the opaque, sense and sound, language and what can't be comprehended by the rational constructs of language— require a different kind of attention than do forms more wholly based in the logic of language. In these terms poetry is seen as a conduit between meaning and being, between the logical-deductive mode and a mode that encompasses a different, more visceral response. How do we respond to dance music? Not the same way we consider an abstract argument. These two poles are present in the poem and in what it expects of us.

Poetry is an additional way of viewing reality that coexists with the rational ways (laws, political principles, philosophies, theories). Its social and political value, as well as its value in terms of the reframing increasingly seen as necessary for the thinking, differentiating, responsible, modern business practitioner, lies in the deeply defamiliarizing potential of the tensions set up by the complex relations between rhythm and language. Derek Attridge, a distinguished British writer on poetry, points up the implications of this with regard to accessing emotion.

> [T]he most powerful rhythmic functions in verse exist at a less conscious level, and it is an attractive thought that the rhythms of poetry may harness those deeper dispositions towards the patterned retardation and release of energy that underlie the expression of emotional states.

Amitai Aviram, in his book *Telling Rhythm*, takes this further: the rhythmical patterns encourage certain sets of expectations and responses that the poem's combination of rhythm and language in tension upsets and confounds. The patterns of expectation that emanate from the rhythmic possibilities vary between cultures.

> [R]hythm is probably like almost every other human activity: it seems to result from the culturally mediated activation, disciplining and cultivation of inherent possibilities . . . rhythm destabilizes language, and with it, the prevailing codes and prejudices of society.

So the rhythms of poetry are important as change agents. The tensions set up between rhythm and language increase your awareness, perhaps at an unconscious level, of the provisional and unstable aspects of the written or uttered word. This makes you more aware of the possibility that *meaning* (which is what language points to or represents) can be unstable and subject to change. In this way poetry encourages a more encompassing and less time bound view of meaning, being, and perhaps of existence itself. Tuning in to the music of what happens, experiencing the relationship between what can be expressed (through language) and what lies beyond, and pulls against and disrupts this language expression, contributes to the horizontal links and new depths of ethical sensibility that Nussbaum's process of "reevaluation" leads to. A. R. Ammons puts it this way: "Definition, rationality and structure are ways of seeing, but they become prisons when they blank out other ways of seeing."

Security

by MICHAEL HAMBURGER

I

So he's got there at last, been received as a Partner—
In a firm going bankrupt:
Found the right place (walled garden), arranged for a mortgage—
But they're pulling the house down
To make room for traffic.

Worse winds are rising. He takes out new policies
For his furniture, for his life,
At a higher premium
Against more limited risks.

2

Who can face the winds, till the panes crack in their frames?
And if a man faced them, what in the end would he do
But look for shelter like all the rest?
The winds too are afraid and blow from fear.

3

I hear my children at play
And recall that one branch of the elm-tree looks dead;
Also that twenty years ago now I could have been parchment
Cured and stretched like a lampshade,
Who now have children, a lampshade
And the fear of those winds.

I saw off the elm-tree branch
To find that the wood was sound;
mend the fences yet again,
Knowing they'll keep out no one,
Let alone the winds.
For still my children play
And shall tomorrow, if the weather holds.

Cross-Wiring:
The Paths Poetry Opens

and the
red, glowing ends burned like the
tiny campfires we lit at night
back at the beginning of the world.

Poetry and Neuroscience

Is there any "hard" evidence that substantiates the relevance of poetry to possibilities, linkages, and fresh intersections? Could there be something in the way poets think, something in the connections they make, that sets them apart—a contemporary justification for Coleridge's assertion that the poet is seer, visionary, a prophet who has the edge over mere mortal men?

Prof. Vilayanur S. Ramachandran, director of the Center for Brain and Cognition at the University of California in San Diego, suggests that this is so. His Reith lectures for the BBC in 2003, "The Emerging Mind," focused on some of his discoveries about the relationship between artistic expression (including poetry) and brain function.

Here is an experiment in the field he rather playfully refers to as "neuro aesthetics" in which he invited the audience to participate.

Ramachandran's Experiment

- Visualize in front of you a bulbous amoeboid shape that has lots of curves on it, undulating curves. And right next to it imagine a jagged shape like a piece of shattered glass with jagged edges.

- This is the Martian alphabet. Just as in English alphabet, *A* is *a*, *B* is *b*, and each shape stands for a particular sound. This is the Martian alphabet, and one of these shapes is kiki and the other is booba.
- Which shape is kiki and which is booba?

Result of the Experiment

- Ninety-eight percent of people say the jagged shape, the shattered glass, is a kiki, and the bulbous amoeboid shape is a booba.

So What?

Lower mammals have a less-developed structure in the brain with which to make this connection than do higher mammals. In higher mammals there's been "explosive development" in this brain area, and it's especially large in humans. Patients with damage in the angular gyrus of the left hemisphere of the brain cannot make these connections. Their answers (over a much wider ranging experiment) were random.

The ability to make these kinds of connections is related to the condition called synesthesia. Synesthesia—a mingling of the senses, a kind of cross-wiring of the brain, so that when you hear a musical note, for example, you experience it as a color—is genetic. One in two hundred people has the peculiarity. Poets, novelists, and artists are seven times more likely than the general population to have synesthesia. These people are also adept at making cross-modal connections, including connections through metaphor.

Cross-modal connection (of which synesthesia is a prime example) is fundamental to abstract thinking. All people, unless they have damage in this area, have synesthetic capability according to Ramachandran. The kiki-booba connection is proof of this. But, crucially, he believes most people are "in denial about it." This means, by extrapolation, that people are missing out on the sensitive, unusual, unexpected, less than obvious connections they could be capable of.

A poem is, generally, a densely metaphoric structure. But more than that, its language is patterned on precisely those cross-modal connections that the kiki-booba experiment was testing. So it follows that in coming to grips with a poem you have to flex your cross-modal thinking capabilities. You have, perhaps, to begin to redress that very "denial" that Professor Ramachandran suggests is endemic.

No one is suggesting that if you read a lot of poems you'll suddenly develop the ability to see ten as red or conceptualize February as purple. But it would be fair to say that an immersion in the poetic method, which centers around the synesthetic cross-modal abstractions Prof Ramachandran has been investigating, could help redress the denial and encourage familiarity with the connections this way of thinking encompasses.

Case Study: Cross-Modal Poetry

Those Winter Sundays
by R O B E R T   H A Y D E N

Sundays too my father got up early
and put his clothes on in the blueblack cold,
then with cracked hands that ached
from labor in the weekday weather made
banked fires blaze. No one ever thanked him.

I'd wake and hear the cold splintering, breaking.
When the rooms were warm, he'd call,
and slowly I would rise and dress,
fearing the chronic angers of that house.

Speaking indifferently to him,
who had driven out the cold
and polished my good shoes as well.
What did I know, what did I know
of love's austere and lonely offices?

The sound patterns of kiki and booba and the associated possibilities of cross-modal engagement are exploited in "Those Winter Sundays." You can't be in denial about them if you're going to make sense of the poem in a full way.

The hard *kuh* sounds in *black, crack, week,* and *thank*—the jagged kiki sounds—are inseparable from the emotional resonance the poem sets out to create. These jagged sounds are counterbalanced by the more bulbous *duh* sounds of *he'd, would, driven, cold, good,* and *did,* sounds more in the register of booba, less sharp, less spiky, in tonal as well as visual terms.

The vowels add to the effect the consonants have. Just as *kiki* has the thin *eee* vowel sound, something akin to the off-key, teeth on edge mode, so in the poem there's the short, sharp, *ah, ah, ah* of *black, crack, hand,* counterpointed by the long, thin *aa* sound of *ached, wake,* the stifled screech of *week.* Just as *booba* has the full *oo* vowel to go with the softer consonants, so the fuller and warmer vowel sounds in the poem—*room, warm, good, shoes, know, lonely*—accumulate to deliver the basic tension on which the poem rests: between childhood indifference and adult appreciation, between immature self-centeredness and a mature apprehension of the nature of love and sacrifice.

What the poem is driving at through its sound patterns plays, in other words, directly to the crossover function Professor Ramachandran was pointing to: the protosynesthetic capability that underlies (a) the making of unusual connections between things and (b) the modalities of abstract thought.

Poetry and the Japanese Garden

Modalities of abstract thought? says my reader. I quite like that one.

She's just come in and is looking a little jet-lagged.

We're in the New Otani hotel in Tokyo. She has been exploring the famous Japanese garden the hotel is situated in. Stones, little arched bridges, tall trees, and waterfalls. She told me she wanted time to think, a space for reflection. She has some important meetings coming up.

You should get out there, she says. It's poetry in miniature. Being out in the garden is like standing in a kind of poem. Each new place you stand you get a different perspective. The new angle, the new placing, gives you a different take on things.

It's one of the things, isn't it, I say, that poetry has to offer? One of the great things, the exciting things—a new space-for-thinking as well as a new thinking-space.

She's been reading quite a lot, some of it poetry but some of it articles and comments about the ways of thinking, the "open-mindedness" (as it's called in some places) that this book is talking about. She's come across something called "postmodern management" that seems to have currency, particularly among academics in business schools.

Does it have any relevance, she asks, to what you're proposing? What I take it to mean, from what I've read so far, is it's something comparable to postmodern architecture or postmodern literature. It's a management style that harnesses paradox and thrives on uncertainty.

I wondered about putting it in, I say. Particularly as it emphasizes how posing and describing a question can be much more valuable in the long run than finding a solution. Its focus away from closure and toward exploration is very much in tune with the mind-set I've been arguing poetry can facilitate.

Isn't it also about how artistic, emotional, and illogical aspects of things can provide important insights? she asks. But maybe you don't need to bring it in because you're already covering that ground from a fresh perspective.

That's the conclusion I've come to. I don't want to corral the idea of what poetry can offer into any preexisting format. I want readers to be able to take what they can from it, to be able to utilize what's in it so it works for them.

I think that's what's happening with me, she says. I've been enjoying it. There's a kind of freedom in having at your fingertips that other way of thinking that poetry is based on.

I tell her I hope my workshop group, just now converging for our poetry session, will feel that way.

You're not nervous, are you? she says. You must have done this so many times. It'll be second nature.

I'm not nervous, exactly, I tell her. But each group is different. Different challenges, different responses.

As I pick up my papers, she smiles. On that quite gray day in central Tokyo I'm glad of her presence. I close the door behind me, just as I hear her call, Good luck!

❧ *Japan*

by BILLY COLLINS

Today I pass the time reading
a favorite haiku,
saying the few words over and over.

It feels like eating
the same small, perfect grape
again and again.

I walk through the house reciting it
and leave its letters falling
through the air of every room.

I stand by the big silence of the piano and say it.
I say it in front of a painting of the sea.
I tap out its rhythm on an empty shelf.

I listen to myself saying it,
then I say it without listening,
then I hear it without saying it.

And when the dog looks up at me,
I kneel down on the floor
and whisper it into each of his long white ears.

It's the one about the one-ton temple bell
with the moth sleeping on its surface,

and every time I say it, I feel the excruciating
pressure of the moth
on the surface of the iron bell.

When I say it at the window,
the bell is the world
and I am the moth resting there.

When I say it at the mirror,
I am the heavy bell
and the moth is life with its papery wings.

And later, when I say it to you in the dark,
you are the bell,
and I am the tongue of the bell, ringing you,

and the moth has flown
from its line
and moves like a hinge in the air above our bed.

A Great View of Downtown Tokyo

I want them to waterski
across the surface of a poem
waving at the author's name on the shore.

Post Poetry

There is a great view of downtown Tokyo from The Bar on the forty-first floor of the New Otani hotel. I am sitting at the window looking down Sotobori-dori Avenue to the round tower with the red flashing light. It could be any city, the tall buildings on the skyline, the car lights running close and busy where the streets meet way down below me, the neon signs—red, green, blue, yellow—flashing off the tops of the shop fronts, the wing lights of an aircraft passing high on the other side of the city.

But it is Tokyo. I can smell and feel its difference, hear and taste the otherness that's underlying all the familiar things you could find in other places: the same brand of drinks and cigarettes, the global icons—McDonalds, BMW. The same flashing symbol on Standard Life.

The workshop has just finished. It is 10:30. We have been talking about poetry for four and a half hours. As we are leaving, Hideaki Imamura says, "I think that went very well. It went much better than I thought it might. I think it has been a very successful evening. I have been inspired to do more in working this way with poetry. Maybe I can take a group away together for a weekend. In June maybe. There is something here now. I am convinced of it."

We prepared quite thoroughly. I went around to Hideaki's office in the afternoon. We agreed that the emphasis of poetry as a "no right answer" ground was paramount. Each contribution to the discussion is valuable. There are shades and interpretations, paths that lead somewhere or nowhere. Each point in the discussion is a place to rest for a moment, a potential vantage point.

At about 4:00 p.m. I look over the Japanese versions with our translator, Shimada San. She is a little surprised by the task confronting her. We'll be conducting the workshop in English, but most of the contributions will be in Japanese. She is to whisper the translations to me as we go along. She is of the opinion that this will not be a particularly easy task. "For two and a half hours," she says. "That is quite a long time."

The aims of the workshop are threefold: (1) to discover whether the discussion of poetry as a means of opening new observational spaces is transferable across cultures, (2) to garner this constituency's view on the applicability of reading poetry to thinking strategically, and (3) to consider what the various interpretations of the poems might reveal about similarities or differences between cultures.

"It is an experiment," Hideaki says. "We have worked with poetry before. But this is a little different."

The table in Trader Vic's is long and thin. Twelve people, in the end, are gathered around it. There is piped music in the background that will have to be worked against. I tune it out.

"I am most grateful," I begin, "to Imamura San for creating this opportunity."

"It is we who are grateful to you," Imamura San responds, "for coming such a very long way."

They want to know what it feels like to work with a poem. They want to know what a poem can offer to someone in their situation. A busy BCG person, focused, practical, energetic, results oriented. Imamura San sets the context. They are invited to tell us what they think the relevance of each poem is. We begin with a poem about reading poems, Billy Collins's "Introduction to Poetry." I ask them what this poem says about what a poem offers. What does it say a poem demands?

Case Study: Introducing Poetry to BCG Tokyo

Introduction to Poetry
by BILLY COLLINS

I ask them to take a poem
and hold it up to the light
like a color slide

or press an ear against its hive.

I say drop a mouse into a poem
and watch him probe his way out,

or walk inside the poem's room
and feel the walls for a light switch.

I want them to waterski
across the surface of a poem
waving at the author's name on the shore.

But all they want to do
is tie the poem to a chair with a rope
and torture a confession out of it.

They begin beating it with a hose
to find out what it really means.

(Introduction to Poetry)

詩とは

ビリー・コリンズ

詩を手にとって
光にかざしてください
カラーのスライドのように

それとも詩の巣箱に耳を当ててみてください

その中にマウスを入れて
出口をさがし出すのを観察するのもいいでしょう

詩の部屋の中に入って
壁を手探りして明かりのスイッチを探して下さい

水上スキーをするのもいいですね
詩上をです
岸に作者の名前が見えたら手をふること

しかし、読者がしたがるのは
ロープでイスに詩を縛りつけて
告白させようと拷問すること

ホースで詩をたたき
本当に意味しているものを見つけようとする

出典： 小泉純一 訳
　　　ビリー・コリンズ詩選集「エミリー・ディキンスンの着衣を剥ぐ」　国文社

The Discussion

C.M.: The poet is asking that you do several things when you read a poem. What kind of things are they?

MR. GOTO: They are very active things. Holding it up. Doing something to it. Going into it.

MR. YAMAMURA: They are things of the senses: looking, hearing, orienting, touching.

MS. WADA: That's the first four things the poet is asking. But what about "water-ski"? I don't see the relevance of that.

MR. OKAYASU: Is he saying go over it quickly; don't go slow and pause too long?

C.M.: That's one of the qualities of water-skiing, speed, yes. But aren't there others?

MS. KITANO: Fun. Water-skiing is about fun and enjoyment.

C.M.: And others?

MS. WADA: Well, you need balance and coordination.

MR. OKAYASU: And flexibility. You can't water-ski if you're stiff and not supple.

MR. KOBAYASHI: There are qualities, too, that are important. Like not being afraid.

C.M.: And what about waving at the author?

MS. KAWAMURA: That means you have to take possession of what you're doing and not try to think there's an absolutely right way that somebody else has dictated.

C.M.: So there's something here that's suggesting a relationship with the poem, one of action and engagement?

MS. HAMANO: Yes, like that "color slide." A color slide is nothing if you don't hold it up at the right angle. You have to do something with it to make anything of it.

MS. KAWAMURA: And for the first two sections the reader is on the outside. But then the reader is asked to be on the inside somehow, through the mouse—like in a maze, with dead ends and maybe circling around a lot until you get out and are free again—and then in the room, which is kind of familiar but unfamiliar because it's dark.

MR. YOKOHAMA: I think it has something to do with rules, too, the last part. And power. The last two sections are very ugly and are about force.

C.M.: The whole approach is very different between the "I" and the "they"?

MS. HAMANO: The "I" person wants to treat the poem with respect and also with curiosity. To take lots of different approaches. The poem isn't one thing; it's many things. So it needs and deserves many different approaches.

MR. OKAYASU: And the "they," the people who don't know what it deserves, they make it one thing only, a prisoner.

MR. KOBAYASHI: What they want is a confession; they are looking for facts. But the "I" person is saying, it's not facts, it's perspectives. It's experiment and observation. That's what you need to bring to this.

MS. WADA: I like the image of the hive particularly. It makes me see the poem as a thing full of activity, growing, a very complex organization, one thing interconnected with another and lots of different ways through it. Like a world in miniature.

Poetry and Culture: Doing It Differently in Civil Society

This is the ground we have for exploring the poems. We have time for two more only. We do not stop at 7:30. The time goes quickly; we have Japanese cocktails, a delicious supper. We discuss "Traveling through the Dark" by William Stafford. The responses fall into a familiar pattern: at first, a polarization between those who blame the speaker for finishing off the deer and those who believe he is a man caught unawares by circumstance. And then, a growing sense that it is not that clear, it is not that easy to say where blame lies. That blame, perhaps, may not even be appropriate.

One new response comes in that I have not heard before, even though I have discussed this poem with more than three hundred people. The largest group I've discussed it with was in a lecture theater at Kuwait University. The air conditioner was very loud, and the acoustics were terrible.

They were a mixed group, some business students, some from the humanities. There was approximately the same split between takes on the moral dilemma there as in discussions in the U.K., U.S., or Germany. The different element that comes in this Tokyo discussion, which is soon taken up and endorsed by the group as a whole, is this: the speaker is thrown back on a place with no rules; he is "outside civil society." We live by the rule of law and custom within civil society; outside its confines we do not know how to behave.

We are getting tired now. It's after 9:00. Three and a half hours is a long time to concentrate on poetry. Which of the remaining two poems should we turn to? We don't have the time, energy, or mental stamina to deal with both.

Imamura San would favor "The Thought Fox." But when we put it to a vote, "Stopping by Woods on a Snowy Evening" comes in first. Is this because it's the shorter poem? There are polite smiles around the table. Then there is silence. Quite a long silence. "Stopping by Woods on a Snowy Evening" isn't as easy as it seems.

Stopping by Woods on a Snowy Evening
by ROBERT FROST

Whose woods these are I think I know.
His house is in the village though;
He will not see me stopping here
To watch his woods fill up with snow.

My little horse must think it queer
To stop without a farmhouse near
Between the woods and frozen lake
The darkest evening of the year.

He gives his harness bells a shake
To ask if there is some mistake.
The only other sound's the sweep
Of easy wind and downy flake.

The woods are lovely, dark and deep.
But I have promises to keep,
And miles to go before I sleep,
And miles to go before I sleep.

(Stopping by Woods on a Snowy Evening)

雪の夜、森のそばに足をとめて

ロバート・フロスト

この森の持ち主が誰なのか、おおかた見当はついている
もっとも彼の家は村のなかだから、
わたしがこんなところに足をとめて、彼の森が
雪で一杯になるのを眺めているとは気がつくまい

小柄なわたしの馬は、近くに農家ひとつないのに、
森と凍った湖のあいだにこうして立ち止まるのを、
へんだと思うに違いない――
一年中でいちばん暗いこの晩に

何かの間違いではないか、そう訊ねようとして、
馬は、馬具につけた鈴をひと振りする
ほかに聞こえるものといえば、ゆるい風と
綿毛のような雪が、吹き抜けていく音ばかり

森がまことに美しく、暗く、そして深い
だがわたしにはまだ、果たすべき約束があり、
眠る前に、何マイルもの道のりがある
眠る前に、何マイルもの道のりがある

I had always taken it for granted that the speaker was on his way home after many years away. Why did I feel that? I don't know, but my reading was unwaveringly in terms of a return, a relearning of familiarity, and a discharge of some duty to the people waiting in the place to be returned to, the community, the family maybe, who had been left many years ago.

My Japanese group took a view that had never been expressed before in any reading of this poem that I've participated in. The speaker, they felt, was leaving what he knew and setting out on a long journey. "This is about mission," one said. "It's about keeping focus on what you have undertaken to do and also about what can distract you. How you feel about that. How it feels to be pulled in two directions."

"I don't want to sound foolish," someone says, "but there is something about Father Christmas here."

"Yes, it's the harness bells and the snow. Like a fantasy."

And the theme arises again, the individual versus society.

"It's about being outside society, being cut adrift. Yes, the tension here is about what happens when you are outside the bounds of civil society. How do you make your choices? There aren't any rules out there, no props anymore, no one to ask for advice. And no one to see if you act well or badly."

They veer away from the "lovely, dark and deep" for some time. Perhaps it is a problem in translation? Certainly, the lullaby effect doesn't come through for them, though the repetition does. But then the idea of action versus inaction begins to gain momentum in the discussion. Is it really something deeper? Could it be? A choice between how you live, maybe even a choice about whether to live at all.

So is every question of "mission" also related to how you choose to live your life more broadly? These are very big questions for quite a small poem. It is getting late. It is time to put poetry away for the moment.

Is there value in discussing it?, I ask. Something so outside the things that you have to deal with? Yes, there is value. As well as making you feel what it's like to be in that situation, it points up the way you try to put your own stories onto things the more they resist you. The poem makes you test your own stories, the way you account for things, and think again about why you have them as your stories. About whether the reasons and answers you give are the best ones or the only ones. That's what discussing this poem can do in a group.

Poetry and Strategy: How They Saw It in Tokyo

When we had put away the poems, each member of the group offered their thoughts on what the value of the evening had been. What could the relationship between poetry and strategy be? What could its value be, based on this experience of poetry discussion, in the business world?

This is a summary of the responses.

- There are many ways to read the same text; this should make us aware of the possibility that clients will read our analyses in many more ways than one, and we can consider the implications of this.
- The precise use of language is vital to getting our meanings across; a very small difference in word usage can make a big difference in the meaning or sense that we impart to our strategies and also how they may be interpreted.
- Words can send different messages in different contexts; reading poems is a trigger that sharpens our sense that we should be careful about the words we use. We can read a word "roughly" or precisely. Being alert to the context and precise meaning of words helps us understand context and use the minimum number of words to greatest effect with clients.
- We use a different aspect of our brain when thinking about how a poem works. With a poem we take a long time to come to no answer. Everyday business requires that we take a short time to come to a single answer. Working with poems reminds us of a valuable alternative way to approach issues.
- Reading poems is enjoyable and valuable. But it's basically not relevant to the business system that corporations operate within. The impressions you get in reading poems are opposite to those of business. That's about the bottom line. Poetry is about different things.
- Reading poems encourages us to harness and use our intuitive sense; the usual business way only harnesses a part of the great power of the brain. If we can get more used to using the intuitive aspects of thinking and harness these for our business issues, that would be powerful.
- The more opaque the poem the more we tend to rely on our own favorite "stories" to fill in the gaps. A discussion of the poem exposes that tendency. It helps show us what our favorite stories are and what others' favorite stories are. We can relate this to how we, and others, respond in addressing strategic situations.
- The poem requires examination and reexamination of hypotheses in light of changing/developing views by oneself and others in the discussion; this may have implications for how we approach the development of our strategies.
- Reading a poem helps us get used to the idea that we can apprehend and understand things that are not immediately susceptible to logic.
- When we analyze, we don't necessarily capture the whole picture in our brains. Analysis gives only part of the picture; reading the poem reveals the need to capture the whole picture in our minds.
- The role of individual judgment in assessing strategic situations and criteria is highlighted through reading poems. *You* have to decide how to look at things. It's up to you to make a counterargument, not just take things at face value.

A Good-bye to My Reader on a Street in a City

Is this it? my reader asks.

Looks like it.

The end of the road? Already?

At the beginning it looked like it was going to be a long haul.

But you haven't covered everything. There's that whole section—you remember, we talked about it. Negative capability. There's a lot going on about it in the academic journals, you said.

That's how it is with books. There's a rise and fall. The fall of this one is here. The point of repose.

But all that stuff about level-five intellectual complexity? Complex, transsystemic, adaptive thinking? Shadow systems in organizational culture?

I'm saving that for next time. Right now I think it's up to the poems. I want to give them a chance to speak for themselves.

I see what you mean, he says. There's quite a lot to take in here already.

Then she tells me something that pleases me immensely.

Not only is she reading poems, but she's also downloading them.

I take a selection with me on my Blackberry, she says. I listen on my iPod, too. Not too many. One a day. Two maybe. I read at night. I listen in the morning. Sometimes on a plane too. Or in the car on the way to the airport.

We shake hands. It is a particular moment. It could be any city. There are lights, winds, the faint sniff of garbage, the taste of petrol rough on the back of your tongue.

From my right, she walks to the cab, gets in. The door clicks. The engine engages. From my left, he waves and hurries off down into the Underground. Just before he disappears he turns, lifts his hand, says something. It's drowned out by the traffic. But his mouth makes a shape and I think I know what he's saying.

I hope I shall see you again.

ɞ *Poetry*

by MARIANNE MOORE

I, too, dislike it: there are things that are important beyond all this fiddle.
   Reading it, however, with a perfect contempt for it, one discovers in
   it, after all, a place for the genuine.
      Hands that can grasp, eyes
        that can dilate, hair that can rise
          if it must, these things are important not because a

high-sounding interpretation can be put upon them but because they are
   useful. When they become so derivative as to become unintelligible,
   the same thing may be said for all of us, that we
      do not admire what
        we cannot understand: the bat
          holding on upside down or in quest of something to

eat, elephants pushing, a wild horse taking a roll, a tireless wolf under
   a tree, the immovable critic twitching his skin like a horse that feels a flea,
                the base-
   ball fan, the statistician—
      nor is it valid
        to discriminate against "business documents and

school-books"; all these phenomena are important. One must make a
                distinction
however: when dragged into prominence by half poets, the result is not
                poetry,

nor till the poets among us can be
   "literalists of
   the imagination"—above
      insolence and triviality and can present

for inspection, "imaginary gardens with real toads in them," shall we have
   it. In the meantime, if you demand on the one hand,
   the raw material of poetry in
      all its rawness and
      that which is on the other hand
        genuine, you are interested in poetry.

Taking It Further: Trying It Out

It is difficult

to get the news from poems
            yet men die miserably every day
                        for lack

of what is found there.

When I Am Asked

by LISEL MUELLER

When I am asked
how I began writing poems,
I talk about the indifference of nature.

It was soon after my mother died,
a brilliant June day,
everything blooming.

I sat on a grey stone bench
in a lovingly planted garden,
but the day lilies were as deaf
as the ears of drunken sleepers
and the roses curved inward.
Nothing was black or broken
and not a leaf fell
and the sun blared endless commercials
for summer holidays.

I sat on a grey stone bench
ringed with the ingenue faces
of pink and white impatiens
and placed my grief
in the mouth of language,
the only thing that would grieve with me.

About "When I Am Asked" and Lisel Mueller

Lisel Mueller's strongly contemporary voice is one from which any request for sympathy seems to be absent. As in Philip Larkin's "Arrival," the speaker of the poem suggests the ultimate loneliness of the individual human, in this case at the extreme moment of grief. The focus of the poem, though, is outward and forward to the business of sharing and to the potentially healing process of placing experience through the medium of artistic expression. The indifference of nature rather than the indifference of humans is a theme here, and Mueller defies the romantic tradition of a synchronicity between human mood and the natural world that characterized much nineteenth- and early-twentieth-century writing. Despite its indifference, though, isn't nature nevertheless an energizing function, the spur to creativity?

Lisel Mueller's *Alive Together: New and Selected Poems* won the Pulitzer Prize of 1997. She was born in Hamburg, Germany, in 1924 and fled with her family to the U.S. at the outbreak of World War II. "When I Am Asked" was a response to her mother's premature death, and marks the beginning of her career as a poet. She has said of writing poetry, "Something just comes to me. Usually it's the juxtaposition of two things. I see something in a new context in which I had not seen it before, and this excites me, and I mind this, try to figure it out in a poem." English is her second language, and she is a translator as well as a poet.

❧ *Jeans Alteration*

by CHANDRAKANT SHAH

The shops and markets have flung open their doors
To alter everything sit here these thousands of tailors

Come bring your jeans that are too long, too short, too broad
Blue jeans that seem brown- or white- or black-skinned
Come, the poor, the hungry, the unemployed
The rich, the high and mighty, the high lifers,
To alter everything sit here these thousands of tailors

The tailors seem familiar, like your uncles, your neighbours
They keep altering your life till you grow old
Gandhi in India and Jesus abroad
Are experts at altering the length, the inseam, the pocket, the zipper

Caste, language, creed and trade
To alter them all sit here these thousands of tailors

Tailors are teachers and tailors are gods
All who visit are altered, none are spared
No other god like them
'Welcome, welcome' resound the markets
To alter everything sit here these thousands of tailors

Physics politics aesthetics medicine Mumbai
Olympics internet NY times IBM E-com
Audiometrician beautician linguistician
Nationhood parenthood sainthood selfhood
Technocracy pornocracy snobocracy
Dancedom filmdom fandom dolldom
Acrobatics biomathematics atmospherics avionics
Zillions gazillions alteration experts sit here here, my friends.

© Translation, 2005, Naushil Mehta and Arundhathi Subramaniam

જીન્સ ઑલ્ટરેશન

ખૂલી છે દુકાનો ખૂલ્યાં છે બજારો
કરી દેવા ઑલ્ટર બધું બધે બેઠા છે દરજી હજારો

લાવો તમારાં જે લાંબાં છે, ટૂંકાં છે પહોળાં છે જીન
બ્લૂ છતાં લાગે છે બ્રાઉન, કોઈક વ્હાઈટ કોઈક બ્લૅક સ્કિન
આવો ગરીબો ઓ ભૂખ્યા બેકારો
તવંગર ને સાહેબો ઓ શાહુકારો
કરી દેવા ઑલ્ટર બધું બધે બેઠા છે દરજી હજારો

દરજીઓ દેખાવે કાકા છે મામા છે આડોશી પાડોશી
જન્મ્યાથી ઑલ્ટર કરે જીવને બની જાએ જ્યાં સુધી ડોસા કે ડોસી
ભારતમાં ગાંધી તો પરદેશે ઈસુ
કરી દેતાં ઑલ્ટર લંબાઈ કે ઝિપ્પર કે inseam કે ખીસું

નાતજાતભાષાને કરી આપે ધર્મોને ધંધાને કરો જો ઈશારો
કરી દેવા ઑલ્ટર બધું બધે બેઠા છે દરજી હજારો

છે માસ્તર પણ દરજી ને દરજી છે દેવો
ઑલ્ટર કર્યા વિના છોડે ના કોઈને
દુનિયામાં નથી કોઈ ઈશ્વર પણ એવો
બજારોમાં ચારે કોર આવો આવોનો દેકારો
કરી દેવા ઑલ્ટર બધું બધે બેઠા છે દરજી હજારો

Physics politics aesthetics medicine mumbai
Olympics Internet NY Times IBM E-Com
Audiometrician, Beautician, linguistician
Nationhood, Parenthood, Sainthood, Selfhood
Technocracy, Pornocracy, Snobocracy
Dancedom filmdom, fandom, dolldum
Acrobatics, biomathematics Atmospherics, Avionics
Zillions Gazillions ના હિસાબે બેઠા છે ઑલ્ટરના એક્સપર્ટો યારો

About "Jeans Alteration" and Chandrakant Shah

The universal twenty-first-century currency of jeans is juxtaposed with the traditions of a non-Western culture to embark on an exploration of cultural identity that is direct and hard-hitting. Could there be some sinister implication in the permeation of all strata of society by the wearing of what has become the symbol of Western democracy and affluence? By putting on the trappings of a different culture you inescapably alter your own, the poem seems to be saying. And in altering your culture do you not also alter the individuals who inhabit it? The mixing of languages in the final stanza of the original is compelling in its potential suggestion of the corrupting nature of one culture over another.

Chandrakant Shah is a Gujarati poet and playwright based in Boston. He is the author of two books of poetry, *Ane Thoda Sapna* and *Blue Jeans,* and a number of plays, in Gujarati and English. He has described himself as "a risk taker" and "a threatening voice." As well as being a poet he is an actor, theater director, producer, and journalist. He was born in 1956.

Mss

by JOHN BARR

Since I start things on the margin
—cocktail napkins, canceled checks,
timetables trying to be reliable—
and since I save it all, I know
there are good words buried and lost
in those fat accordion files, words
that sounded good at the time,
that I promised to get back to,
rhyme trains that never left Grand Central,
monikers that chattered like silverware
at 30,000', sounds struck
sheer of sense—coin of a realm—
from a currency of air, pronounced
like blessings on an express world,
soul puffs, plain mistakes,
angels, working definitions of.

About "Mss" and John Barr

This poem—unpublished until now—was written by John Barr in the early stages of his career as a merchant banker. It captures the challenges faced by the creative mind in a busy executive existence in which precious moments of clarity and insight have to be snatched from the "express world." The speed and excitement of that world is captured in the punching rhythms that complement the images of restaurants, meetings, and traveling from place to place. Whether the alluring opportunities of life in the world can co-exist satisfactorily with the hope and frustration of creativity is one of the questions the poem addresses. Will the one be opted for at the expense of the other? Will the exigencies of business allow for creative expression, for those "working definitions of" that are the stuff of creative thought?

John Barr is president of the Poetry Foundation, which publishes *Poetry* magazine. He worked for eighteen years as a managing director at Morgan Stanley, and has brought his executive experience to bear in furthering the reach and appreciation of poetry in the U.S. and internationally. He has published six collections of poetry, and his work has been characterized as "deliciously thick with language and facts." A number of his poems reflect his five years of service as a naval officer on destroyers and the three cruises he made to Vietnam.

ᕽ The Economy

by ISHIGAKI RIN

The phrase "economic animal"
I suppose is already fairly old.
Quite a gap exists between
The time when they said we seem that way
And now when we are that way.
Now then we economic animals
Will think about the economy.
From the time that I was born I've just been counting money.
That was what we were taught in the home
By the state.
People only count the time they have left
When it has started to run out.
We live terribly impoverished lives.
We die terribly lonely deaths.

© Translation, 2005, Leith Morton

About "The Economy" and Ishigaki Rin

Ishigaki Rin is known as "the bank clerk poet," and this poem is clearly influenced by her immersion in the banking profession. The central focus on whether there is more to life than making money is clear and is certainly not a new preoccupation. Its expression, though, in such stark terms may come as a shock, particularly as the individual seems to be portrayed as powerless to change things. There is no argument in the poem, merely a series of statements juxtaposed. But isn't there a kind of relentless progression between the term being coined, its enforcement by the state, and the outcome of a life wasted? It has been suggested that beyond the impoverished lives and lonely deaths can be seen, perhaps, the disintegration of the social and familial ties that formerly characterized Japanese culture.

Ishigaki Rin was born in Tokyo in 1920 and worked for nearly forty years as a bank clerk with the Industrial Bank of Japan, where she became active in trade unionism. Rin's translator, Leith Morton, has commented on the power and simplicity of the poet's language. "Ishigaki's words ring out like the beating of a drum," Morton says, "sometimes the rhythm is gentle, almost comforting, but sometimes it breaks the silence like the cracking of whip." She published four major collections of poetry between 1959 and 1984, as well as several volumes of essays. She died in December 2004.

(The Economy)

経済

石垣　りん

エコノミック・アニマル
という言葉は既に古いかもしれない。
そう見える、と言われたころと
そうなってしまった、いまとでは
だいぶ差がある。
そこでアニマル自身
ケイザイについて考える。
生まれてこのかたオカネばかり数えてきた。
それは私たち国家の
家庭内におけるシツケだった。
ヒトビトは命数について
いつも足りなくなったときだけ指を折る。
とても貧しく生きてしまう。
とても寂しく死んでしまう。

出典：　「やさしい言葉―石垣りん詩集」　童話屋

∽ *Shifting the Sun*

by DIANA DER-HOVANESSIAN

When your father dies, say the Irish,
you lose your umbrella against bad weather.
May his sun be your light, say the Armenians.

When your father dies, say the Welsh,
you sink a foot deeper into the earth.
May you inherit his light, say the Armenians.

When your father dies, say the Canadians,
you run out of excuses. May you inherit
his sun, say the Armenians.

When your father dies, say the French,
you become your own father.
May you stand up in his light, say the Armenians.

When your father dies, say the Indians,
he comes back as the thunder.
May you inherit his light, say the Armenians.

When your father dies, say the Russians,
he takes your childhood with him.
May you inherit his light, say the Armenians.

When your father dies, say the English,
you join his club you vowed you wouldn't.
May you inherit his sun, say the Armenians.

When your father dies, say the Armenians,
your sun shifts forever.
And you walk in his light.

About "Shifting the Sun" and Diana Der-Hovanessian

The repetitions of "Shifting the Sun" give rise to an almost incantatory feel, making room for a gentle humor that guides this exploration of loss and consolation. The statements made in each stanza are deceptively simple, like folklore, revealing at once the idiosyncrasies of cultural difference and the universality of the effects of bereavement. The poem addresses, perhaps, questions of inheritance and change, as well as loss and longing, and reflects the poet's desire to bring Armenian literary culture into the spotlight.

Diana Der-Hovanessian is a New England poet of Armenian descent, and her translations have revealed the depth and breadth of Armenian poetry and history to a new readership. She has published more than twenty-two volumes of poetry and translation and has won many awards, including from the National Endowment for the Arts and the Poetry Society of America. Her work has been praised for being "subtle, humorous and vividly tragic."

Summer Solstice, New York City

by SHARON OLDS

By the end of the longest day of the year he could not stand it,
he went up the iron stairs through the roof of the building
and over the soft, tarry surface
to the edge, put one leg over the complex green tin cornice
and said if they came a step closer that was it.
Then the huge machinery of the earth began to work for his life,
the cops came in their suits blue-grey as the sky on a cloudy evening,
and one put on a bullet-proof vest, a
black shell around his own life,
life of his children's father, in case
the man was armed, and one, slung with a
rope like the sign of his bounden duty,
came up out of a hole in the top of the neighboring building
like the gold hole they say is in the top of the head,
and began to lurk toward the man who wanted to die.
The tallest cop approached him directly,
softly, slowly, talking to him, talking, talking,
while the man's leg hung over the lip of the next world
and the crowd gathered in the street, silent, and the
hairy net with its implacable grid was
unfolded near the curb and spread out and
stretched as the sheet is prepared to receive at a birth.
Then they all came a little closer
where he squatted next to his death, his shirt
glowing its milky glow like something
growing in a dish at night in the dark in a lab and then
everything stopped
as his body jerked and he
stepped down from the parapet and went toward them
and they closed on him, I thought they were going to
beat him up, as a mother whose child has been
lost will scream at the child when it's found, they
took him by the arms and held him up and
leaned him against the wall of the chimney and the
tall cop lit a cigarette
in his own mouth, and gave it to him, and
then they all lit cigarettes, and the
red, glowing ends burned like the
tiny campfires we lit at night
back at the beginning of the world.

About "Summer Solstice, New York City" and Sharon Olds

The matter-of-fact tone and the unfolding sequence of events make this poem, from Sharon Olds's 1987 collection *The Gold Cell,* seem in many respects more like a story. And yet the dramatic moment of decision between life and death has all the resonance and richness that the density of the poetic form can bring to it. Critics have pointed to the huge vistas the poem opens, leading out from the social mechanisms of contemporary society to distant historical and existential realms. Whether the poem is a refreshing reinforcement of the positive aspects of civil society—help, succor, order, support—or a comment on the individual desperation that exists as a substratum of such a society is open to question. Perhaps in that final image of the flickering campfire, the essential comradeship of mortal human beings is alluded to, the fragility common to all existence on earth.

Sharon Olds was born in San Francisco and educated at Stanford and Columbia universities. Her work has appeared in more than one hundred anthologies and has been characterized in the *New York Times* as having "a robust sensuality, a delight in the physical that is almost Whitmanesque." She lives in New York City, where she held the position of state poet from 1998 to 2000.

✍ *Rice*

by A M A N O   T A D A S H I

Pick up these grains of rice
scattered about the wet railroad tracks,
will you?
It's a sort of rice-bomb sack
thrown out of the train window near the station.

Rice grains spilled from the sack.
Pick up those rain soaked grains
scattered around the tracks, will you?
Bring me the woman bearer
who was manhandled and hauled away a little while ago,
and please ask her, her husband forced into the front lines
and killed, how she managed
to raise her children, no money or anything else.
And ask if her children
had ever had enough rice to eat.
Ask her gently, before God and man.
These rice grains shining in the rain and mud
were raised up by some
stupidly honest, poor Japanese peasant.
Pick up those grains of rice, will you?

Pick them up one by one,
silently.

About "Rice" and Amano Tadashi

The anger informing this poem's exhortation to attend the plight of a dis-
possessed woman, and thereby perhaps a whole sector of society, is palp-
able. The repeated invitation to pick up the grains of rice, halfway between
an instruction and a question, frames the stark message the speaker does
not hesitate to express. Is the world of deprivation that comes into focus
along with the rice grains one the reader would want, or be able, to enter?
It could be that an imaginative engagement with the process of picking up
the grains one by one, as the woman or another hungry person may have to

(Rice)

米

天野忠

この
雨に濡れた鉄道線路に
散らばった米を拾ってくれたまえ
これはバクダンといわれて
汽車の窓から駅近くなって放り出された米袋だ
その米袋からこぼれ出た米だ
このレールの上に　レールの傍に
雨に打たれ　散らばった米を拾ってくれたまえ
そしてさっきの汽車の外へ　荒々しく
曳かれていったかつぎやの女を連れてきてくれたまえ
どうして夫が戦争に引き出され　殺され
どうして貯えもなく残された子供らを育て
どうして命をつないできたかを　たずねてくれたまえ
そしてその子供らは
こんな白い米を腹一杯喰ったことがあったかどうかをたずねてくれたまえ
自分に恥じないしずかな言葉でたずねてくれたまえ
雨と泥の中でじっとひかっている
このむざんに散らばったものは
愚直で貧乏な日本の百姓の辛抱がこしらえた米だ
このうつくしい米を拾ってくれたまえ
何も云わず
一粒ずつ拾ってくれたまえ。

出典：　「単純な生涯―天野忠詩集」　コルボオ詩話会

do, is the challenge the poem ultimately proposes. And perhaps the question that lingers is one concerning the ability to empathize.

Amano Tadashi was a noted Japanese poet of the twentieth century. He was born in Kyoto, the eldest son of a traditional craftsman, and lived from 1909 to 1993. He was blacklisted by the Special Political Police in the late 1930s, and his production of poetry was interrupted for twelve years until 1949. While working as a clerk in the Nara Women's University Library he published a number of collections of poetry, including *Tanzyunna Shogai* (*A Simple Life*) in 1958, from which "Rice" comes. Although his work won several awards, he remained poor throughout his life and wrote in a tiny study only five meters square. His work has appeared in the anthology *Like Underground Water: Poetry of Mid-Twentieth-Century Japan,* edited by Edward Lueders and Naoshi Koriyama.

ᔕ *Could Have*

by WISLAWA SZYMBORSKA
(trans. Stanislaw Baranczak and Clare Cavanagh)

It could have happened.
It had to happen.
It happened earlier. Later.
Nearer. Farther off.
It happened, but not to you.

You were saved because you were the first.
You were saved because you were the last.
Alone. With others.
On the right. The left.
Because it was raining. Because of the shade.
Because the day was sunny.

You were in luck—there was a forest.
You were in luck—there were no trees.
You were in luck—a rake, a hook, a beam, a brake,
A jamb, a turn, a quarter-inch, an instant . . .

So you're here? Still dizzy from
another dodge, close shave, reprieve?
One hole in the net and you slipped through?
I couldn't be more shocked or
speechless.
Listen,
how your heart pounds inside me.

Wszelki Wypadek (Could Have)
by WISLAWA SZYMBORSKA

Zdarzyć się mogło.
Zdarzyć się musiało.
Zdarzyło się wcześniej. Później. Bliżej. Dalej.
Zdarzyło się nie tobie.

Ocalałeś, bo byłeś pierwszy.
Ocalałeś, bo byłeś ostatni.
Bo sam. Bo ludzie. Bo w lewo. Bo w prawo.
Bo padał deszcz. Bo padał cień.
Bo panowała słoneczna pogoda.

Na szczęście był tam las.
Na szczęście nie było drzew.
Na szczęście szyna, hak, belka, hamulec,
Framuga, zakręt, milimetr, sekunda.
Na szczęście brzytw pływała po wodzie.

Wskutek, ponieważ, a jednak, pomimo.
Co było to było gdyby ręka, noga,
O krok, o włos
Od zbiegu okoliczności.
Więc jesteś?
Prosto z uchylonej jeszcze chwili?
Sieć jednooka, a ty przez to oko?
Nie umiem się nadziwić, namilczeć się temu.
Posłuchaj
Jak mi prędko bije twoje serce.

About "Could Have" and Wislawa Szymborska

This poem comes from Szymborska's *View with a Grain of Sand,* published in 1996, the year she was awarded the Nobel Prize "for poetry that with ironic precision allows the historical and biological context to come to light in fragments of human reality." The fragment at the heart of "Could Have" seems to be the miraculous avoidance of disaster of some kind, no doubt informed by the poet's long experience of political upheaval (she was born in Poland in 1923). The issue of empathy is here, just as it is in "Rice," but very differently configured. Isn't there perhaps a sense of guilt, or even horror, that one individual survives, possibly at the expense of others? The poet's comment, from her Nobel acceptance speech, seems to throw light on this. "All imperfection," she said, "is easier to tolerate if served up in small doses."

Wislawa Szymborska has lived in Kraków, Poland, since 1931. She has published more than ten collections of poetry, for which she has received many honors and awards. In speaking of inspiration, she has said, "There is, has been, and will always be a certain group of people whom inspiration visits. It's made up of all those who've consciously chosen their calling and do their job with love and imagination. [For these people] difficulties and setbacks never quell their curiosity. A swarm of new questions emerges from every problem they solve. Whatever inspiration is, it's born from a continuous 'I don't know.'"

In My Craft or Sullen Art
by DYLAN THOMAS

In my craft or sullen art
Exercised in the still night
When only the moon rages
And the lovers lie abed
With all their griefs in their arms,
I labour by singing light
Not for ambition or bread
Or the strut or trade of charms
On the ivory stages
But for the common wages
Of their most secret heart.

Not for the proud man apart
From the raging moon I write
On these spindrift pages
Nor for the towering dead
With their nightingales and psalms
But for the lovers, their arms
Round the griefs of the ages,
Who pay no praise or wages
Nor heed my craft or art.

About "In My Craft or Sullen Art" and Dylan Thomas

The music of language is central to this 1946 poem, published in the collection *Deaths and Entrances,* whose somber tones reflect the recently ended World War II. The vocation of the poet is a central theme, and the rich sensual and emotional fabric attests to Thomas's debt to the romantic tradition and his rejection of the cooler tones of reason that were popular among English poets at the time. Those sensuous and impassioned images, the lovers, the griefs, the towering dead, form the context for an assertion of the ultimate value of artistic expression, that it occurs in spite of the indifference or unknowingness of those for whom it is intended.

Dylan Thomas was perhaps the most feted Welsh poet of the twentieth century, and his short but legendary life of passion and excess has become almost mythical. He was a renowned reader of his work, delivering his poems in a highly charged, rhetorical manner whose drama endeared him to American audiences when he toured the U.S. in the early 1950s. According to the *New York Times,* "Dylan Thomas's voice has added a new dimension to literary history. He will surely be remembered as the first in modern literature to be both a maker and speaker of poetry."

Acknowledgments

"Under Which Lyre," copyright ©1976 by Edward Mendelson, William Meredith, and Monroe K. Spears, Executors of the Estate of W. H. Auden, "Stop All the Clocks," copyright 1940 and renewed 1968 by W. H. Auden, "The Unknown Citizen," copyright 1940 and copyright renewed 1968 by W. H. Auden, from *Collected Poems by W. H. Auden.* Used by permission of Random House, Inc., and Faber and Faber Ltd.

"You Reading This, Be Ready," copyright 1998. The Estate of William Stafford. Reprinted from *The Way It Is: New and Selected Poems* with the permission of Graywolf Press, Saint Paul, Minnesota.

Billy Collins, "Introduction to Poetry," from *The Apple That Astonished Paris.* Copyright 1988, 1996 by Billy Collins. Used by permission of the University of Arkansas Press, www.uapress.com.

"Jim Desterland," by Hyam Plutzik, reprinted with the permission of Tanya Plutzik.

"Dirge," reprinted by the permission of Russell & Volkening, Inc., as agents for the author. Copyright 1934 by Kenneth Fearing, renewed in 1972 by the Estate of Kenneth Fearing.

"The Road Not Taken," "Stopping by Woods on a Snowy Evening," and "Mending Wall" from *The Poetry of Robert Frost,* edited by Edward Connery Lathem. Copyright © 1916, 1923, 1969 by Henry Holt and Company. Copyright 1944, 1951, 1958 by Robert Frost. Copyright 1967 by Lesley Frost Ballantine. Reprinted by permission of Henry Holt and Company, LLC.

Judith Wright, "Legend," from *A Human Pattern: Selected Poems* (Sydney: ETT Imprints, 1996).

"Hawk Roosting," from *Selected Poems, 1957–1994,* by Ted Hughes. Copyright ©2002 by The Estate of Ted Hughes. Reprinted by permission of Farrar, Strauss and Giroux, LLC, and Faber and Faber Ltd.

"Ars Poetica," from *Collected Poems, 1917–1982,* by Archibald MacLeish. Copyright 1985 by the Estate of Archibald MacLeish. Reprinted by permission of Houghton Mifflin Company. All rights reserved.

"Postscript," by Seamus Heaney, from *The Spirit Level*. Copyright 1996, reprinted by permission of Faber and Faber Ltd.

"Traveling through the Dark," copyright 1962, 1998. The Estate of William Stafford. Reprinted from *The Way It Is: New and Selected Poems* with the permission of Graywolf Press, Saint Paul, Minnesota.

"Rough Country," copyright 1991 by Dana Gioia. Reprinted from *The Gods of Winter* with the permission of Graywolf Press, Saint Paul, Minnesota.

"Penitence," from *A Normal Skin*, by John Burnside, published by Jonathan Cape. Reprinted by permission of the Random House Group Ltd.

"In Memory of Henry West," from *Prince Rupert's Drop*, by Jane Draycott ©1999, is reprinted with permission from Carcanet Press Limited.

"The Door: Anticipation of Wisdom," from *Someone Else's Life*, by Kapka Kassabova, ©2003. Used by permission of Bloodaxe Books, Kapka Kassabova, and Aukland University Press.

Permission to reprint "Snow" by Louis MacNeice from *Collected Poems*, published by Faber and Faber, is granted by David Higham Associates Limited.

"the door," by Miroslav Holub, from *Poems Before and After: Collected English Translations*, trans. Ian and Jarmila Milner et al., ©2006. Used by permission of Bloodaxe Books.

"How These Words Happened," copyright 1991, 1998. The Estate of William Stafford. Reprinted from *The Way It Is: New and Selected Poems* with the permission of Graywolf Press, Saint Paul, Minnesota.

"The Thought Fox," by Ted Hughes, from *The Hawk in the Rain: Poems*, reprinted by permission of Faber and Faber Ltd.

"The Islanders," from *Lifelines*, by Philip Booth, copyright ©1999 by Philip Booth. Used by permission of Viking Penguin, a division of Penguin Group (USA), Inc.

"Executive," from *A Nip in the Air*, by John Betjeman. Copyright ©1974 by John Betjeman. Used by permission of W. W. Norton and Company, Inc.

"Anecdote of the Jar," copyright 1923 and renewed 1951 by Wallace Stevens. "Notes toward a Supreme Fiction," copyright 1954 by Wallace Stevens and renewed 1982 by Holly Stevens, from *The Collected Poems of Wallace Stevens*, by Wallace Stevens. Used by permission of Alfred A. Knopf, a division of Random House, Inc., and Faber and Faber Ltd.

Photo of T. S. Eliot in his London office, January 19, 1956, is used by permission of AP/Wide World Photos.

"The Diver" by E. L. Mayo, is reprinted with permission from the Mayo family.

The image on page 132 is from *The Forgotten Half of Change*, by Luc de Brabandere (Dearborn Trade Publishing, 2005), 52.

Permission to reprint "The Listeners," by Walter de la Mare, granted by the Literary Trustees of Walter de la Mare and the Society of Authors as their representative.

"Leda and the Swan" is reprinted with the permission of Scribner, an imprint of Simon and Schuster Adult Publishing Group, from *The Collected Works of W. B. Yeats*, vol. 1: *The Poems, Revised*, edited by Richard J. Finneran. Copyright ©1928 by the Macmillan Company, copyright © renewed 1956 by Georgie Yeats. All rights reserved. And with the permission of A. P. Watt Ltd on behalf of Gráinne Yeats.

Permission to reprint "The Makers" and "Life Cycle of the Common Man," by Howard Nemerov, granted by Margaret Nemerov.

"Found in a Storm," Copyright 1962, 1998, the Estate of William Stafford. Reprinted from *The Way It Is: New and Selected Poems*, with the permission of Graywolf Press, Saint Paul, Minnesota.

"Night-time: Starting to Write," by Bernard Spencer, reprinted by permission of Hodder and Stoughton.

"The Fish," from *The Complete Poems, 1927–1979*, by Elizabeth Bishop. Copyright ©1979, by Alice Helen Methfessel. Reprinted by permission of Farrar, Strauss and Giroux, LLC.

"Arrival," from *Collected Poems*, by Philip Larkin. Copyright ©1988, 2003 by the Estate of Philip Larkin. Reprinted by permission of Farrar, Strauss and Giroux, LLC, and Faber and Faber Ltd.

"Shopper," from *Choosing to Be a Swan*, by Connie Bensley, ©1994. Used by permission of Bloodaxe Books.

"Traders' Call to Arms," by Eugene Schlanger, originally published in *September 11 Wall Street Sonnets and Other New York City Poems* (Paris: Éditions Underbahn), © 2006 Eugene Schlanger. Reprinted by permission of the poet.

"Asphodel, That Greeny Flower," by William Carlos Williams, from *Collected Poems, 1939–1962*, vol. 2, copyright © by William Carlos Williams. Reprinted by permission of New Directions Publishing Corp. and Carcanet Press Limited.

"Dulce et Decorum Est," by Wilfred Owen, from *The Collected Poems of Wilfred Owen*, copyright ©1963 by Chatto and Windus Ltd. Reprinted by permission of New Directions Publishing Corp.

"Animals," from *The Collected Poems of Frank O'Hara*, by Frank O'Hara, edited by Donald Allen, copyright ©1971 by Maureen Granville-Smith, Administratrix of the Estate of Frank O'Hara. Used by permission of Alfred A. Knopf, a division of Random House, Inc.

Heather McHugh, "The Oven Loves the TV Set," in *Hinge & Sign: Poems*, ©1994 by Heather McHugh and reprinted with permission from Wesleyan University Press.

"Easter 1916" is reprinted with the permission of Scribner, an imprint of Simon and Schuster Adult Publishing Group, from *The Collected Works of W. B. Yeats*, vol. 1: *The Poems, Revised,* edited by Richard J. Finneran. Copyright ©1924 by the Macmillan Company; copyright © renewed by Bertha Georgie Yeats. All rights reserved. And with the permission of A. P. Watt Ltd on behalf of Gráinne Yeats.

"Security" is taken from *Michael Hamburger: Collected Poems, 1941–1994*, published by Anvil Press Poetry in 1995.

"Those Winter Sundays." Copyright ©1966 by Robert Hayden, from *Collected Poems of Robert Hayden*, by Robert Hayden, edited by Frederick Glaysher. Used by permission of Liveright Publishing Corporation.

"Japan," from *Picnic, Lightning*, by Billy Collins, ©1998. Reprinted by permission of the University of Pittsburgh Press.

"Introduction to Poetry," by Billy Collins, was translated into Japanese by Junichi Koizumi and originally published by Kokubunsha in *Emily Dickinson no Chakui wo Hagu.*

The Japanese translation of "Stopping by Woods on a Snowy Evening," by Robert Frost, is reprinted by permission of the translator, Koji Kawamoto, and the publisher, Iwanami Shoten.

"Poetry," from *The Poems of Marianne Moore*, by Marianne Moore, edited by Grace Schulman, copyright ©2003 by Marianne Craig Moore, Executor of the Estate of Marianne Moore. Used by permission of Viking Penguin, a division of Penguin Group (USA), Inc.

"When I Am Asked," reprinted by permission of Louisiana State University Press from *Alive Together*, by Lisel Mueller. Copyright ©1996 by Lisel Mueller.

Permission to reprint "Jeans Alteration," by Chandrakant Shah.

"Mss," by John Barr, is printed by kind permission of the author.

Permission to reprint the translation of "The Economy," by Ishigaki Rin, by Leith Morton, translator. Permission to reprint the original Japanese granted by Fumi-taka Sekiya.

Permission to use "Shifting the Sun," by Diana der Hovanessian, granted by the poet.

"Summer Solstice: New York City," from *Strike Sparks: Selected Poems, 1980–2002*, by Sharon Olds, copyright ©2004 by Sharon Olds. Used by permission of Alfred A. Knopf, a division of Random House, Inc.

"Rice," by Amano Tadashi, is reprinted by permission of Thomas Fitzsimmons, Katydid Books. I was unable to locate the Japanese publisher of the original poem from 1958.

"Could Have" from *View with a Grain of Sand*, copyright © 1993 by Wislawa Szymborska. English translation by Stanislaw Baranczak and Clare Cavanagh copyright © 1995 by Houghton Mifflin Harcourt Publishing Company and Faber and Faber Ltd. Printed by permission of the publishers. The original Polish version is reprinted with permission of Wislawa Szymborska.

"In My Craft or Sullen Art," by Dylan Thomas, from *The Poems of Dylan Thomas*, copyright © by New Directions Publishing Corp. Reprinted by permission of New Directions Publishing Corp. and by David Higham Associates Limited.

Notes

PART I, CHAPTER I

1. The discussion of representation versus narration is indebted to Marjorie Perloff, "In Defense of Poetry," http://bostonreview.net/ BR24.6/perloff.html, in which the quote from Aristotle is cited.

PART I, CHAPTER 4

The discussion of sharpeners versus levelers is indebted to Else Frenkel-Brunswick, "Intolerance of Ambiguity as an Emotional and Perceptual Variable," *Journal of Personality* xviii (1) (1949): 108–43; and Richard Ohmann, "Modes of Order," in *Linguistics and Literary Style*, edited by Donald C. Freeman (New York: Holt, Rinehart and Winston, 1970), pp. 209–42, cited by Reuven Tsur at http://www2.bc.edu/ ~richarad/lcb/fea/tsurin/tsurmain.html.

1. J. C. C. Smart's quotation cited by Reuven Tsur (http://www2.bc.edu/ ~richarad/lcb/fea/tsurin/tsurmain.html).

PART I, CHAPTER 5

1. The quotations from Socrates are cited in C. C. W. Taylor, *Socrates: A Very Short Introduction* (Oxford: Oxford University Press, 2000). The opening discussion of Socrates is indebted to this text.

2. The discussion of the precategorical realm is indebted to Reuven Tsur's exposition of the pre-categorial in "Aspects of Cognitive Poetics," http://www2.bc .edu/~richarad/lcb/fea/tsur/cogpoetics.html; and Howard Leventhal, "Toward a Comprehensive Theory of Emotion," in L. Berkowitz, ed., *Advances in Experimental Social Psychology*, vol. 13, pp. 139–207 (1980), cited in John Fudjack and Patricia Dinkelaker, "The Five Levels of the Feeling Function: A Brief Phenomenological Description," http://tap3x.net/ENSEMBLE/mpage3f.html. Grateful acknowledgment is made to Reuven Tsur, in whose work on cognitive poetics the term *poetic competence* was first encountered.

PART 2, CHAPTER 1

1. The discussion of Wittgenstein is indebted to John Heaton and Judy Groves, *Wittgenstein for Beginners* (Cambridge: Icon Books, 1994).

2. Yuri Lotman's study of automatic perception is cited in Phil Roberts, *How Poetry Works* (Harmondsworth: Penguin, 2000).

PART 2, CHAPTER 2

1. The quotations are from *Businessweek*, August 1, 2005 (unattributed Special Report).

PART 2, CHAPTER 4

1. Ryan's summation of Foucault's position appears in Michael Ryan, *Literary Theory: A Practical Introduction* (Oxford: Blackwell, 1999), quoted at p. 71, emphasis added.

PART 2, CHAPTER 5

The term *hot cognition* was first encountered in Willie van Peer, "Towards a Poetic of Emotion," in *Emotion and the Arts*, edited by Mette Hjort and Sue Laver, pp. 215–24 (Oxford: Oxford University Press, 1997).

1. The discussion of form, including references to Viktor Schklovsky, is indebted to P. Gifford and B. Stimpson, eds., *Reading Paul Valéry: Universe in Mind* (Cambridge: Cambridge University Press, 1998); and Gerald L. Bruns, *Modern Poetry and the Idea of Language* (Normal, IL: Dalkey Archive Press, 2001), who summarizes Schklovsky's argument in "Art as Technique" (1917).

2. Quotation no. 1 is from James Hillman, "Emotion: A Comprehensive Phenomenology of Theories and Their Meanings for Therapy" (Evanston, IL: Northwestern University Press, 1960), p. 244, cited in John Fudjack and Patricia Dinkelaker, "The Five Levels of the Feeling Function," http://tap3x.net/ENSEMBLE/mpage3f.html. Quotation no. 2, unattributed, is cited in Fudjack and Dinkelaker, "The Five Levels of the Feeling Function," p. 1. Quotation no. 3 is from Jacques Hadamard, *Psychology of Invention in the Mathematical Field* (Princeton: Princeton University Press, 1945), p. 10, cited in Fudjack and Dinkelaker, "The Five Levels of the Feeling Function."

3. This case study is discussed in Steven Pinker, *The Language Instinct* (London: Penguin, 1994), pp. 97–101.

PART 2, CHAPTER 6

1. The discussion of the use of poetry at Accor is indebted to "Accor Cultivates its 'Jardin Extraordinaire,'" *H.T.R.* (Hotel, Tourism, and Restaurant Industry), pp. 100–102, no. 124/5, May–June 2005.

2. The discussion of new versus old is indebted to *Business Week*, July 25, 2005.

PART 2, CHAPTER 7

1. The discussion of creativity is indebted to Margaret A. Boden, *The Creative Mind* (London: Routledge, 2003).

2. The Bruner quote is from J. Bruner, *On Knowing: Essays for the Left Hand* (New York: Athenaeum, 1965).

3. The discussion of Saussure is indebted to Deborah Cameron, *Feminism and Linguistic Theory* (Basingstoke: Macmillan, 1985).

PART 3, CHAPTER 2

1. Richards's quotation is from I. A. Richards, *Science and Poetry* (London: Kegan, Paul, Trench, Trubner, 1926), reprinted as *Poetries and Sciences* (New York: Norton, 1970), pp. 58–60.

2. David Hume, *A Treatise of Human Nature*, rpt. (Oxford: Oxford University Press, 2000), p. 419.

3. T. S. Eliot, "Hamlet and His Problems," in *The Sacred Wood: Essays on Poetry and Criticism* (London: Faber and Faber, [1919] 1997), p. 103.

PART 3, CHAPTER 3

1. General Lennox's quotes are from William James Lennox Jr., "Romance and Reality," http://www.poetryfoundation.org/journal/feature.html?id=146660 (accessed May 2006).

PART 3, CHAPTER 5

1. The discussion of Martin Heidegger is indebted to David Cooper, *Metaphor* (Oxford: Blackwell, 1989), quoted at pp. 253–54. The Nietzsche quotation is from Friedrich Nietzsche, *Ecce Homo*, translated by Anthony M. Ludovici (Mineola, NY: Courier Dover Publications, 2004), p. 75.

Selected References

Abbs, Peter, ed. *The Symbolic Order: A Contemporary Reader on the Arts Debate*. Basingstoke: Falmer Press, 1989.

"Accor Cultivates Its 'Jardin Extraordinaire.'" *H.T.R.* (Hotel, Tourism, and Restaurant Industry) no. 124/5, May–June 2005.

Adamson, Jane, Richard Freadman, and David Parker. *Renegotiating Ethics in Literature, Philosophy, and Theory*. Cambridge: Cambridge University Press, 1998.

Annas, Julia. *Plato: A Very Short Introduction*. Oxford: Oxford University Press, 2003.

Ammons, A. R. "A Poem Is a Walk." In *Claims for Poetry*, edited by Donald Hall, 1–8. Ann Arbor: University of Michigan Press, 1982.

Attridge, Derek. *The Ryhthms of English Poetry*. London and New York: Longman, 1982.

Aviram, Amitai. *Telling Rhythm: Body and Meaning in Poetry*. Ann Arbor: University of Michigan Press, 1994.

Badaracco, Joseph L., Jr. "Leadership in Literature." *Harvard Business Review*, March 2006.

Becker, Carol, ed. *The Subversive Imagination: Artists, Society, and Social Responsibility*. New York and London: Routledge, 1994.

Belbin, Meredith. *Management Teams: Why They Succeed or Fail*. London: Heinemann, 1987.

Bierwisch, Manfred. "Poetics and Linguistics." In *Linguistics and Literary Style*, edited by Donald C. Freeman, 97–115. New York: Holt, Rinehart and Winston,1970.

Boden, Margaret A. "Précis of 'The Creative Mind: Myths and Mechanisms.'" *Behavioral and Brain Sciences* 17, no. 3 (1994): 519–70. http://www.bbsonline.org/Preprints/OldArchive/bbs.boden.html (accessed March 2006).

Boden, Margaret A. *The Creative Mind*. London: Routledge, 2003.

Boyle, Mary-Ellen, and Edward Ottensmeyer. "Solving Business Problems through the Creative Power of the Arts: Catalyzing Change at Unilever." *Journal of Business Strategy* 26, no. 5 (2005): 14–21.

Brown, Richard Harvey. *A Poetic for Sociology: Toward a Logic of Discovery for the Human Sciences*. Chicago: University of Chicago Press, 1977.

Bruner, J. *On Knowing: Essays for the Left Hand.* New York: Athenaeum, 1965.

Bruns, Gerald L. *Modern Poetry and the Idea of Language.* Normal, IL: Dalkey Archive Press, 2001.

Buswick, Ted, Alastair Creamer, and Mary Pinard. "(Re)Educating for Leadership: How the Arts Can Improve Business." http://www.absa.org/uk/render.aspx ?siteID=1&navIDs=1,150,085.

Cameron, Deborah. *Feminism and Linguistic Theory.* Basingstoke: Macmillan, 1985.

Case, Peter. "Management Education and the Philosophical Life." *Management Learning* 37, no. 3 (2006): 283–89.

Caulkin, Simon. "Big Business Brought to Book." *Observer,* November 21, 2004.

Coleridge, Samuel Taylor. *Biographia Literaria.* Princeton: Princeton University Press, 1983.

Collins, James C., and Jerry I. Porras. *Built to Last: Successful Habits of Visionary Companies.* 2nd ed. London: Random House, 1998.

Constable, John. "Science in Poetry." *Kyoto Seika University Review,* no. 6 (1994): 24–30.

Cooper, David E. *Metaphor.* Oxford: Blackwell, 1989.

Damasio, Antonio. *Descartes' Error: Emotion, Reason, and the Human Brain.* New York: Avon Books/HarperCollins, 1994.

Damasio, Antonio. *The Feeling of What Happens: Body, Emotion, and the Making of Consciousness.* London: Heinemann, 1999.

Damasio, Antonio. *Looking for Spinoza: Joy, Sorrow, and the Human Brain.* New York: Harcourt Inc., 2003.

Darsø, Lotte. *Artful Creation: Learning-Tales of Arts-in-Business.* Frederiksberg, Denmark: Samsfundlitteratur, 2004.

Davis, Stan, and David McIntosh. *The Art of Business.* San Francisco: Berrett-Koehler, 2005.

Day Lewis, C. *The Poetic Image.* Los Angeles: Jeremy P. Tarcher, 1984.

de Brabandere, Luc. *The Forgotten Half of Change.* Chicago: Dearborn, 2005.

Dissanayke, Ellen. *Art and Intimacy: How the Arts Began.* Seattle: University of Washington Press, 2000.

Dissanayake, Ellen. *Homo Aestheticus.* Seattle: University of Washington Press, 1995.

Earthman, Elise Ann. "The Lonely, Quiet Concert: Readers Creating Meaning from Literary Texts." PhD diss., Stanford University, 1989.

Eaton, Marcia Muelder. *Merit, Aesthetic, and Ethical.* Oxford: Oxford University Press, 2001.

Eisner, Elliot W. *The Arts and the Creation of Mind.* New Haven: Yale University Press, 2002.

Eldridge, Richard. *Beyond Representation: Philosophy and Poetic Imagination.* Cambridge: Cambridge University Press, 1996.

Eliot, T. S. *On Poetry and Poets.* London: Faber and Faber, 1986.

Eliot, T. S. *The Sacred Wood: Essays on Poetry and Criticism.* Rpt. London: Faber and Faber, 1997.

Eliot, T. S. *The Use of Poetry and the Use of Criticism.* London: Faber and Faber, [1933] 1964.

Empson, William. *Seven Types of Ambiguity.* Harmondsworth: Penguin, [1930] 1965.

Farson, Richard. *Management of the Absurd: Paradoxes in Leadership.* New York: Simon and Shuster, 1996.

Fauconnier, Gilles, and Mark Turner. *The Way We Think.* New York: Basic Books, 2002.

Fergusson, Francis, and S. H. Butcher. *Aristotle: Poetics.* New York: Hill and Wang, 1961.

Fudjack, John, and Patricia Dinkelaker. *The Dimensions of Human Space.* http://tap3x.net/ENSEMBLE/main.html#1 (accessed November 2003).

Fudjack, John, and Patricia Dinkelaker. "The Five Levels of the Feeling Function: A Brief Phenomenological Description." http://tap3x.net/ENSEMBLE/mpage3f.html (accessed September 2003).

Gagliardi, Pasquale. *Symbols and Artifacts: Views of the Corporate Landscape.* New York: Aldine de Gruyter, 1992.

Gardner, Howard. *Changing Minds: The Art and Science of Changing Our Own and Other People's Minds.* Cambridge: Harvard Business School Press, 2004.

Gardner, Howard. *Intelligence Reframed.* New York: Basic Books, 1999.

Gardner, Howard, Mihaly Csikszentmmihalyi, and William Damon. *Good Work: Where Excellence and Ethics Meet.* New York: Basic Books, 2001.

Garvey, Bob, and Bill Williamson. *Beyond Knowledge Management.* Harlow, England: Prentice-Hall, 2002.

Gibbs, Raymond. *The Poetics of Mind.* Cambridge: Cambridge University Press, 1994.

Gifford, P., and B. Stimpson, eds. *Reading Paul Valéry: Universe in Mind.* Cambridge: Cambridge University Press, 1998.

Gioia, Dana. *Can Poetry Matter?* Saint Paul: Graywolf Press, 1992.

Goleman, Daniel. *Emotional Intelligence: Why It Can Matter More than IQ.* New York: Bantam, 1995.

Grisham, Thomas. "Metaphor, Poetry, Storytelling, and Cross-Cultural Leadership." *Management Decision* 44, no. 4 (2006): 486–503.

Grant, David, and Cliff Oswick, eds. *Metaphor and Organizations.* London: Sage Publications, 1996.

Green, Keith, and Jill LeBihan. *Practical Theory and Practice: A Coursebook.* London: Routledge, 1996.

Hadamard, Jacques. *Psychology of Invention in the Mathematical Field.* Princeton: Princeton University Press, 1945.

Harré, Rom, and Grant Gillet. *The Discursive Mind.* London: Sage Publications, 1994.

Heaton, John, and Judy Groves. *Wittgenstein for Beginners.* Cambridge: Icon Books, 1994.

Hendry, John. "Educating Managers for Post-bureaucracy: The Role of the Humanities." *Management Learning* 37, no. 3 (2006): 267–81.

Hillman, James. *Emotion: A Comprehensive Phenomenology of Theories and Their Meanings for Therapy.* Evanston, IL: Northwestern University Press, 1960.

Hjort, Mette, and Sue Laver. *Emotion and the Arts.* Oxford: Oxford University Press, 1997.

Hofstadter, Douglas R. *Le Ton beau de Marot: In Praise of the Music of Language.* New York: Basic Books, 1997.

Hume, David. *A Treatise of Human Nature*. Rpt. Oxford: Oxford University Press, 2000.

Iser, Wolfgang. "The Reading Process: A Phenomenological Approach." *New Literary History* (winter) 3 (1972): 279–99.

Janaway, Christopher. *Images of Excellence Plato's Critique of the Arts*. Oxford: Oxford University Press, 1998.

Karmiloff-Smith, A. "Precis of *Beyond Modularity: A Developmental Perspective on Cognitive Science*." *Behavioral and Brain Sciences* 17, no. 4 (1994): 693–745.

Keats, John. *Selected Letters*. Edited by Jon Mee. Oxford: Oxford World's Classics, 2002.

Kemal, Salim, and Ivan Gaskell. *Explanation and Value in the Arts*. Cambridge: Cambridge University Press, 1993.

Kepner, C., and B. Tregoe. *The New Rational Manager*. Princeton: Princeton Research Press, 1981.

Kermode, Frank. *Romantic Image*. London: Routledge and Kegan Paul, 1986.

Kivy, Peter. *Philosophies of Arts: An Essay in Differences*. Cambridge: Cambridge University Press, 1997.

Lakoff, G., and M. Johnson. *Metaphors We Live By*. Chicago: University of Chicago Press, [1980] 2003.

Le Doux, Joseph. *The Emotional Brain*. New York: Simon and Schuster, 1996.

Lennox, William James. "Romance and Reality." http://www.poetryfoundation .org/journal/feature.html?id=146660 (accessed May 2006).

Lucie-Smith, Edward. *British Poetry since 1945*. Harmondsworth: Penguin, 1987.

March, James G. "Poetry and the Rhetoric of Management." *Journal of Management Enquiry* 15, no 1 (2006): 70–72.

McKenzie, Jane, and Christine van Winkelen. *Understanding the Knowledge Organization*. London: Thompson, 2004.

Morgan, Clare, Kirsten Lange, and Ted Buswick. "Poetry in the Boardroom: Thinking beyond the Facts." *Journal of Business Strategy* 26, no. 1 (2005): 34–40.

Morgan, Clare, Jane McKenzie, Nick Woolf, and Christine van Winkelen. "Cognition in Strategic Decision-Making: A Model of Nonconventional Thinking Capacities for Complex Situations." *Journal of Management Decision*, vol. 47, no. 2 (2009): 209–32.

Nemerov, Howard. *Figures of Thought*. Boston: David R. Godine, 1979.

Newton, K. M. *Twentieth-Century Literary Theory: A Reader*. Basingstoke: Macmillan, 1988.

Nussbaum, Martha C. *Poetic Justice: The Literary Imagination and Public Life*. Boston: Beacon Press, 1995.

Nussbaum, Martha C. *Upheavals of Thought: The Intelligence of Emotions*. Cambridge: Cambridge University press, 2001.

Ortenblad, Anders. "Educating Everyone in Humanities for both Post-bureaucracy and Bureaucracy." *Management Learning* 37, no. 3 (2006): 291–94.

Perloff, Marjorie. "In Defense of Poetry." http://bostonreview.net/BR24.6/perloff .html (accessed December 2003).

Perloff, Marjorie. *Wittgenstein's Ladder: Poetic Language and the Strangeness of the Ordinary*. Chicago: University of Chicago Press, 1996.

Pierer, Heinrich von, and Bolko von Oetinger. *A Passion for Ideas*. West Lafayette, IN: Purdue University Press, 2002.

Pinker, Steven. *The Language Instinct*. London: Penguin, 1994.

Press, John. *A Map of Modern English Verse*. Oxford: Oxford University Press, 1969.

Raffman, Diana. *Language, Music, and Mind*. Cambridge: MIT Press, 1993.

Ramachandran, Vilayanur S. "The Emerging Mind." BBC Reith Lectures, 2003. http://www.bbc.co.uk/radio4/reith2003/ (accessed September 2005).

Richards, I. A. *The Philosophy of Metaphor*. Oxford: Oxford University Press, 1971.

Richards, I. A. *Science and Poetry*. London:. Kegan, Paul, Trench, Trubner, 1926. Reprinted as *Poetries and Sciences*. New York: Norton, 1970.

Ricks, Christopher. *The Force of Poetry*. Oxford: Oxford University Press, 1984.

Roberts, Phil. *How Poetry Works*. Harmondsworth: Penguin, 2000.

Root-Bernstein, Robert, and Michèle Root-Bernstein. *Sparks of Genius*. Boston: Houghton Mifflin, 1999.

Ryan, Michael. *Literary Theory*. Oxford: Blackwell, 1999.

Sartre, Jean-Paul. *The Emotions: Outline of a Theory*. New York: Philosophical Library, [1948] 1976.

Saunders, Leslie. "'Something Made in Language': The Poet's Gift?" *Management Decision* 44, no. 4 (2006): 504–11.

Schein, Edgar H. "The Role of Art and the Artist." *Reflections* 2, no. 4 (2001): 81–83.

Serres, Michel, with Bruno Latour. *Conversations on Science, Culture, and Time*. Ann Arbor: University of Michigan Press, 1995.

Shelley, Percy Bysshe. *A Defense of Poetry and Other Essays*. Lenox, MA: Hard Press, 2006.

Sidney, Philip. *An Apology for Poetry*. London: Thomas Nelson and Sons, 1967.

Sternberg, Robert J., and Janet E. Davidson. *The Nature of Insight*. Cambridge: MIT Press, 1995.

Sutcliffe, Kathleen M., and Klaus Weber. "The High Cost of Accurate Knowledge." *Harvard Business Review*, May 1, 2003: 82.

Sternberg, Robert J., ed. *Handbook of Creativity*. Cambridge: Cambridge University Press, 1998.

Szirtes, George. "The Sweetest Sound of All." "Comment." *Guardian*, November 21, 2005.

Taylor, A. E. *Aristotle*. New York: Dover, 1955.

Taylor, C. C. W. *Socrates: A Very Short Introduction*. Oxford: Oxford University Press, 2000.

Tsur, Reuven. "Aspects of Cognitive Poetics." http://www2.bc.edu/~richarad/lcb/fea/tsur/cogpoetics.html (accessed February 2003).

Tsur, Reuven. "On Cognitive Style." http://www2.bc.edu/~richarad/lcb/fea/tsurin/cogstyle.html (accessed November 2004).

Tsur, Reuven. *Toward a Theory of Cognitive Poetics*. Amsterdam: Elsevier, 1992.

Tsur, Reuven. "What Can We Know about the Medieval Reader's Response to Rhyme?" http://www.tau.ac.il/~tsurxx/What_can_we_2b.html (accessed May 2008).

Tsur, Reuven. *What Makes Sound Patterns Expressive? The Poetic Mode of Speech Perception*. Durham: Duke University Press, 1992.

Tsur, Reuven, and Beth Bradburn. "An Interview with Reuven Tsur." http://www2.bc.edu/~richarad/lcb/fea/tsurin/tsurmain.html (accessed November 2004).

von Ghyczy, Tihamer. "The Fruitful Flaws of Strategy Metaphors." *Harvard Business Review*, September, vol. 81, no. 9 (2003): 86–94.

von Ghyczy, Tiha, Bolko von Oetinger, and Christopher Bassford. *Clausewitz on Strategy*. New York: John Wiley and Sons, 2001.

von Oetinger, Bolko. *Hansel und Gretel und die Kuba Krise*. Munich: Hanser, 2006.

von Oetinger, Bolko, and Martin Reeves. "Size Obliges." *HarvardBusinessmanager*, January 2007.

Wallas, Graham. *The Art of Thought*. London: Jonathan Cape, 1926.

Wendt, Ronald F. "The Sound of One Hand Clapping." *Management Communication Quarterly* 11, no. 3 (1998): 323–71.

Wilson, Robert N. *Man Made Plain: The Poet in Contemporary Society*. Cleveland: Howard Allen, 1958.

Wittgenstein, Ludwig. *Philosophical Investigations*. Oxford: Blackwell, [1958] 1994.

Whyte, David. *The Heart Aroused: Poetry and the Preservation of the Soul in Corporate America*. New York: Currency Doubleday, 1994.

Index